The Social Semiotics of Populism

Bloomsbury Advances in Semiotics

Series Editor: Paul Bouissac

Bloomsbury Advances in Semiotics publishes original works applying semiotic approaches to linguistics and non-verbal productions, social institutions and discourses, embodied cognition and communication, and the new virtual realities of the digital age. It covers topics such as socio-semiotics, evolutionary semiotics, game theory, cultural and literary studies, human-computer interactions, and the challenging new dimensions of human networking afforded by social websites.

Titles published in the series:
Semiotics of the Christian Imagination, Domenico Pietropaolo
Computational Semiotics, Jean-Guy Meunier
Cognitive Semiotics, Per Aage Brandt
The Semiotics of Caesar Augustus, Elina Pyy
The Social Semiotics of Tattoos, Chris William Martin
The Semiotics of X, Jamin Pelkey
The Semiotics of Light and Shadows, Piotr Sadowski
Music as Multimodal Discourse, edited by Lyndon C. S. Way and Simon McKerrell
Peirce's Twenty-Eight Classes of Signs and the Philosophy of Representation, Tony Jappy
The Semiotics of Emoji, Marcel Danesi
Semiotics and Pragmatics of Stage Improvisation, Domenico Pietropaolo
Critical Semiotics, Gary Genosko

The Social Semiotics of Populism

Sebastián Moreno Barreneche

BLOOMSBURY ACADEMIC
LONDON • NEW YORK • OXFORD • NEW DELHI • SYDNEY

BLOOMSBURY ACADEMIC
Bloomsbury Publishing Plc
50 Bedford Square, London, WC1B 3DP, UK
1385 Broadway, New York, NY 10018, USA
29 Earlsfort Terrace, Dublin 2, Ireland

BLOOMSBURY, BLOOMSBURY ACADEMIC and the Diana logo are trademarks of
Bloomsbury Publishing Plc

First published in Great Britain 2023
Paperback edition published 2024

Copyright © Sebastián Moreno Barreneche, 2023

Sebastián Moreno Barreneche has asserted his right under the Copyright, Designs and
Patents Act, 1988, to be identified as Author of this work.

Cover design: Tjaša Krivec
Cover image © Daria Moroz / Alamy Stock Vector

All rights reserved. No part of this publication may be reproduced or transmitted in any
form or by any means, electronic or mechanical, including photocopying, recording,
or any information storage or retrieval system, without prior permission in writing
from the publishers.

Bloomsbury Publishing Plc does not have any control over, or responsibility for, any third-
party websites referred to or in this book. All internet addresses given in this book were
correct at the time of going to press. The author and publisher regret any inconvenience
caused if addresses have changed or sites have ceased to exist, but can accept no
responsibility for any such changes.

A catalogue record for this book is available from the British Library.

A catalog record for this book is available from the Library of Congress.

ISBN: HB: 978-1-3502-0539-0
PB: 978-1-3502-0543-7
ePDF: 978-1-3502-0540-6
eBook: 978-1-3502-0541-3

Series: Bloomsbury Advances in Semiotics

Typeset by Deanta Global Publishing Services, Chennai, India

To find out more about our authors and books visit www.bloomsbury.com and
sign up for our newsletters.

This book is dedicated to my grandmother 'Pompona', in gratitude for teaching me the passion for books and everything that comes with them.

Contents

List of Figures		ix
Preface		x
1	The Populist Moment	1
	1.1 Populism: A concept to describe our political present	1
	1.2 The challenges of populism as a political phenomenon	4
	1.3 Populism studies: Historic overview	8
	1.4 Towards a general theory of populism	12
	1.5 About this book	14
2	What Is Populism?	19
	2.1 Conceptual definitions in the social sciences and humanities	19
	2.2 The challenge of defining populism	22
	2.3 Accounts on populism	24
	2.4 On the compatibility of these accounts	34
3	Social Semiotics and the Study of 'Meaning in Action'	39
	3.1 Semiotics and the 'semiotic outlook'	39
	3.2 Greimas and Eco	43
	3.3 Social Semiotics and the study of 'meaning in action'	47
	3.4 Studying populism from a socio-semiotic perspective	55
4	Politics as a 'Contest over Meaning'	59
	4.1 The conflictive nature of the political	59
	4.2 The political as a discursive field	63
	4.3 Collective identities in political discourse	72
	4.4 Politics as a 'contest over meaning'	78
5	'The People' and Its 'Other(s)'	81
	5.1 The populist dichotomization of society	82
	5.2 The discursive construction of 'the people'	87
	5.3 'The people's other'	94

6	The Populist Leader	101
	6.1 The role of the leader in politics	102
	6.2 The populist leader: A semiotic discussion	104
	6.3 Donald Trump	108
	6.4 Matteo Salvini	112
	6.5 Hugo Chávez	115
7	Right-Wing Populism	121
	7.1 What is right-wing populism?	121
	7.2 Populism and nationalism	125
	7.3 Right-wing populism in Europe: Marine Le Pen and the Front National	128
	7.4 Right-wing populism in the United States: Donald Trump revisited	134
	7.5 Right-wing populism in South America? Jair Bolsonaro	138
8	Left-Wing Populism	143
	8.1 What is left-wing populism?	144
	8.2 Left-wing populism, neoliberalism and globalization	147
	8.3 Left-wing populism in South America: The challenge of distinguishing between populist and popular politics	150
	8.4 Left-wing populism in Europe: Podemos	157
	8.5 Left-wing populism in the United States? Bernie Sanders	162
Conclusion		169
Notes		177
References		190
Index		208

List of Figures

1	Towards a theory of populism	12
2	The semiotic square	44
3	Landowski's interactional regimes	50
4	Meaning as a cultural unit	64
5	Types of political regimes	69
6	The populist dichotomization of the social space	83
7	The semiotic construction of 'the people' and its 'other' in populist discourse	86
8	'The people' as part and as a whole of society	91
9	The 'other' as a single collective identity	97
10	The discursive construction of 'the people's other' in positive terms	99

Preface

This book is a revised version of my doctoral thesis, which was accepted by the Ludwig-Maximilians-Universität München in 2022.

Over the past decade, the references to populism and populist political actors, parties and movements became ubiquitous around the globe. My first contact with the concept from an academic perspective occurred in 2017 in Munich, in a seminar on populist parties and anti-establishment politics in Europe at the Geschwister Scholl Institute of Political Science of the Ludwig-Maximilians-Universität. I volunteered to deliver the first presentation of the seminar, on the concept of populism, and was fascinated by the challenges of defining and making sense of this elusive, chameleonic and contested political phenomenon.

While preparing that presentation, I found myself confronted with a concept whose proper comprehension required – so I believed – the use of theoretical tools not only from the fields of political science, theory and philosophy but also from what at the time I used to refer to as 'narrative and cultural studies'. To pass that seminar, I wrote a paper entitled 'Defining populism: A contribution to the debate from narrative and cultural studies', where I employed concepts and tools that I had acquired in my undergraduate studies – in communications, philosophy and literature – to approach the concept of populism. Although populism was a political phenomenon, my intuition at the time was that it had a strong discursive component that could be examined using these tools.

While writing that paper, I felt particularly attracted by the fact that discursive accounts of populism – such as those of Ernesto Laclau and the Essex school – did not include in their reflections any references to authors such as Vladimir Propp, Jerome Bruner, Umberto Eco, Paul Ricoeur, Hayden White and Gerard Genette, among other theorists interested in studying narratives and the role they play in how individuals make sense of reality. Why did discourse-theoretical scholars not conceive of populism as a story – a narrative – composed of a main character – 'the people' – who has an enemy – 'the elite' – and needs a helper – the populist leader – to achieve its collective goals? Why did nobody write about the conflictive narrative plot that populist leaders establish between 'the people' and 'the elite' in their discourses and performances? Why did discursive accounts of populism remain at such a high level of abstraction, making of empirical work with concrete discourses and performances something secondary to theoretical speculation?

Immediately after finishing that exploratory paper, I prepared a project for a doctoral dissertation and, following the convener of the seminar's advice, I discussed it with Prof. Dr Karsten Fischer, Chair of Political Theory at the Geschwister-Scholl-Institut für Politikwissenschaft of the University of Munich, who enthusiastically agreed to supervise it. Since that first meeting from 2017, I have been working in trying to make sense of the phenomenon of populism as something that due to its inherent discursive component transcends the academic boundaries of (comparative) political science and that needs of Semiotics to be properly grasped and understood. This book is my attempt to argue for that thesis.

After my stay in Munich, I spent a brief period of 2017 at the University of Bologna, Italy, where I had the opportunity of taking a deep dive into semiotic theory thanks to the lectures of prominent semioticians such as Patrizia Violi, Maria Pia Pozzato and Claudio Paolucci, who introduced me with rigour into the works of Umberto Eco and Algirdas Greimas, the two popes of contemporary Semiotics. It was in Bologna that, finally, the concepts and tools I possessed in my eclectic personal toolbox thanks to my undergraduate studies – which I used to refer to as 'narrative and cultural studies' – gained theoretical consistency and could be placed within the bigger picture of the 'sciences of language' and, more precisely, within the discipline, research field or outlook called *Semiotics*. It was also during my time in Bologna that the working title of the doctoral dissertation changed to *The Social Semiotics of Populism*.

It was with that updated working title that, in November 2019, during a conference organized by the Hellenic Semiotics Society in Thessaloniki, Greece, I presented the project to Paul Bouissac, editor of Bloomsbury's 'Advances in Semiotics' series, who enthusiastically and generously agreed to receive a book proposal from me and forward it to Bloomsbury's editorial team. From that moment, I started writing a dissertation to obtain a doctoral degree in political theory and, at the same time, a book of Semiotics. This was a quest that posed some interesting challenges, particularly regarding the 'model reader(s)' of what I was writing. I hope that the final result fulfils the expectations of both semioticians and political theorists/scientists. Given that my major overarching goal in conducting research is to overcome disciplinary boundaries within the social sciences and humanities, I hope this book can be a good example of interdisciplinary dialogue.

Since 2019, the ideas and arguments presented in this book have been discussed in a number of seminars, colloquia and conferences, such as the 2021 edition of the annual congress of the Italian Society of Political Science (SISP); a colloquium on left-wing populism in October 2021 at the University of Liège, Belgium; one of the sessions of Prof. Dr Fischer's colloquium at the Ludwig-Maximilians-Universität Munich; one of the seminars of the DESIRE research group organized by Benjamin De Cleen and Jana Goyvaerts at the Vrije Universiteit Brussels; a session of the seminar 'Las Ciencias de la Comunicación desde una perspectiva Semiótica' organized at the Universidad Nacional Autónoma de México in May 2022; the international conference 'The Role of Emotions in Populist Movements', organized by the Comenius University of Bratislava also in May 2022; the conference HEPP3 (Third Helsinki Conference on Emotions, Populism and Polarisation), organized by the Helsinki Hub on Emotions, Populism and Polarisation of the University of Helsinki, Finland, in June 2022; the international seminar 'The internationalization of populism. Populism beyond the nation state?', at the University of Aalborg, in June 2022; and the 15th World Congress of Semiotics 'Semiotics in the Lifeworld', organized by the International Association for Semiotic Studies in Thessaloniki, Greece, in September 2022. In April 2021, Paul Bouissac offered me the opportunity of presenting my ideas on populism in one of the very first sessions of *Smart Semiotics*, a series of e-seminars on Semiotics. In the virtual seminar I received invaluable comments on the project from Jef Verschueren, Jan Zienkowski, Vasileios Adamidis and Peer Age Brandt, who sadly passed away. Moreover, a handful of papers on the topics addressed in this book were published since 2019 in Latin American and European journals on Semiotics and discourse studies, such as *DeSignis* and *Punctum*. Many of those were kindly read by Prof. Dr Fischer, whose comments have always been not only of invaluable help in clarifying my ideas but, most important, reassuring.

This book focuses on populism and it does so from a semiotic perspective. As such, it aims at bringing together political science and Semiotics, two research fields that, albeit having been in contact for years, in 2022 are still trying to become close friends. I regard this close friendship as crucial in the attempts of understanding how the political field of the social world functions. I hope readers versed in political theory – and particularly in populism studies – can find the semiotic content of the book relevant, interesting and inspiring. Symmetrically, I hope that readers versed in Semiotics consider this case study – in a way, this book is an exercise of applied Semiotics – a fruitful contribution to the development of our discipline by examining a relevant and challenging phenomenon of our time.

This is not only my doctoral dissertation but also my first book. As such, in writing it I had doubts, insecurities and even questioned the whole project more than once. Thankfully, colleagues and friends located in the two margins of the Atlantic Ocean were kind enough to support me with their reassuring comments and feedback. Chapters and passages of the book were read and commented on by Paul Bouissac, Gastón Cingolani, Jacopo Custodi, Mariano Dagatti, Benjamin De Cleen, Paolo Demuru, Lucrecia Escudero Chauvel, Óscar García Agustín, Jana Goyvaerts, Samuele Mazzolini, Grigoris Paschalidis, Alain Perusset and Andreas Ventsel. I take the opportunity to thank them for their time, interest and comments, which certainly helped me in clarifying ideas and, most important, in gaining clarity when putting them in writing.

Belgium and Uruguay, 2022

1

The Populist Moment

1.1 Populism: A concept to describe our political present

In the first sentence of the Introduction to the volume *Populism and the Mirror of Democracy* that he edited in 2005, Francisco Panizza (2005: 1) wrote that 'it has become almost a cliché to start writing on populism by lamenting the lack of clarity about the concept and casting doubts about its usefulness for political analysis'. More than fifteen years after that statement was written, it is still not possible to begin any scholarly work on the political phenomenon referred to as 'populism' celebrating its conceptual clarity and its usefulness for political analysis.

This is the case because the vast number of books, edited volumes, journal articles and book chapters that have been published within the social sciences and the humanities – particularly during the last two decades – that revolve around this elusive contemporary political phenomenon has not contributed to finding a solution for the fundamental issue of working with a clear, precise and consensual concept of populism. This is the first necessary task in any scholarly enterprise: finding common ground among researchers regarding what it is that they are studying and writing about (Pappas, 2019b). In this sense, the conceptual history of populism is prototypical of the challenges linked to any scientific enterprise, particularly within the social sciences and the humanities.

This book puts Semiotics' conceptual and theoretical apparatus to the test with the purpose of finding out if it can be of use in clarifying the nature of populism. Irrespective of what its genus might be – an ideology, a discourse, a performance, a cognitive frame, a political strategy – populism is a *social* phenomenon; that is, it is something carried out by human beings. Then, it has a constitutive discursive dimension linked to meaning-making and signification. This dimension is evidenced not only in the production and consumption of social discourses but also in the interactions that occur between political actors. Semiotic theory will serve not only to analyse textual products by political actors said to be populist but also to clarify the nature of populism as a discursive practice that occurs in the political domain. The originality of this book is that it examines populism from a scholarly perspective that until now has been used only sporadically.

Over the last years, there have been myriad references around the globe to 'populism' and 'populist' parties, candidates, movements and political actors in the media and in the public sphere of dozens of countries. Together with these references, a high number of researchers, scholars and political commentators working in various disciplines within the social sciences and the humanities – such as political theory, political science, discourse studies, linguistics, economics and others – have published works on populism with the aim of making sense of this chameleonic and contested political phenomenon. The growing interest for populism evidences its usefulness as a concept to refer to a phenomenon that seems to be characteristic of our political present:[1] we, the citizens of a globalized world, live in an era where politics evidences certain traits that were not present in previous eras like Antiquity and the Middle Ages. The emergence and normalization of populist politics seems to be one of those traits. Populism would then be a symptom of contemporary politics.

Is populism actually a political phenomenon limited to our contemporary era? Vasileios Adamidis (2021) argues that populism can already be found in ancient Greece. This statement would deny the consensual idea that populism is a phenomenon linked to contemporary, industrial, globalized, modern and mediatized societies. For Jan-Werner Müller (2016: 101), populism did not exist in ancient Athens: 'demagoguery perhaps, but not populism, since the latter exists only in representative systems'. Müller's statement supports the thesis that populism is a contemporary phenomenon because it is in this age that political systems became representative. Moreover, his statement thematizes the frequent confusion between *populism* and *demagoguery*. It can be seen how even a simple factual question, such as if populism existed in eras other than the contemporary, sparks controversies.[2]

However, even if populism existed in the Antiquity, it is out of discussion that our contemporary political present has seen a rise of phenomena labelled as 'populist'. This has led researchers to put an emphasis on the concept of populism. In 2004, Cas Mudde (2004), one of the most prominent voices within populism studies, identified a 'populist *Zeitgeist*'. Fourteen years later, he argued that populism is 'the concept that defines our age' (Mudde, 2018). In 2006, Pierre Rosanvallon (2006) identified a 'populist turn' and argued in 2020 that the twenty-first century will be 'the century of populism', that is, one characterized by a political culture that is original (Rosanvallon, 2020). In 2007, Ivan Krastev (2007) wrote that the world was living a 'populist moment' that he assessed as a dangerous rise around the world of illiberalism within democratic systems. For Krastev (2007: 2), populism 'captures the nature of the challenges that liberal democracy faces today'. Ten years later, Chantal Mouffe (2018: 6) argued that Europe was experiencing a 'populist moment', which she conceived of as 'the expression of a set of heterogeneous demands' that in her view do not pose a threat to democracy but can rather strengthen it. Also in 2018, Francis Fukuyama (2018a) diagnosed a 'populist surge' and argued that 'the term "populism" has been used very loosely [. . .] to describe a wide range of phenomena that don't necessarily go together'. More recently, and in line with Krastev's thesis, Takis Pappas (2019a: 36) equalled populism with 'democratic illiberalism' and claimed that populism is 'the major historical phenomenon of our times'. Statements like these open up the field for two possible interpretations: on the one hand, it could be argued that we have been living in a populist moment for a long time; on the other, it evidences that some contemporary diagnoses might forget to reflect on the history of the concept.

The explosive interest for populism and populist political actors, parties and movements both in the academia and the civil society – media, citizens, political commentators and so on – does not seem to be unjustified. Over the last two to three decades – at least – observers and commentators have labelled numerous politicians and parties around the world as 'populist', an adjective that has been the source of more semantic controversies than of conceptual clarity. In 2022, populism is a global phenomenon still in development that can be found in many political contexts.[3] As a result, references to populism were not as common in the past as they have been over the last twenty to thirty years.

In Europe, Jean-Marie Le Pen and his daughter Marine, both part of the Front National (in France), Geert Wilders and the Pim Fortuyn List (in the Netherlands), Matteo Salvini and the Lega (Nord), together with Beppe Grillo and the Movimento Cinque Stelle (in Italy), the party Alternative für Deutschland (in Germany), Nigel Farage and UKIP (in the United Kingdom), Viktor Orbán and Fidesz (in Hungary), Spanish Vox, Swiss SVP, Austrian FPÖ and Portuguese Chega, among a long list of many other politicians, parties and actors, have been frequently identified as – and even accused of – being right-wing populists (Akkerman, de Lange & Rooduijn, 2016; Betz, 1994; Mudde, 2007).

Symmetrically, the same occurred with politicians and parties regularly located within the group of the left-wing populists, such as Alexis Tsiptras and SYRIZA (in Greece), Pablo Iglesias and Podemos (in Spain) and Jean-Luc Mélenchon and La France Insoumise (in France), just to mention a handful of examples of what scholars have identified as populism on the left side of the political spectrum (Damiani, 2020; García Agustín, 2020; Katsambekis & Kioupkiolis, 2019). As is argued in this book, the fact that 'populism' and 'populist' are labels that can be applied to political actors both from the left and the right sides of the political spectrum – this is where its chameleonic nature lies – has posed significant challenges for theorists of populism.

In the Americas, before and after his election as the president of the United States in November 2016, Donald Trump was widely accused of being a right-wing populist, while Bernie Sanders was frequently labelled as a left-wing populist. In South America, scholarship on populism is usually organized according to three populist moments or 'tides' which correlate with historical occurrences of populism. The first tide developed during the 1930s and 1940s and saw charismatic politicians, such as Juan Domingo Perón (in Argentina), Getúlio Vargas (in Brazil) and Lázaro Cárdenas (in México) in power. The second tide occurred in the 1990s, when populism and neoliberal economic policies were brought together by Carlos Menem (in Argentina) and Alberto Fujimori (in Peru), among others.[4] Finally, the third populist wave is more recent and includes politicians such as Hugo Chávez and Nicolás Maduro (in Venezuela), Evo Morales (in Bolivia) and Cristina Fernández de Kircher (in Argentina), among others, all usually labelled as left-wing populists. María Esperanza Casullo (2019) locates the third wave of South American populism – usually referred to as 'the pink tide' [*ola rosa*] – between 1998, when Hugo Chávez rose to power in Venezuela, and 2012, when Paraguayan president Fernando Lugo was impeached.

Shortly put, by taking into account only Europe and the Americas – the continents the author is familiar with due to his biography – the conclusion seems to be that the labels 'populism' and 'populist' are instruments that are handy for observers to use in their attempts to make sense of our political present, even if they lack the clarity that is expected of any concept for it to be capable of shedding more light than shadow on social phenomena. This occurs because the concept of populism and its derived words are *meaningful* to them, even if it is in negative terms to express 'all kinds of political anxieties [. . .], with the word *populism* being used for many political phenomena that appear at first sight to be mutually exclusive', as Müller (2016: 7) proposes. Therefore, even if scholars might still have not reached an agreement regarding what the noun *populism* and the adjective *populist* mean, denote or imply – in logical terms, what are its intension and extension – populism has 'become the buzz word in almost any discussion about, or analysis of, contemporary politics', as argued by Pappas (2019a: 1). Unsurprisingly, Cas Mudde and Cristóbal Rovira Kaltwasser (2017: 1) open their *Very Short Introduction* to populism stating that 'populism is one of the main political buzzwords of the 21st century'.

When did the salience of populism as one of the traits that define our political present begin? From an academic perspective, populism has been studied since the late 1960s, mainly with a focus on two historical movements – one in the United States and the other in Russia – from the nineteenth century (Ionescu & Gellner, 1969; Canovan, 1981; Müller, 2016). During the twentieth century, it has also been of interest for scholars based in South America who tried to understand political movements in their countries of origin or residence, such as Gino Germani (1965; 1973) and Torcuato di Tella (1965; 1973) in Argentina.

However, the interest for populism was renewed after the transition from the twentieth to the twenty-first century. Particularly, if a year is needed to locate what could be labelled a 'populist hype' – that is, the time in which the words 'populism' and 'populist' made it into the vocabulary of ordinary people – then 2016 seems to be the answer. It was in 2016 that, in June, citizens of the United Kingdom voted in favour of Brexit and, in November, Donald Trump was elected as the president of the United States. In these two cases, something called *populism* (concretely, a type of discourse and of doing politics that appealed to 'the people' and that challenged politics as usual through the use of bad manners, lies and demagoguery) was identified as one of the major causes for these electoral results. In the first case, Nigel Farage was one of the main targets of the accusations of populism following his mode of campaigning in favour of Brexit. In the second, Trump himself was labelled a populist candidate in a presidential race in which other candidates – namely, Bernie Sanders – were also described as populist. Therefore, as Manuel Anselmi (2017) proposes, 2016 will certainly be remembered as the year of populism. Unsurprisingly, Cambridge University Press made of 'populism' its Word of the Year in 2017.[5]

1.2 The challenges of populism as a political phenomenon

The rise of 'populism' as a concept to make sense of our political present brought with it a number of problems and issues. As will be discussed in the following chapter, one of the major problems linked to the study of populism is related to its definition. What does the term 'populism' mean, encompass and refer to? What type of phenomenon is it – a political ideology, a strategy to mobilize the electorate and conquer power, a discursive practice, a political logic, a communicative or discursive style, a cognitive frame, a political regime, a social movement and so on? Which are its defining features? What do all manifestations of populism – past and present, right-wing and left-wing – have in common? Do they have something in common at all? What is the relationship of populism with classic – or 'major' (Alexander, 2015) – political ideologies ended in *-ism*, such as liberalism, socialism and conservatism?

Questions like these have been addressed by scholars working in the social sciences and humanities, including empirically oriented political scientists that employ comparative methodologies (Mudde, 2004; Pappas, 2019a; 2019b; Hawkins, 2009); researchers approaching politics from a discursive perspective (Laclau, 1977; 2005a; 2005b; Mouffe, 2005b: 2018; Panizza, 2005; De Cleen, 2017; 2019; Zienkowski & Breeze, 2019); scholars interested in political communication and rhetoric (Aalberg et al., 2017; Jagers & Walgrave, 2007; Mazzoleni, Stewart & Horsfield, 2003) and, most recently, semioticians (Landowski, 2018; 2020; Sedda & Demuru, 2018a; Demuru, 2021a; 2021b; Cervelli, 2018; Addis, 2020; Fontanille, 2020). This book aims at adding to the scholarly debate on populism from the last perspective. Here, populism is defined as a *discursive practice* based on the use of a specific *narrative structure* that can be analysed through the conceptual toolbox of Semiotics.

Besides the disagreement regarding the conceptual definition, the words 'populism' and 'populist' have been extensively used with an axiological value, that is, loaded with connotations that make of it 'an analytical attribution rather than a term with which most political actors would willingly identify', as Panizza (2005: 1) argues. The concept has usually been employed pejoratively, as a mode of discrediting and denigrating political opponents, particularly in public political debates and by the media (Stavrakakis, 2017). Since 2016, the terms 'populism' and 'populist' have been 'imposed by the media to disqualify all those who oppose the status quo', as Mouffe (2018: 10) argues. Therefore, *being a populist* is neither a compliment nor a predicate that political actors seem to conceive of as one to use actively when trying to boost their electoral chances. Although populist political actors tend to speak about 'the people' in their discourses and performances, they hardly use the words 'populism' and 'populist' to refer to their own political proposals. That is why observers were taken aback when, in June 2016, former US president Barack Obama declared during a press conference: 'I suppose that makes me a populist.'[6]

Although this rule might have a number of exceptions, like when French politician Jean-Luc Mélenchon declared in an interview '*Populist, moi? J'assume!*',[7] Obama's utterance reflects how, back in 2016, the concept of populism might still have not been as value-loaded as it is nowadays. Otherwise, Obama's self-identification as a populist would have been hard to make sense of due to the negative and pejorative connotations of the term. This brings to the fore the vagueness that is a salient feature of the terms 'populism' and 'populist'. Individuals can recognize these words as acceptable within the English language. They might even translate them into other languages, such as *populismo* in Spanish, Italian and Portuguese, *Populismus* in German and *populisme* in French. Nevertheless, these linguistic facts are far from solving the issue of meaning, which remains unclear and contested. How can one explain the meaning of these words? These challenges are related to the broad possibilities linked to what the words 'populism' and 'populist' could mean in different political, national, linguistic and historical contexts. Hence, it was interesting to see a public figure like Obama trying to load these terms with a *positive* connotation, contrary to the negative connotations usually linked to them both in the contemporary public sphere (media, journalists, political actors, etc.) and in a vast part of the academic literature.

Independently of what they might actually mean or refer to, the words 'populism' and 'populist' normally carry a *normative baggage* with them (Aslanidis, 2016): while some use these words as neutral labels in their attempts to describe a political phenomenon in an allegedly objective manner, others use them loaded with connotations, that is, implying other meanings, such as appraisal or reprobation. This 'connotative gain' stands in a relation that is inversely proportional to the denotative function of the words, as is argued in a subsequent chapter.

Together with their conceptual non-clarity and the implicit normative load, a third problematic aspect with the words 'populism' and 'populist' is that they have been used to refer to politicians, actors and parties both from the right and from the left sides of the political spectrum. Due to this alleged *chameleonic* nature, since its emergence as a concept of interest for political theorists and scientists, populism has challenged the dichotomic opposition that is normally assumed to exist between the two standard ideological poles: Left versus Right, a theoretical construct that has been central in political theory at least since the French Revolution (Bobbio, 1994).

Nevertheless, this issue seems to have been solved: as is argued in these pages, populist actors and movements need to select the specific contents of their discourses and performances from *outside* the signifying system called *populism*. This is what a group of scholars has in mind when arguing that populism is better understood as a 'thin-centred' ideology, that is, not a full-fledged ideology, such as socialism, conservatism and liberalism, but a more modest and less solid articulation of ideas that needs to be combined with other contents (see Section 2.3.1). As is argued in this book, the idea of a 'thin-centred' ideology does not differ much from the conception of populism as a cognitive frame, that is, as a particular way of articulating pre-existing political contents taken from the cultural encyclopaedia of a political community.

Finally, a fourth challenge of populism studies has become evident during the last two decades, when *populism* became a 'hot topic' in the social sciences and the humanities (in particular within political science and theory). This has been the case mainly due to the relationship that has been established between populism and (liberal) democracy (Abts & Rummens, 2007; Akkerman, 2003; Albertazzi & McDonnell, 2008; Arditi, 2007; Bang & Marsh, 2018; Finchelstein & Urbinati, 2018; Krastev, 2007; Mouffe, 2018; Rovira Kaltwasser, 2012; Müller, 2016; Urbinati, 1998). According to Pappas (2019a: 2), 'current interest in populism is driven, first and foremost, by growing disquiet about democracy and liberalism, their delicate interplays and possible failures'.

Unsurprisingly, for a vast majority of scholars who have dealt with this complex relationship, populism poses *a threat* to (liberal) democracy and, in particular, to party politics and pluralism. According to Panizza (2005: 22), 'in populist discourse, politics and political parties are often considered as divisive institutions that should be eliminated, or at least purified of factions and particularistic interests, to allow the people to become united'. For Krastev (2007: 2), '"populism" captures the nature of the challenges that liberal democracy faces today.' According to the author, these 'emanate [. . .] from dangerous mutations within liberal democracies themselves'. Arditi (2005; 2007) argues that populism is an 'internal periphery' of liberal-democratic politics.

Besides the semantic challenges linked to the definition of the concept, populism is a phenomenon of interest for a discipline like Semiotics because it renders visible several mechanisms of politics *as a social activity with a constitutive discursive component*. Politics is an activity carried out by human beings embedded in the 'webs of signification' usually referred to as *culture* (Geertz, 1973). Therefore, it has an inescapable discursive dimension that renders the production of sense and meaning possible (Verón, 1988). As Panizza (2005: 20) argues, 'at the heart of populist narratives is populism's relation with the political.' This is an aspect also central in Laclau's (2005a) account of populism. According to Panizza (2005: 20), 'populism both depoliticizes and hyper-politicizes social relations' and, in doing so, it blurs 'the public-private dividing line' by bringing 'into the political realm both individual and collective desires that previously had no place in public life' (Panizza, 2005: 24).

To sum up, there are several issues that make of populism a challenging phenomenon to deal with and one that is not neat to grasp theoretically. The most salient of these issues is the multiplicity of uses and layers of hidden meaning that the word brings with it when used in different political, national and linguistic contexts. Challenges like these might explain the proliferation of populism studies over the last two decades and, since 2016, in the global public sphere. This book is another contribution to this already vast pile of studies. Its particularity is that it contributes to the scholarly debate on populism by examining the phenomenon through a specific outlook: that of Semiotics, that is, the discipline that studies meaning-, sense-making and signification. Although semioticians have shown some interest in populism, until now comprehensive studies do not exist besides a handful of articles and a few special issues of well-known Semiotics journals, such as *Actes Sémiotiques* (2018) and *DeSignis* (2019).[8]

As is argued in the following chapters, a semiotic account of populism will propose that populism is better understood when conceived of as a discursive practice that implies the use of a specific narrative structure that allows political actors – individual and collective – using it to fill its empty categories with specific meanings taken from the political contexts they are embedded in. As such, populism is a paradigmatic object of study for Semiotics, and in particular for *social* Semiotics, the branch of the discipline interested in studying 'meaning in action', that is, in making sense of how social actors produce meaning through the manipulation of semiotic resources of different modality – linguistic, visual, auditory and so forth – that can range from signs to practices. Therefore, if the content of this book had to be summarized in one sentence, it would be that it approaches populism from a semiotic perspective. It might not be unrealistic to state that this is the first monograph dealing with populism from a declared semiotic perspective.

As broad and void as this one-sentence summary might sound, it states in a clear manner the two areas of the social sciences and humanities that constitute the theoretical ground of the chapters that follow: on the one hand, Semiotics, a broad but somehow consistent discipline, outlook or research field that grew and achieved a certain degree of autonomy during the twentieth century; on the other hand, political science and theory, with a focus on the research area of *populism studies*.

1.3 Populism studies: Historic overview

Why does scholarship on populism need a new contribution just because its perspective is different from what has been published so far in the field? To answer this question, a brief historic overview of populism studies must be presented. Luckily, this retrospective will not take us far back in time since the systematic scholarship on populism – at least in English – begins in the late 1960s. Besides, the first historical occurrences of populism that have obtained consensus among scholars date from the late nineteenth century. This section presents a succinct history of populism studies and discusses concisely the first historical occurrences of populism.

Panizza (2005: 2) argues that 'there is little purpose in attempting to summarise the many studies of populism in the already existing vast academic literature on the topic'. This claim is still valid in 2023. However, every scholarly effort to understand the phenomenon of populism should trace the history of the concept, even if it does so minimally. This is specifically relevant when taking into account the diagnostics that were presented in Section 1.1. In spite of the theses that argue that in the first quarter of the twenty-first century the world is experiencing a populist moment, surge, turn or whatever analysts might call it, populism is not a concept that burst into the social sciences as a result of this salience: it is an old concept that originated in specific historical political movements.

Pappas (2019a: 14ff) segments the history of populism studies in three 'generations': the Pioneers, the Classics and the Contemporaries. According to Pappas, the first generation of 'the Pioneers' consists of scholars who participated in the interdisciplinary conference organized in May 1967 at the London School of Economics by the journal *Government and Opposition* and chaired by Isaiah Berlin. Some of the papers presented in the conference were compiled by Ghita Ionescu and Ernest Gellner in the book *Populism. Its Meanings and National Characteristics*, published in 1969. The book is probably the mandatory starting point for any study of populism.[9] It is organized in two parts: one with a geographical scope that includes chapters on populism in North America (Hofstadter, 1969), Latin America (Hennessy, 1969), Russia (Walicki, 1969), Eastern Europe (Ionescu, 1969) and Africa (Saul, 1969), and the second with a conceptual focus, where populism is approached as an ideology (MacRae, 1969), a syndrome (Wiles, 1969), a political movement (Minogue, 1969), a phenomenon with social roots (Stewart, 1969) and a concept (Worsley, 1969).

As the editors explain in the Introduction, the purpose of the conference was to define populism and to find out 'whether populism is a unitary concept, regardless of the variety of its incarnations, or whether it is simply a word wrongly used in completely heterogeneous contexts' (Ionescu & Gellner, 1969: 3). The use of the concept in posterior contexts surely added to the complexity of such an initial exploratory task. However, the editors stress that, in 1969, populism was *a phenomenon of the past* that had disappeared as such and canalized into stronger movements or ideologies, such as socialism, nationalism and peasantism (Ionescu & Gellner, 1969: 4). The first generation of populism scholars expanded into the 1970s and 1980s, although it 'failed to provide a commonly agreed definition of populism, causing instead conceptual stretching and empirical confusion', as argued by Pappas (2019a: 16). Although in their essays a few hints can be found that might be relevant for Semiotics, the discursive, performative and meaning-making aspects of populism are almost absent in the work of 'the Pioneers'.

The second generation – 'the Classics' – consists mainly of scholars who saw populist movements emerge and consolidate in their surroundings, mainly natives or residents in South American countries, such as Gino Germani and Torcuato di Tella, two authors who are inescapable for anyone interested in studying the Latin American manifestations of populism both in the middle and in the end of the twentieth century: while the first tide of South American populism consisted of authoritarian leaders such as Perón in Argentina, Vargas in Brazil and Cárdenas in México, the posterior form of Latin American populism consisted in an articulation of a type of politics that resembled that of the 'first tide' with neoliberal economic policies. Alan García and Alberto Fujimori in Peru, Carlos Menem in Argentina and Fernando Collor de Mello in Brazil are illustrative examples of this second populist tide. Pappas (2019a: 17) calls scholars of this generation 'the Classics' because it was them who 'even more than either their predecessors or their immediate successors, and by virtue of the pure quality of the cases they studied, reached conclusions of lasting worth'. For Pappas (2019a: 19), this second generation identified two of populism's main features: its mass movement character and the importance of charismatic leadership. As is argued in this book, none of these features are constitutive of populism when approached from a semiotic perspective. Nevertheless, Semiotics can be of help in making sense of them.

Finally, the third group of scholars is that of 'the Contemporaries'. According to Pappas (2019a: 20), 'largely based on the idea that a powerful populist zeitgeist, evident already by the early 1990s, has overwhelmed Western democracies [. . .], a global army of scholars has undertaken to analyze every nook and cranny of whatever one may term "populism"'. This third generation is characterized by four traits: (1) the attempt to find 'ever-innovative definitions with general applicability', (2) the expansion of the comparative scope to encompass more cases (countries, political parties etc.), (3) the anchorage in quantitative methods reflecting a sort of 'obsession' in *measuring* populism and (4) the articulation of empirical findings with the normative debate on the decay of democracy and liberalism (Pappas, 2019a: 20–1). It is within this third generation that the discursive and performative accounts of populism became prominent.

Pappas's classification of populism studies in three generations is useful to have a first approach to scholarship on populism. However, it is the segmentation of a comparative political scientist interested in developing a general theory of populism. For discursive accounts like that of Semiotics, the group of 'the Classics' would probably not include authors such as Germani and di Tella, two authors who came up with sociologist, economist, functionalist and organizational accounts of populism; instead, it would include scholars like Ernesto Laclau, who since the 1970s studied populism by examining its discursive component, and Margaret Canovan. Laclau and Canovan were pioneers in dealing with populism with the aim of making sense of this contested political phenomenon from a conceptual perspective. In fact, their works are usually at least mentioned by any scholar working on populism.

Laclau (1977: 143–4) begins the essay 'Towards a Theory of Populism' – included in the book *Politics and Ideology in Marxist Theory. Capitalism-Fascism-Populism* – writing:

> Populism is a concept both elusive and recurrent. Few terms have been so widely used in contemporary political analysis, although few have been defined with less precision. We know intuitively to what we are referring when we call a movement or an ideology populist, but we have the greatest difficulty in translating the intuition into concepts. This has often led to an *ad hoc* kind of practice: the term continues to be used in a merely allusive way and any attempt to ascertain its content is renounced. [. . .] The result is a vagueness which contributes little to a scientific analysis of any political phenomena.

Canovan (1981), for her part, was a pioneer in mapping different types of populism and proposing a coherent typology. In the book, Canovan (1981: 3) argues that the term 'populism' is 'exceptionally vague and refers in different contexts to a bewildering variety of phenomena', such as popular initiatives and dictatorships such as that of Perón in Argentina. Therefore, her contribution aimed not at proposing a 'single essentialist definition' of populism, but rather at creating a typology 'capable of accommodating a wide range of different phenomena seen from different analytical viewpoints' (Canovan, 1981: 12–13). This typology consists of seven types of populisms grouped in two broad families: agrarian (farmers radicalism, peasant movements and intellectual agrarian socialism) and political (populist dictatorship, populist democracy, reactionary populism and politicians' populism). Since Canovan argued that 'the types suggested are analytical constructs' and hence 'real-life examples may well overlap several categories' (Canovan, 1981: 13), her proposal was criticized by posterior scholarship (Laclau, 2005a: 5–7).

Working on a strand of research that gives discourse a central position in making sense of populism, Panizza (2005) identifies three main forms in which scholars have approached this political phenomenon. In the first place, there is an *empiricist* approach consisting of the study of *cases* of populism with the aim of listing their defining properties. Wiles's (1969) essay included in Ionescu and Gellner's book is a good example of this methodology: in the chapter, Wiles lists twenty-four characteristics of populism. Second, Panizza identifies a *historicist* approach, which links populism to specific historical contexts and that is not interested in developing anything like a general theory of populism. Finally, there is what he calls a '*symptomatic* reading of populism'.

When looking at the concrete cases that scholars refer to when dealing with populism, one thing seems clear: populism is a *contemporary* phenomenon; that is, it begins after the liberal revolutions of the nineteenth century, both in Europe and in the Americas. As Ionescu and Gellner wrote in 1969, 'the present relevance of populism has [. . .] brought about a revival interest in some half-forgotten nineteenth-century currents which bore, or were given, the same name'.

According to Tarragoni (2021), populism has three founding historical experiences. The first of those cases is the American farmers' protest movement that took place between 1877 and 1896 in the United States and the US People's Party it gave place to in 1892 (Tarragoni, 2021; Canovan 1981: 17–58). In their efforts to protest against the modernization of the US economy (capitalism, trusts, banks and financial companies etc.), these indebted farmers organized themselves following a logic that divided society discursively in two groups: the countryside and the city (Minogue, 1969). As Krastev (2007: 2) points out, with this movement a first 'original ideological meaning' emerged 'as the expression of agrarian radicalism'.

Second, also dating from the nineteenth century, between the 1860s and 1890s, the *narodnitchestvo* movement occurred in tsarist Russia (Tarragoni, 2021; Canovan, 1981: 59–97). This movement consisted of a group or urban and middle-class students and intellectuals who tried to mobilize peasants to oppose the tsarist regime. These were the *narodniki*, that is, the 'friends of the people', 'popular' or 'populists',[10] who saw in the peasantry a pure group, untouched by capitalism, that could be the source of emancipation against tsarist oppression. As Rovira Kaltwasser et al. (2017: 19) argue, 'in their celebration of the untainted nature of the peasantry and with the unbridled sense that the establishment needed overturning, these Russian students shared some themes with the populists in the US'.

These American and Russian movements were non-urban and probably for that reason were considered two manifestations of the same political phenomenon, partly because of the translation of the words *narod* and *narodni* into English as 'a people' or 'the people'. However, the basis for the conceptions that these two movements had of what is 'the people', who belongs to that collective identity and what is its role in society were different. However, these two movements seem to attract consensus within historians of populism regarding the origins of the term 'populism'. As discussed, some argue that populism could also be found in ancient Greece, even if the term did not exist to refer to the discursive practice currently named *populism*.

Normally, after introducing the cases of the US People's Party and the Russian *narodniki*, scholars differ in the inclusion of other historical movements of the twentieth century as being occurrences of populism. For example, Rovira Kaltwasser et al. (2017) refer to French Boulangism as a third relevant movement that gave rise to the scholarly interest in the phenomenon. Krastev (2007) includes movements in Latin America during the 1960s and 1970s that took the form of a neocaudillism and that were predominantly urban movements linked to mass migration of farmers and peasants to the industrialized cities. According to Krastev, neocaudillism could be regarded as a form of populism. Hence, populism has been usually connected with modernization and with a type of politics that is characteristic of the contemporary era. Also Tarragoni (2021) sees national-popular regimes in South America (1930–60) as one of populism's three 'founding political experiences', since it was here that populist political actors rose to power, generally with policy programmes oriented towards a better inclusion of the popular masses of dispossessed individuals.

In any case, when studying the history of the concept of populism and scholarship around it, it is clear that, following Tarragoni (2021: 3), 'the concept's history coincides with its unlimited expansion to include a multitude of political actors whose appeals to the people are ideologically incompatible, because their "peoples" have nothing in common, apart from being opposed to the same establishment'. For Tarragoni, 'this common opposition hardly gives them a common political identity'.

1.4 Towards a general theory of populism

Jan-Werner Müller (2016: 2) begins his book *What Is Populism?* arguing that 'we simply do not have anything like a *theory* of populism, and we seem to lack coherent criteria for deciding when political actors turn populist in some meaningful sense'. This statement, which is still partially valid in 2022, addresses the challenges of dealing with populism when the academic community does not dispose of a theory to explain and predict the emergence and development of populism within the political field.

In a brief article entitled 'On Populism, Planets, and Why Concepts Should Precede Definitions and Theory-Seeking', Pappas (2019b) discusses how a comprehensive theory of populism would look like. Such a theory would allow scholars predict the context for the emergence of populism. For Pappas, such an enterprise should include the following levels (Figure 1).

For Pappas, the first step to achieve a theory of populism is to agree on a *minimal definition* of what populism is. This is an issue that has been problematic within scholarship on populism since its origins, as discussed in the following chapter. Even if a general consensus between scholars regarding how to define populism – and, in particular, regarding the genus of this political phenomenon – has not been achieved,

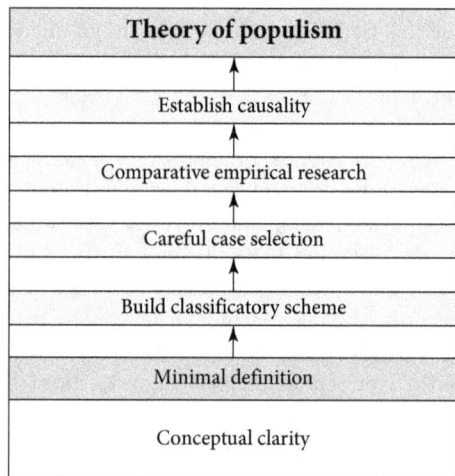

Figure 1 Towards a theory of populism. Source: Own elaboration based on Pappas (2019b: 20). The level of 'conceptual clarity' was added to Pappas's proposal by the author.

scholars have nevertheless been successful in formulating a minimal definition. This definition has allowed them to measure populism in an empirical and comparative manner, a task that is central for comparative political scientists. As a second step, it is necessary to establish *a criterion to distinguish populist from non-populist parties and actors*. What concepts are the opposites of populism? Mudde (2004), Müller (2016) and Schoor (2021) argue that populism's opposite concepts are *elitism* and *pluralism*. Therefore, populist political actors and parties are by default *antielitist* and *antipluralist*. For Schoor (2021), elitism and pluralism are populism's opposite concepts, but the three of them share a core structure. As a third step towards a theory of populism, Pappas argues that researchers must *select empirical cases* so that, in a fourth step, they can conduct a *systematic comparative study* of them.

As of the fourth level, methodology plays a crucial role. How should populism be empirically measured? A good example of how to implement that fourth step can be found in a research article by Akkerman, Mudde and Zaslove (2014: 1331), where they use the following indicators to measure populist (POP), pluralist (PLU) and elitist (E) attitudes in the Dutch electorate:

POP1 The politicians in the Dutch parliament need to follow the will of the people.
POP2 The people, and not politicians, should make our most important policy decisions.
POP3 The political differences between the elite and the people are larger than the differences among the people.
POP4 I would rather be represented by a citizen than by a specialized politician.
POP5 Elected officials talk too much and take too little action.
POP6 Politics is ultimately a struggle between good and evil.
POP7 What people call 'compromise' in politics is really just selling out on one's principles.
POP8 Interest groups have too much influence over political decisions.
PLU1 In a democracy it is important to make compromises among differing viewpoints.
PLU2 It is important to listen to the opinion of other groups.
PLU3 Diversity limits my freedom.
E1 Politicians should lead rather than follow the people.
E2 Our country would be governed better if important decisions were left up to successful business people.
E3 Our country would be governed better if important decisions were left up to independent experts.

It goes without saying that these questions measure populism, pluralism and elitism as conceptualized and defined by the authors of the study. Therefore, the results of empirical studies like this one will depend on how those concepts are defined and which indicators are chosen to measure them. For example: Is the POP5 indicator actually a good one to detect populism when surveying citizens?

Pappas (2019b: 20) believes that once that the empirical analyses have been conducted, 'causal patterns will emerge that are common among the cases, which may then lead to interesting propositions, which, after been tested, may give rise to a sound theoretical framework addressing the major questions in the study of populism'. It is, therefore, based on empirical work driven by a clear and precise concept that a theory of populism can emerge. Therefore, any study of populism cannot avoid combining a conceptual and an empirical approach to make sense of this political phenomenon.

1.5 About this book

Pappas (2019b: 20) argues that 'no definition of modern populism is possible without a clear conceptualization of this phenomenon in its various interactions with contemporary political reality'. Therefore, the 'scientific road' towards a theory of populism includes another level that underlies the minimal definition and that defines whatever is done afterwards: the *conceptual level*, as represented in Figure 1. There cannot be a minimal definition of populism useful for empirical purposes if scholars do not agree on what type of phenomenon populism is and which its defining features are. It is in this conceptual level that a majority of the discursive approaches to populism have intervened.

This book is not an exception to this, although it also includes a number of case studies (in Chapters 6, 7 and 8) to anchor the theoretical digressions into real discourses and performances by political actors labelled as 'populist'. The book's main objective is *to shed new light on the challenging phenomenon of populism by examining how meaning-making occurs in populist political actors' discourses and performances*. In light of that objective, it seeks to extend the interdisciplinary dialogue between political theory, comparative political science and Semiotics, together with other research fields interested in language and meaning. Although this dialogue already exists, it is still not as systemic and as fluid as it should be in an era of mediatized, personalized and networked politics (Cosenza, 2018) to fully grasp the discursive dimension inherent to any social phenomenon based on intersubjectivity. The thesis presented in the book is the result of such an interdisciplinary dialogue.

In this book, populism is dealt with as a concept created and used by scholars through the inclusion of disparate political events, discourses and performances that are regarded as sharing some common features. Therefore, the word 'populism' serves to refer to an abstraction that was inductively created based on real and actual political events, discourses and performances (cf. Canovan, 1981). This premise is aligned with Umberto Eco's (1968) idea of an *absent structure* that can be postulated methodologically – not ontologically – to make sense of sociocultural events as being shaped with the same mould. The assumption is, therefore, that all populist movements, parties and actors share *something* that motivates analysts to identify them as occurrences of the concept of populism. *The thesis of this book is that it is the identification in empirical case studies of the presence of that shared absent structure what justifies to legitimately label political actors, movements and parties as 'populist'*. That 'absent structure' must be present for a political movement, actor or party – actual or historic – to be legitimately populist.

This book argues that that *something* is a discursive articulation in the form of a specific narrative structure in which the collective identity 'the people' is discursively constructed through the opposition to an 'other' with whom they coexist within the social space in a relationship of antagonism, that is, that 'other' is *an enemy*. Even if it is true that populism occurs within the political field, that it is strategically used to produce specific political effects such as mobilizing the masses and that it tends to revolve around personalistic and charismatic leaders that usually challenge the political system and politics as usual, the thesis of this book is that what defines populism and makes of it a *distinct* political phenomenon is the presence of a specific narrative structure: the *Populist Narrative Structure*.

Conceiving of populism as a discursive practice that is enacted and brought to life by political actors in diverse political contexts, the thesis of this book is that *populism is better understood when conceived as the discursive practice of producing meaning by using the Populist Narrative Structure. This structure is used to frame political contents in narrative terms by embracing a conception of the social space as divided into two groups: 'the people' and 'the people's other'*. These two empty categories – to be found in the 'deep' level of the semio-narrative structures (Greimas, 1966; 1970) – take different figurative and discursive forms depending on the specific contents that are relevant in a given political context. Therefore, they are 'empty positions' that are filled with specific content through discursive practices, performances and procedures that can only be properly grasped when theorized from a semiotic perspective, that is, by looking at meaning-making and signification.

According to this conception, populism is a phenomenon that occurs within the political field and that is evidenced in the discourses and performances of political actors in which meaning-making is grounded in the use of the Populist Narrative Structure. Hence, populism needs to be identified empirically through a scrutiny of discourses and performances, and it is an analytical construction created and used by researchers – and also by the media, political actors and the people in general – to make sense of something that occurs within the political field and that implies a series of commonalities between different events.

The conception of populism as a discursive practice should also not forget to examine another discursive practice: that of using the term 'populism' to make sense of disparate events within the political domain. As an analytical construction, populism is a category based on a segmentation of events that is mediated by language. It is here where many of the challenges linked to the concept of populism emerge: particularly over the last two decades, the concept has been used to make sense of phenomena within the political domain of societies around the world that still do (or did) not have a name, such as the use of social media to generate the illusion of a closeness between the political leaders and their audiences, or the use of manners and forms of communication that are not standard in the political domain.

Besides the challenges linked to the pragmatics of the term 'populism' – that is, how it is used – its semantics do not help: *populism* refers to a unit of meaning that is linguistically – and hence culturally – segmented and determined, that does not have a reference in the world outside discourse – such as the reference of the word 'unicorn' does not exist outside discourse – and whose meaning varies depending on the context in which the term is used. This analytical abstraction that groups disparate political phenomena has a *discursive nature*: this book poses that *the word 'populism' denotes a specific discursive practice – understood in a broad sense as an articulation of semiotic modes of meaning-making and not only as linguistic utterances – that is enacted by political actors – both individual and collective – in various contexts as a strategy to achieve specific effects of sense in their respective electorates*. It is precisely in those acts of bringing the 'populist absent structure' to life by filling it with specific contents that populism gains its complexity and diversity. It is also the same logic that explains why one could agree with the existence of populism in ancient Greece, even if it is normally theorized as a modern or contemporary phenomenon.

The conception of populism embraced in this book as a discursive practice certainly emerges from the three founding historical occurrences of populism: the US People Party, the *narodniki* movement and the Latin American governments from the first half of the twentieth century. These three original occurrences of populism were left-wing, socially inclusive and had a clear anti-elite component (Tarragoni, 2021). As time passed, the narrative structure that was in the base of the ideological articulations of political actors from those movements in their attempts to include the marginalized sections of society – peasants, farmers, working classes – was used in combination with other type of political contents, giving place to right-wing populism as a political phenomenon that can also be described with the term 'populism'. Another of the theses presented in this book is that, *if right-wing and left-wing populism can be conceived as manifestations of the same political phenomenon – that is why they are referred to as 'populisms' – it is because they share the presence of the Populist Narrative Structure*. The contingent emancipation of the Populist Narrative Structure from the historical manifestations of populism implies that the discursive core of what sociologists and political scientists regard as a political ideology was decontextualized and used to make sense of new political events and situations. As is argued here, that discursive core shared by populist movements, actors and parties on the right and on the left is the Populist Narrative Structure.

By examining various dimensions of populism and discussing examples from Europe, the United States and South America, the book is conceived of as a systematic approach to the multifaceted phenomenon of populism from a semiotic perspective with the aim of building bridges between disciplines, traditions of scholarship and geographical latitudes.

Chapter 2 introduces the research field of populism studies. It maps the existing accounts on populism and argues why a semiotic perspective could help make those accounts compatible: if populism is conceived of as the discursive practice of using an empty narrative structure that political actors must fill with specific context-dependent political contents, then the ideological, discursive, strategic and performative dimensions are all constitutive of this political phenomenon. In the chapter, particular attention is given to the *discursive* or *ideational* accounts of populism since these constitute the solid ground where the conceptualization presented in this book will stand.

Chapter 3 introduces Semiotics as a discipline – or research field – with a specific focus on *social* Semiotics, that is, the branch of general Semiotics that studies 'meaning in action'. Due to the dynamic and open nature of meaning- and sense-making within the political field, social Semiotics is in a privileged position to shed light on it. The chapter also discusses what a semiotic approach will pay attention to when studying populism. The concepts presented in this chapter constitute the methodological framework for the analytical work conducted in the following chapters.

Chapter 4 focuses on the political field. By bridging political theory and Semiotics, it demonstrates how social Semiotics can shed light in the attempts to grasp the specific dynamics of the political field. The chapter takes Ernesto Laclau and Chantal Mouffe's discourse theory as its departure point because it is the standard theory when studying populism – and, more generally, the political domain – from a discursive perspective. Since Laclau and Mouffe's discourse theory is filled with semiotic insights, the chapter bridges their theory with Eliseo Verón's theory of social discourses and with the work of other semioticians that studied the political field. Besides the interdisciplinary discussion, the chapter argues how identity is a key variable when dealing with populism, formulates a hypothesis regarding the formation of collective identities in political discourse and discusses how politics could be conceived as a 'contest' over the fixation of meaning.

Chapter 5 presents the Populist Narrative Structure as the 'absent structure' shared by texts and products of populist politicians, movements and parties. By drawing on the work of Laclau, Mouffe and their followers – the standard scholarship when approaching populism from a discursive perspective – the chapter analyses the structure of the Populist Narrative Structure through the examination of its defining features: the discursive construction of the collective identity 'the people' through an opposition with an 'other' with whom it coexists in an antagonistic relationship. The chapter demonstrates how the semiotic account of populism is already present in existing scholarship.

Chapters 6, 7 and 8 revolve around case studies with the aim of illustrating the theoretical argument presented in the previous chapters. Chapter 6 focuses on populist leaders as a crucial – albeit not necessary – figure in bringing the Populist Narrative Structure to life in their discourses and performances. The cases of Donald Trump (United States), Matteo Salvini (Italy) and Hugo Chávez (Venezuela) are studied for this purpose.

Chapter 7 focuses on right-wing populism, that is, the result of combining the Populist Narrative Structure with right-wing political contents. The cases of Marine Le Pen (France) and Donald Trump (United States) are used to illustrate the theoretical argument. The chapter also discusses the case of Jair Bolsonaro (Brazil) to show how populism can be used to make sense of political phenomena that are not necessarily populist in the sense put forward in this book.

Finally, Chapter 8 focuses on left-wing populism. The paradigmatic case of Podemos (Spain) is used to illustrate the combination of the Populist Narrative Structure with left-wing political contents. Moreover, the chapter discusses the challenges of distinguishing between populist and popular politics in South America. It also focuses on Bernie Sanders (United States) as an interesting case of left-wing politics in the United States, usually labelled as 'populist'.

In our study of populism, some discussions that are central in the field of populism studies are deliberately left aside. In the first place, sociological, economic and structural approaches are not discussed. The conditions of emergence of populism constitute a topic of utmost interest for researchers committed to achieving Pappas's final step of a theory of populism. They will not be addressed here because they fall beyond the scope of Semiotics. Many causal hypotheses have been put forward over the last five decades to explain how, why and when populism can be expected to emerge. To fill this void, the following working hypothesis taken from Panizza (2005: 9) will be assumed:

> populist practices emerge out of the failure of existing social and political institutions to confine and regulate political subjects into a relatively stable social order. It is the language of politics when there can be no politics as usual: a mode of identification characteristic of times of unsettlement and de-alignment, involving the radical redrawing of social borders along lines other than those that had previously structured society. It is a political appeal that seeks to change the terms of political discourse, articulate new social relations, redefine political frontiers and constitute new identities.

Panizza's argument is in line with that of Eric Landowski, one of the most active semioticians of our current time. According to Landowski (2018; 2020), populism reveals a crisis of confidence [*crise fiduciaire*] between the electorate and their political representatives. Also Wiles's (1969: 167) statement about populism arising 'precisely when a large group, becoming self-conscious, feels alienated from the centres of power' is valid to point out this aspect of a *feeling of exclusion* that certain social actors might experience in a given context. This feeling can make populist discourse look like a possible solution.

A second aspect left aside in this book concerns populists in power and the policies they implement. Although this is an issue of utmost relevance for political scientists, it is not so relevant for semioticians. This is the case because the discursive dimension of policy tends to be less interesting than that of the strategies that political actors use in the 'contest over meaning' that is the political activity. In any case, the conclusions of this book should also be capable of explaining what populists do once they have been elected and taken office. Particularly, they should be able to explain how they frame those policies in discursive terms.

Finally, also normative discussions regarding the threat that populism poses to democracy or, by contrast, its function in strengthening democracy are left aside. Even if Semiotics has an alleged transformative and critical aim (Bitonte, 2008; Demaria, 2019; Landowski, 2019), its way of proceeding is primarily and above all descriptive, empirical and theory-driven. Normative debates fall beyond its scope. Without further ado, then, let us proceed to the study of the phenomenon of populism from a semiotic perspective.

2

What Is Populism?

The previous chapter introduced in a broad manner the phenomenon of populism. This chapter approaches populism from an academic perspective and discusses how populism has been conceptualized by researchers since the 1970s. After discussing the challenges of defining concepts in the social sciences and by listing some of the specific challenges linked to the definition of populism, it presents three of the main accounts on populism: the ideological, the discourse-theoretical and the performative. These are the most relevant for a social Semiotics of populism. Finally, the chapter argues how these accounts are compatible from a semiotic perspective and highlights the core features of populist discourse.

2.1 Conceptual definitions in the social sciences and humanities

Before approaching any type of phenomenon – be it natural, social, discursive and so on, if distinctions like this still make sense – from a scientific perspective, a previous and necessary step consists in defining in a precise and univocal manner the concepts that will be employed. As an example, when studying the process of 'democratic erosion' or 'democratic backsliding', a clear definition of what these labels refer to is needed (Moreno Barreneche, 2020a): What are the defining features of this process of political change? How can researchers identify a case of democratic erosion or backsliding? Which indicators serve to measure it empirically?

Precise and univocal concepts are a necessary step in research because 'reality' – that is, the facts that a researcher is interested in studying with objectivity – will be apprehended, modelled and dealt with through the mediation of those concepts. Language mediates the relationship between 'reality' – natural, social, discursive and so on – and the researchers' cognitive apparatus. Concepts are the building blocks of the theoretical building that science tries to construct (Goertz, 2006). Depending on how a researcher defines what they understand by a term, the conclusions that can be extracted.

In the case of populism, the various and disparate events from numerous political contexts around the world and historical moments that researchers might identify as being occurrences of populism will certainly depend on what the academic community understands under the term 'populism'. As argued in the previous chapter, 'populism' is a term that refers to a concept used to refer to an 'absent structure' that is present in multiple political manifestations and contexts.

As a term, the word 'populism' can be found in dictionaries. The definitions presented there will be the concept the term refers to. Based on this definition, the English term 'populism' can be translated as *populismo* in Spanish and *Populismus* in German. What does this eight-letter noun mean? To what type of phenomenon does it refer to? Which traits need a political phenomenon evidence to be a manifestation of the concept of populism? How can researchers identify populism in the world? What do populisms around the world and across history have in common? Do they have anything in common at all? Questions like these are fundamental when studying populism. They constitute the first step in researching the subject.

The research area of 'populism studies' is an informal federation of disciplines interested in the same phenomenon, as is the case with 'memory studies' or 'gender studies'. Although researchers have engaged in discussing the concept of populism for decades, only recently a sort of consensus seems to have been achieved regarding what is defining of this political phenomenon. Defining populism is challenging because the noun *populism* and the adjective *populist* have been usually used not only to make sense of disparate and heterogeneous political phenomena and events from various political contexts but also with a normative load. The specific case of populism does not differ from other concepts in the social sciences such as democracy, ideology and nationalism, whose conceptual definitions have been a matter of discussion and contestation over decades.

Concepts are linguistic abstractions that have an impact on cognition. They are normally formulated inductively based on the scrutiny of a set of events from 'the real world'. After being analysed and compared, the properties that are identified as shared by those events will constitute the definitional core of the concept. In this process, what is in play is *a relationship of the particular with the universal*, an idea that is to be found already in ancient philosophy – for example, in Plato – and that has also been of utmost relevance for semioticians, who have studied with interest the distinction between *type* and *token* (Eco, 1976).

Once a concept has been created based on induction, it is normally used to make sense of new events based on the identification of a similarity of its traits with the ones that constitute the core of the concept. If the concept of *democratic erosion* is defined as the process of weakening of democratic institutions over time towards authoritarianism, whenever a political event E in a political context C presents these 'symptoms', researchers will most probably tend to identify what is happening as an occurrence of *democratic erosion* and read that particular event through the lens of this concept.

Conceptual clarification has always been a common challenge for social scientists because empirical work depends on the operationalization of concepts, that is, on their 'translation' into indicators that allow identifying them in the world. At the beginning of the twenty-first century, political scientists and sociologists are challenged by new forms of political participation that were inexistent when the standard concept of *political participation* was created to make sense of what people do in the political arena. Currently, online political participation challenges that concept. Hence, the concept had to be reviewed and discussions started among scholars regarding what type of online actions can be considered modes of political participation (Theocharis, 2015; Van Deth, 2004).

The challenges of conceptual definitions attracted the attention of social scientists such as Giovanni Sartori (1970; 1984), David Collier (Collier & Mahon, 1993; Collier & Gerring, 2009), Gary Goertz (2006) and John Gerring (2012). These scholars made significant efforts to help social and political scientists develop solid conceptual definitions before proceeding with the empirical work. In a well-known article dealing with the role of concepts in comparative politics, Sartori (1970: 1040) argues that 'things conceived or meaningfully perceived, i.e., concepts, are the central elements of propositions, and – depending on how they are named – provide in and by themselves guidelines of interpretation and observation'. As the researchers' grasping of the social reality is inescapably mediated by language, the labels they use to build their theories depend on how reality is segmented and made sense of in conceptual terms. Sartori (1970: 1035) was also aware of the dangers of *concept stretching*, a common practice in the history of political science in which 'our gains in extensional coverage tend to be matched by losses in connotative precision'. When including forms of online political participation into the concept of political participation, stretching is taking place.

Within the social sciences, and in particular within political theory, Sartori's work has been the starting point for further reflections regarding defining concepts. Collier and Mahon (1993: 845) picked up Sartori's work on conceptual travelling and stretching and argued that 'stable concepts and a shared understanding of categories are routinely viewed as a foundation of any research community'. For his part, in a book where he argues that theory should always guide methodology, Gary Goertz (2006: 1–2) identifies Sartori and Collier as the 'dominating figures in the work on concepts' and argues that a concept 'involves a theoretical and empirical analysis of the object or phenomenon referred to by the world' (Goertz, 2006: 4).

More recently, John Gerring (2012: 113) argued that social scientists 'make lexical and semantic choices as they write and thus participate, wittingly or unwittingly, in an ongoing interpretative debate' as a result of science being dependent on language, which always plays a mediating role in how researchers grasp reality. The author also points out the challenges of the tendency within the social sciences of concepts being 'variously employed in different fields and subfields, within different intellectual traditions, among different writers, and sometimes – most alarmingly – within a single work' (Gerring, 2012: 113). He proposes three strategies of concept formation – minimal, maximal and cumulative – which are usually addressed by social scientists dealing with conceptual definitions (Gerring, 2012: 134–8).

The role of concepts is crucial in doing social theory and research, especially when embracing a constructivist premise, that is, one that assumes that the social world is partially constructed by researchers through the concepts they employ. When looking at concepts, researchers deal with semantics, that is, with meaning within language. Why did researchers feel at some point the need to create and/or employ a new concept such as *populism* to refer to political phenomena? What specific events are covered by that concept? Which are the core traits that need to be found in a specific political event or situation to be considered as an occurrence of the concept? How has the concept of populism been 'stretched' over the past decades to encompass new phenomena? These questions are related to how scientists – and other social actors – perceive, grasp and make sense of reality. This is a process in which linguistic – and, with it, conceptual – mediation is inescapable.

2.2 The challenge of defining populism

Although the question 'What is populism?' is straightforward and easy to grasp linguistically, the task of answering it does not share these features. As argued, this complexity is not exclusive of the concept of populism: myriad other concepts pose similar challenges. Nevertheless, the concept of *populism* presents some traits that make it particularly difficult to deal with. To begin with, the noun ends with the suffix *–ism*. This is a morphological mechanism that languages have to create new words drawing on the meaning of already existing words. *Marxism* and *liberalism* constitute good examples of this lexical mechanism: the former originates in the proper name *Marx*, which refers to a specific individual with a real historical existence, and the latter on the adjective *liberal*, which is derived from the noun *liberty*. Although it might be difficult to define what *Marxism* and *liberalism* are, at least the departure point for the conceptual analysis seems to be clear.

The noun *populism* is another example of the mechanism of 'yoking the suffix "-ism" to certain key concepts with the intention to signify a distinct pattern of thinking', as Ben Stanley (2008: 100) argues. However, contrasting with the cases of *Marxism* and *liberalism*, the word it uses as its base is not any longer in use in English: the base *popul-* originates in the Latin word *populus*, a word that is not used in the vast majority of languages that have in their lexical repertoire a word to refer to the concept of *populism*. In spite of this challenge, the root of the concept of populism in the Latin word *populus* gives some hints regarding the phenomenon being examined: it is grounded on that entity that the Romans referred to as *populus*, a lexical unit usually translated as *the people* in English; *das Volk* in German; *el pueblo* in Spanish; *le peuple* in French; *il popolo* in Italian and *o povo* in Portuguese, just to list a few examples.[1] In all these languages, different meanings coexist linked to these words: in Spanish, for example, 'the people' can be translated both as *el pueblo* and *la gente*.

In all the Romanic languages listed earlier – as well as in English – the persistence of Latin can be identified in the words that are currently used to refer to what the Romans called *populus*. To begin with, they all begin with the letter *p* followed by a vowel. Etymology helps in trying to set some boundaries to the extension of what the concept of populism might be about: a (political) movement – an *-ism* (Kurunmäli & Marjanen, 2018) – related to that what is denoted by the noun *populus*, whatever that might mean nowadays. As is evident, despite being a good start, this lexical analysis is not enough to clarify our contested concept.

Another challenge of defining populism is grounded in the cacophony around the concept, that is, the multiple uses it has been subject of during the last decades. This is the case because not only scholars and political scientists deal with populism: journalists, politicians and citizens also use the term to make sense of the political field. As discussed in the previous chapter, the noun *populism* and the adjective *populist* have been used in ordinary language pejoratively (Stavrakakis, 2017) to refer to political attitudes and events regarded as anti-democratic, a feature that might not be 'populist' in the sense of the term dominant in the social sciences. The research line that has dealt with populism as a threat to democracy has not been helpful in separating the wheat from the chaff.

The definition of *populism* as a concept has been a common challenge since the term started being used by scholars in a systematic manner (the symposium at the London School of Economics probably is the beginning of that). As Abts and Rummens (2007: 407) argued in 2007, 'the conceptualization of populism is a matter of confusion in contemporary political analysis'. These challenges and confusions are already present in Ionescu and Gellner's book from 1969. In the introduction, the authors write that the aim of the conference that gave place to the book was to conduct 'an assessment of whether populism is a unitary concept, regardless of the variety of its incarnations, or whether it is simply a word wrongly used in completely heterogeneous contexts' (Ionescu & Gellner, 1969: 3).

This hypothesis – unfortunate for academic research – seems to be frequent in the uses of the concept in everyday life: *populism* and *populist* are often used as synonyms for *demagoguery* and *demagogue*. In 2005, Benjamín Arditi (2005: 75) argued that 'the conceptual contours of the term [*populism*] remain fuzzy, and its theoretically contested status unabated'. As a result, 'any precise description [of *populism*] faces a real and perhaps insurmountable limit'. For Pappas (2019a: 31), 'the failure to agree on a common understanding of modern populism is related to our mixing up, and studying together, different kinds of populism, which in turn has caused several methodological pitfalls'.

In spite of these challenges, it is not impossible to deal with populism from a conceptual point of view. As Worsley (1969: 219) argues, 'since the word *has* been used, the existence of verbal smoke might well indicate a fire somewhere'. Stanley (2008: 95), for his part, argues that 'in spite of its reputation for persistently escaping the nets of theory, populism is a distinct concept'. To this claim he adds that 'the term "populism" has a history of usage in political discourse and although the meaning of the term has proven controversial in the literature, the persistence with which it has recurred suggests the existence at least of an ineliminable core: that is, that it refers to a distinct pattern of ideas' (Stanley, 2008: 100). It is precisely to this 'distinct pattern of ideas' that the suffix *-ism* refers to.

The challenges posed by the concept of populism are linked to its irruption into the social sciences. During the twentieth century, it was used to refer to political events from different countries, such as a farmers' movement in the United States, the *narodniki* in Russia and Latin American politics for the masses. According to Ionescu and Gellner (1969), the flexible translatability of the Russian concept *narodni* as *the people* in English led to the term 'populism' becoming a concept useful to make sense of these disparate political events as sharing a number of features.

Kenneth Minogue (1969: 197) argued that the US farmers' movement and the Russian *narodniki* were 'two brief historical episodes in Russia and America' that 'presented themselves as movements against established power by or on behalf of little men living on the land; and both placed great emphasis upon the "people" as the oppressed agents of future changes'. However, he believed that these were 'radically different experiences', although they share a name as the result of the Russian word *narodnik* being translated into English as *populist*. According to Minogue (1969: 197), besides the designation, these two historical moments shared 'one or two suggestive analogies on which an edifice of theory might be constructed'. Successively, researchers identified new political events as being further occurrences of populism, a concept constructed by establishing an analogy between two concrete historical episodes. As Minogue (1969: 197) points out, 'what has followed parallels the wine industry: new products have crowded in under the established name'.

To sum up: as a concept pertaining to the social sciences, *populism* has been subject of a number of theoretical challenges, particularly in terms of its definition. To begin with, it is not clear what the lexical base *popul-* refers to: can it be translated simply as *the people*? How to explain the multiple possible meanings of *the people* in languages such as Spanish, where the word *pueblo* [the people] has multiple meanings (*pueblo* as the *demos* of democracy; *pueblo* as the popular classes, *pueblo* as a nation, etc.)? Moreover, there has been a cacophonic use of the concept by various social actors, normally to refer to different types of phenomena (e.g. as a synonym of *demagoguery*) and, usually, with a pejorative normative load. Finally, populism studies have dealt with the concept from multiple theoretical perspectives, descriptive and normative, condemning and celebratory, what has not been helpful in coming up with a precise, clear and uncontested definition of what populism is.

2.3 Accounts on populism

In light of the challenges presented in the previous sections, scholarship on populism has witnessed throughout history the emergence of various accounts on what populism is. All these accounts have *competed* over the years within populism studies to establish a hegemonic definition. That competition is characterized by the fact that the multiple existing definitions are usually product of different research traditions and disciplines. This might explain the apparent incompatibilities between the different existing accounts. This section presents those accounts with the aim of mapping the research field of populism studies.

When mapping existing definitions of populism, analysts usually pay attention to the *genus* ascribed to populism. In 1977, Laclau argued that one could 'single out four basic approaches to an interpretation of populism', three of which consider it 'simultaneously as a movement and as an ideology', and a fourth that 'reduces it to a purely ideological phenomenon' (Laclau, 1977: 144). In 2005, Francisco Panizza (2005: 2–3) listed three accounts of populism that go in a different direction: empiricist approaches, historicist approaches and symptomatic readings. The following three subsections examine some

2.3.1 Populism as an ideology

Cas Mudde (2017: 46–7) proposes that although the concept of populism 'has been defined in many different ways, the ideational approach has almost always been at least part of the study of populism'. The author claims that 'a majority of scholars of European populism employ explicitly or implicitly ideational definitions' and mentions the works of Abts and Rummens (2007) and Stanley (2008), among others, as examples of this approach to what populism is. The researchers listed by Mudde are indeed those that constitute the 'canon' of the account of populism as an ideology. For Mudde (2017: 47), 'though it is still far too early to speak of an emerging consensus, it is undoubtedly fair to say that the ideational approach to populism is the most broadly used in the field today', even by scholars who do not explicitly declare that their conception of populism is related to ideas and ideology.

We will come back to the idea of an 'ideational approach' to populism in the last section of this chapter. For the moment, we could agree with Mudde's proposal: the conception of populism as an ideology – which emerged within research in comparative political science – is quite extended nowadays, at least within comparative political science. Proof of this – to mention an example – is that Oxford University Press' 'Very Short Introductions' volume on populism – authored by Mudde and Rovira Kaltwasser (2017) – defines populism as an ideology. However, this seems to be limited to the domain of political science and is not the case in other disciplines, such as discourse theory and communication science, which also deal with populism and prefer other type of conceptualizations (see 2.3.2).

The conception of populism as an ideology can be found already in Ionescu and Gellner's book from 1969. In the chapter entitled 'Populism as an Ideology', Donald MacRae (1969) argued that populism is an 'a-political ideology'. According to Mudde (2017: 48), this was probably the first definition of populism as an ideology. In his 1977 essay on populism, Laclau (1977: 147) also identifies a conception of populism as ideology, whose typical features would be 'hostility to the status quo, mistrust of traditional politicians, appeal to the people and not to classes, anti-intellectualism, and so on'. As Laclau points out, for those who subscribe to the ideological account of populism, this particular articulation of ideas can be 'adopted by social movements with different bases, according to concrete historical conditions about which it is impossible to formulate any a priori generalization' (Laclau, 1977: 147). In 2002, Canovan argued that populism is an ideology in the sense of the term proposed by Michael Freeden, that is, as 'a conceptual map of the political world' which prioritizes some core concepts over others (Canovan, 2002: 30–3). According to Canovan, those central concepts are 'the people', 'democracy', 'sovereignty' and the 'majority rule'. More recently, Tarragoni (2021: 7) argued that populism is 'a political ideology that appears in contexts of democratic crisis and that mobilizes a socially heterogeneous plebe against a ruling elite accused of robbing democracy'.

In an article from 2004, Mudde introduced his definition as a way of overcoming the intuitive interpretations of populism that according to him were dominant at the time: one that regarded populism as 'a highly emotional and simplistic discourse that is directed at the "gut feelings" of the people' and another that conceived of it as a type of 'opportunistic policies with the aim of (quickly) pleasing the people/voters' (Mudde, 2004: 542). According to Mudde, these interpretations are better covered by the concepts of *demagogy* and *opportunism*, respectively, and do not 'go to the core of what is generally considered as populism' (Mudde, 2004: 543). Mudde's aim in the article was to overcome these widespread interpretations and to present a new definition that could reflect the dominant interpretations within the academic community.

For Mudde (2004: 543), 'most definitions of populism have at least two points of reference in common: 'the elite' and "the people"'. Populism would be something related to the *relationship* between these two social groups. As we will see later on, this will be the common feature that almost all the existing accounts on populism share. However, accepting this does not contribute to clarify what type of *thing* populism is. To solve this deficit, Mudde (2004: 543) proposes that populism is 'an ideology that considers society to be ultimately separated into two homogeneous and antagonistic groups, "the pure people" versus "the corrupt elite", and which argues that politics should be an expression of the *volonté générale* (general will) of the people'. When defined in this fashion, populism opposes to elitism and pluralism: to the former, because it privileges the interests of 'the people' over those of 'the elites'; to the latter, because it proposes that only one voice should be present in taking care of political issues: that of 'the people'.

However, Mudde acknowledges that populism is not a *full-fledged* ideology, such as liberalism, socialism and conservatism are. Krastev (2007: 2) shares that opinion: he believes that populism is 'too eclectic to be an ideology in the way that liberalism, socialism, or conservatism are'. Drawing from the work of Michael Freeden (1996) on the concept of ideology, Mudde argues that populism is a *thin-centred ideology*. In Freeden's account, thin-centred ideologies exhibit 'a restricted core attached to a narrower range of political concepts' and can be easily combined with other ideologies (Mudde, 2004: 544). In the case of populism, the core would be 'the people'. This is a proposal that makes sense given the roots of this core concept in the Latin *populus*. According to this account, populism would then be the (thin-centred) ideology that puts 'the people' at the centre of the political domain.

Mudde (2004: 544) also argues that populism is 'moralistic rather than programmatic'. As such, it is not only highly normative – it believes that the source of legitimacy in politics is the general will of 'the people' – but also holds a Manichean outlook that simplifies reality into *friends* and *foes*. Moreover, Mudde acknowledges a feature of 'the people' that is crucial when dealing with populism from a semiotic perspective: 'the people in the populist propaganda are neither real nor all-inclusive, but are in fact a mythical and constructed sub-set of the whole population' (Mudde, 2004: 546). This statement will be discussed in Chapters 4 and 5.

In defining populism as in ideology, Mudde focuses on the *content* of populism. However, in the conclusion of the article he writes that 'populist *discourse* has become mainstream in the politics of contemporary western democracies' (Mudde, 2004: 562, my emphasis). Is populism an ideology or is it a discourse? What is the relationship between ideology and discourse? What is the point in making an effort to justify that populism is an ideology if then ideology and discourse will be used as interchangeable concepts? Do discourses express ideologies? Are ideologies constructed in discourse? Are ideologies other than discourses? What would be the point of defining populism as an ideology if its material manifestation occurs in the form of discourse? As is argued next, Semiotics has some insights to answer these challenges.

Further on the account of populism as an ideology, in an article in which they theorize the relationship of populism with democracy, Abts and Rummens (2007: 408) argue that populism 'provides a thin-centered ideology concerning the structure of power in society' and not 'a comprehensive vision of society'. The authors list the following as its defining features: (1) 'a central antagonistic relationship between "the people" and "the elite"'; (2) an attempt to 'give power back to the people and restore popular sovereignty' and (3) a conceptualization of 'the people' as 'a homogeneous unity' (Abts & Rummens, 2007: 408). Also Stanley (2008) sees in populism a thin-centred ideology and points out that it 'should be regarded as a distinct ideology in that it conveys a particular way of constructing the political in the specific interaction of its core concepts' (Stanley, 2008: 95). For Stanley (2008: 102), populism is 'an ideology dedicated to identifying the people as the privileged subject of politics and justifying their place on this pedestal'. The author lists four core components of the thin-ideology of populism: (1) 'the existence of two homogeneous units of analysis: "the people" and "the elite"'; (2) 'the antagonistic relationship between the people and the elite'; (3) 'the idea of popular sovereignty' and (4) the positive valorization of 'the people' and denigration of 'the elite'.

When arguing for the morphological account of ideology, Stanley (2008: 100) writes that the conceptual core of any ideology is 'a product of the empirical practices of political actors' and that 'establishing the core concepts of a particular ideology requires empirical observation of what its exponents have thought and said'. The link between discourse – as the product of enunciation – and ideology once again seems central. This is evident when the author argues that 'to Laclau's formal logic I counterpose a concept of populism as an ideology articulated by political agents in the attempt to mobilise "the people"' (Stanley, 2008: 98). He also claims that 'ideologies, as logically and culturally elaborated frameworks of interpretations, provide compelling, convincing and heuristically useful organizations of interpretative possibilities' (Stanley, 2008: 99).

When scrutinizing these accounts, a question arises: what is the difference between ideology and discourse when ideology is conceived following Freeden's semantic or morphological account? Why have these political scientists insisted in distinguishing discourse from ideology when these two concepts refer to articulations of ideas that occur *in discourse*? The confusion seems to reflect a problem linked to the travelling of concepts between disciplines: if for discourse-theoretical scholars, such as Laclau and Mouffe, discourse is not restricted to linguistic utterances only, comparative political scientists seem to have more trouble in accepting that the concept of discourse can also include practices and other non-linguistic phenomena. For Semiotics – as well as for other 'sciences of language', such as Critical Discourse

Analysis – the concept of *discourse* covers a broad spectrum of meaning-making phenomena that normally have an ideological component (cf. Hodge & Kress, 1993; Verschueren, 2012).

On the conceptualization of populism as an ideology, Paris Asladinis (2016) argues that grounding the definition of a contested concept like *populism* in another contested concept like *ideology* is not a safe move. This is the case because the concept of *ideology* has also posed challenges to social scientists for decades (Knight, 2006). However, the 'sciences of language' – and, among them, Semiotics – have shown that ideology and discourse are two sides of the same coin: ideologies can only be expressed as discourse and discourse is always ideological (Eco, 1976; Bianchi, 2016; Escudero Chauvel, 2016). Hence, what Canovan, Mudde, Abts and Rummens, Stanley and others have defined as *ideology* might in fact be *discourse* understood not as mere linguistic utterances but in a broad sense (as discussed in Chapters 3 and 4).

2.3.2 Populism as discourse

Within the 'sciences of language' and other disciplines interested in language, meaning and discourse, populism has been broadly conceived as a type of discourse (Wodak, 2015; Wodak, KhosraviNik & Mral, 2013; Charaudeau, 2011). In these studies, the term 'discourse' has been used not in the sense of a collection of linguistic utterances that can be mapped through content and discourse analysis – a limited conception of what discourse is – but in a broad sense, that is, as it is conceived by Semiotics (Verón, 1988), discourse analysis (Charaudeau, 2014; Dagatti, 2012), Critical Discourse Analysis (Wodak & Fairclough, 2013; Wodak & Meyer, 2001), discursive pragmatics (Verschueren, 2001) and other sciences focused on language, communications and syncretic – or multimodal – meaning-making. To mention an example, Ruth Wodak (2015), one of the founders of Critical Discourse Analysis, studied the discourse of right-wing populist parties and actors in Europe and identified a 'politics of fear' as a type of social discourse that is at the basis of these actors' performances in the political arena. Wodak's work deals with discourse not only in descriptive terms but also has a critical aim.

Within populism studies, the discursive account is strongly anchored in the work of Ernesto Laclau. In fact, it seems almost impossible to approach populism with a focus on discourse without discussing his work. In 1977, Laclau included the chapter 'Towards a Theory of Populism' in the book *Politics and Ideology in Marxist Theory. Capitalism – Fascism – Populism*. There, Laclau advances some of the ideas that will be central in his subsequent work on discourse, such as that political movements are grounded on an articulation of the demands of social actors. For Laclau (1977: 162), 'it is not in the presence of determinate *contents* of a discourse but in the articulating principle which unifies them that we must seek the class character of politics and ideology'. In the chapter, he also introduces some key elements of his theory of populism, such as the idea that 'the people' is the main subject of this political discourse and that it is presented in an antagonistic relationship with 'the power block'. Aslanidis (2016: 98) believes that 'Laclau pioneered efforts to discard nonessential dimensions (economic, social, etc.) that contaminated the literature and focused on the discursive construction of populist appeals'.

In 1985, Laclau published with Chantal Mouffe *Hegemony and Socialist Strategy*, a book that became a reference for discursive studies within political theory and that was the starting point of a research group referred to as 'the Essex school of discourse analysis'. These scholars usually assume the theoretical premises of that book in their analyses of discursive phenomena within the political, including populism (Glynos & Howarth, 2007; Howart, Norval & Stavrakakis, 2000). The edited volume *Populism and the Mirror of Democracy* (Panizza, 2005) is representative of this mode of approaching the political. As an example, in one of its chapters Yannis Stavrakakis (2005: 233) argues that 'if populism exists it can only refer to all discourses in which "the people" functions as a *point de capiton*, discourses that include "the people" in the set of their master-signifiers', where *point de capiton* and *master-signifiers* are concepts stemming from Laclau and Mouffe's book.

In the introduction to an edited volume entitled *Discourse Theory and Political Analysis*, David Howarth and Stavrakakis (2000: 2) refer to the assumptions underlying discourse theory. Among them they mention the assumption that 'all objects and actions are meaningful, and that their meaning is conferred by historically specific systems of rules', as well as that 'meaning depends on the orders of discourse that constitute its identity and significance'. In the foreword of the volume, Laclau (2000: xi) refers to a 'displacement of the research emphasis from mainly sociologistic categories, which address the group, its constitutive roles and its functional determinations, to the underlying logics that make these categories possible'. The influence of Laclau and Mouffe's work in this strand of research is evident.

In 2005, Laclau published two works that constitute a more elaborated and exhaustive account of populism: the chapter 'Populism: What's in a Name?' (2005b) and the book *On Populist Reason* (2005a). Since then, his account of populism became the inevitable point of reference when dealing with populism from a discursive perspective. In particular, his views regarding the discursive construction of 'the people' as being part of a specific political logic that structures the political domain have been broadly embraced by discourse analysts and communication scientists. However, Laclau's approach to populism was not purely descriptive but also celebratory: one of the conclusions of *On Populist Reason* is that populism is somehow equivalent to politics and hence positive for democracy (Laclau, 2005a: 47). This is a normative stance that has been questioned by some of his followers and that is not acceptable for a descriptive discipline like Semiotics (at least in principle).

Even if in his work Laclau frequently employs concepts relevant for semioticians such as *empty signifiers, discourse, articulation* and *fixation of meaning,* his tangential incursion into the field of discourse studies and Semiotics seems more like a step needed in his strongly theoretical and abstract system to justify some normative theses rather than a discipline-oriented step. In fact, even if Laclau and Mouffe make sense of the political through the use of the concepts of *discourse* and *meaning*, they do not draw on the work of semioticians (with the exception of Ferdinand de Saussure).[2]

In general terms, discourse-theoretical accounts argue that populism is 'an anti-status quo discourse that simplifies the political space by symbolically dividing society between "the people" (as the "underdogs") and its "*other*", as Panizza (2005: 3) proposes. For Panizza (2005: 3), 'needless to say, the identity of both "the people" and "the *other*" are political constructs, symbolically constituted through the relation of antagonism, rather than sociological categories'. For his part, Oscar Reyes (2005: 111) believes that 'it is only with the successful *articulation* of a series of issues into a coherent (if contradictory) discourse that we can properly speak of populism'.

According to the discourse-theoretical account, populism is not defined by the specific ideological contents it proposes, but by *the logic inherent to its discourse*. For Mouffe (2018: 11), populism 'is not an ideology and cannot be attributed a specific programmatic content. Nor is it a political regime. It is a way of doing politics that can take various ideological forms according to both time and place, and is compatible with a variety of institutional frameworks'. This thesis is aligned with the one presented in this book, where populism is regarded not as a phenomenon defined by the specific political contents it proposes but by the use of the Populist Narrative Structure as the formal frame used for meaning- and sense-making.

For David Howarth (2005: 203), populism consists of 'a loose set of features that permits a range of "family resemblance" phenomena to be connected or derived'. It has three basic features: (1) 'populist discourses appeal to "the people" as the privileged subject of interpellation'; (2) they are 'grounded on the construction of an underdog/establishment frontier which, if successful, opposes the people to its political enemy – say the elite or the power holders'; (3) 'populist discourses are necessarily predicated on a certain passage through the universal', meaning that 'there is [. . .] an appeal to *all* the people within a delimited sphere or domain' (Howarth, 2005: 204). In line with the main Laclauian theoretical assumptions, Howarth (2005: 204) identifies a fourth feature: 'the political orientation and character of a populist movement depends upon the kinds of hegemonic articulation available and practiced within a given historical context'.

More recently, scholars like Benjamin De Cleen (2017; 2019), Jan Zienkowski and Ruth Breeze (2019) and others have used the Essex school's discourse-theoretical approach more pragmatically, that is, without spending much time in dealing with the ontological assumptions usually discussed by the researchers of the Essex school. De Cleen (2019: 19) argues that the best way to grasp the populist process of discursive construction of 'the people' is by conceiving it as a *discursive political logic*, that is, as 'a particular way of formulating political demands in the name of "the people" and of interpellating citizens as members of "the people"'. In an edited volume entitled *Imagining the Peoples of Europe,* Zienkowski and Breeze (2019) present a series of chapters that analyse how different populist political parties and actors construct 'the peoples' of their respective political contexts.

Recently, a 'post-Laclauian' approach to populism has been proposed.[3] It bridges Laclau's conception of populism as a political logic with a sociocultural approach (Ostiguy, 2017; Ostiguy, Panizza & Moffitt, 2021). This account focuses on the study of the performances and discourses used by populist political actors to relate with their audiences by shaping popular identities discursively. The volume edited by Ostiguy, Panizza and Moffitt (2021) is presented as a contribution to a relational and performative approach to populism as a phenomenon that is inherently social, that is, enacted by political actors in their interactions with the electorate. This strand of research is close to the socio-semiotic account presented in these pages, at least in its conception of how the political field works based on interactions and performativity.

Also part of a discursive account of populism, but in an overlap with the communicative accounts (section 2.3.3), there is a conception of populism as a *frame*, that is, a discursive structure used to make sense of political situations. Aslanidis (2016) doubts of the conceptual foundations of the notion of 'thin-centredness' used by Mudde and other scholars and, within a discursive approach still anchored in Laclau's theory, introduces the cognitive dimension of discourse as a way of developing 'a more productive methodological vantage point than discourse analysis' (Aslanidis, 2016: 99). Aslanidis (2016: 102) proposes a formal approach to populism, one 'in which structural elements of populist discourse account for perceived patterns among populist instances, with differences explained by the circumstantial content of the constructed subjectivities of the "people" and the "elites"'. In a similar argumentative line, María Esperanza Casullo (2019) sees the discursive and cognitive core of populism in an empty narrative structure that she calls *the populist myth* and that consists of an opposition between a hero and a villain. Even if they do not frame their arguments in semiotic terms, Aslanidis's and Casullo's accounts are closely related to how populism is approached in this book.

2.3.3 Populism as a style

The conceptualization of populism as a style is closely related to the discursive account but prefers to leave the theoretical digressions of the Laclauian account aside and focus on the tangible and pragmatic dimension of discourse through the study of specific cases (Jagers & Walgrave, 2007; Moffitt & Tormey, 2014; Moffitt, 2014; 2016). References to populism as a style can be found in the works of Taguieff (1995), Knight (1998) and Canovan (1984; 1999), among others. For Taguieff (1995: 9), populism 'does not embody a particular type of political regime, nor does it define a particular ideological content. It is a political style applicable to various ideological frameworks'. Canovan (1999: 5) argues that populism is a 'rhetorical style' and that 'populist appeals to the people are characteristically couched in a *style* that is "democratic" in the sense of being aimed at ordinary people'. For Knight (1998: 223), populism is 'a political *style* characteristically involving a proclaimed rapport with "the people", a "them-and-us" mentality, and (often, though not necessarily) a period of crisis and mobilization'. Moffitt (2016: 41) argues that 'these authors' distinct contributions to understanding populism as a political style cannot be underestimated: they have each tried to push beyond dominant approaches to populism by highlighting the centrality of its communicative (and at times, performative) appeal'.

It was after the turn of the century that the account of populism as a style became more prominent. Inspired by Canovan, Jagers and Walgrave (2007: 322) distinguish between a 'thick' and a 'thin' definition of populism. While the former consists of a combination of references to the people, anti-establishment ideas and an exclusion of certain categories of the population, the authors regard the latter as 'a political communication style of political actors that refers to the people', or as 'a communication frame that appeals to and identifies with the people, and pretends to speak in their name'. According to the authors, defining populism in such a 'thin way' depoliticizes the concept: they argue that 'it is colourless and can be of the left and of the right' (Jagers & Walgrave, 2007: 323). Their account is close to Aslanidis's in conceiving populism as a frame that revolves around 'the people' and that is used by political actors in their communication strategies to produce specific effects of sense in the audiences they address. The reference to the concept of 'style' would imply looking at the performative dimension resulting from the use of that frame as the ground for meaning-making.

Also Moffitt and Tormey (2014: 387) see populism as a political style and focus on its performative dimension. As they argue, they prefer to conceive it as a *political* rather than as a *communicative* style to 'move beyond the purely communicative and rhetorical elements [. . .], and emphasise the performative and relational elements of political style' (Moffitt & Tormey, 2014: 387). With this move, the authors broaden the restricted premise of linguistic accounts focused on language use and include non-linguistic resources used in meaning-making that are relevant for a semiotic perspective, such as how closeness between political actors and the electorate is constructed on social media through the use of images and live online streaming, or the music used in electoral spots to produce specific effects of sense.

For Moffitt and Tormey (2014: 394), the analytical category of *political style* denotes 'a repertoire of performative features which cuts across different political situations that are used to create political relations'. According to the authors, in a context of growing mediatization of politics, performativity is crucial in understanding how political discourse is meaningful discourse. The subtitle of Moffitt's book *The Global Rise of Populism* (2016) is *Performance, Political Style, and Representation*. There, Moffitt (2016: 46) defines *political style* as 'the repertoires of embodied, symbolically mediated performance made to audiences that are used to create and navigate the fields of power that comprise the political, stretching from the domain of government through to everyday life'.

Also relevant from a semiotic perspective is the study of how populist political actors construct in discourse and perform the idea of crisis (Moffitt, 2014). If populism emerges in contexts where a crisis of trust in representative democracy is prevalent, then populist political actors will create in their discourses the effect of sense of a crisis. As Moffitt (2014: 190) argues, 'populist actors actively participate in the "spectacularization of failure" that underlies crisis, allowing them to pit "the people" against a dangerous other, radically simplify the terms and terrain of political debate and advocate strong leadership and quick political action to stave off or solve the impending crisis'. For Moffitt (2014; 2016), crises are neither given nor external nor neutral phenomena: they are mediated by the performances of certain social actors.

More recently, a group of communication scientists (Reinemann et al., 2017) approached populism as a form of political communication with some defining traits. For the authors, 'populism is mostly reflected in the oral, written, and visual communication of individual politicians, parties, social movements, or any other actor that steps into the public sphere' (Reinemann et al., 2017: 13). Therefore, populism can be approached by examining the 'communicative messages that have their roots in – or resonate with – the goals, motives, and attitudes of political actors, the media, or citizens' (Reinemann et al., 2017: 14). According to the authors, populist political communication presents three core traits: (1) a construction of 'the people'; (2) anti-elitism and (3) an exclusion of out-groups. They explicitly exclude from their conceptualization of populism other aspects identified in previous scholarship as constitutive of the phenomenon, such as charismatic leadership, references to crisis and threat, the use of colloquial language, harshness with opponents, simplicity and directness, among others.[4] In contrast, Moffitt and Tormey (2014) and Moffitt (2016) argue that the three defining features of populism as a political style are: (1) an appeal to 'the people' as opposed to 'the elite'; (2) the use of bad manners and (3) the sense of a crisis, breakdown or threat.

Although Reinemann et al. (2017) do not make of *performance* or *style* central categories in their analyses, they coincide with performative scholars in approaching populism through the study of its communicative dimension. Over the decades, various studies have focused on how populist actors use language and communicate with their audiences. This *communicative*, *pragmatic* or *performative* turn in populist research broadened the conception of discourse to encompass semiotic resources other than linguistic utterances. As evidenced in this chapter, as a political phenomenon embedded in the cultural webs of signification that characterize a specific political context – its *political culture* – populism is more than a simple strategic use of linguistic utterances to produce meaning in the audiences. Although linguistic utterances are crucial to identify and make sense of populism as a social phenomenon, it is naïve to reduce its complexity to its linguistic dimension only. In this sense, performative and communicational accounts opened the field for a semiotic account of populism, which focuses on the role that language, but also images, performances, the body, music, attitudes and other meaningful resources and practices play in meaning-making, both in cognitive and affective terms.

The performative and communicative accounts of populism focus on what populist political actors say and do. Therefore, in semiotic terms, they focus on the dimension of the *expression*. A semiotic approach to populism will certainly examine the dimension of the expression with great interest and also that of the *content*, that is, how populist discourse structures and hence constructs the social world in a particular manner. Chapters 4 and 5 focus on examining this aspect of populism.

2.3.4 Other accounts

The three accounts presented previously – ideology, discourse and style – are relevant for Semiotics and other disciplines interested in discourse, sense- and meaning-making. Nevertheless, other accounts exist besides these within populism studies. For the sake of an exhaustive mapping of the conceptual debate, some other accounts must be at least mentioned.

To begin with, populism has been conceived of as a *political movement*. This definition makes sense when taking into account the noun's suffix *-ism*, which is usually used to mean a movement or a trend (not only in politics but also in the arts and in fashion, like in *impressionism* or *cubism*). In Ionescu and Gellner's book, Minogue (1969: 197) argues that populism is a political movement and stresses the importance of identifying the *structure of feelings* that moves people to take action in the name of something greater than themselves.[5] Minogue (1969: 204) believes that modern politics is a matter of *movements* and *associations*: while a movement 'demands that its members should surrender their individuality and become "vehicles" of a cause', an association is 'primarily as an alliance between individualities' (Minogue, 1969: 204). According to Minogue (1969: 205), 'every movement creates an ideology, which is the thought of the movement', where *ideology* stands for 'the thought of a movement [that] outlines the radical changes which the movement seeks to bring about'. For Minogue (1969: 206), 'the actual ideology of populism has few features which distinguish it from the products of any other movement'. From a semiotic perspective, it is interesting to examine how ideas and discourses can encourage people to mobilize politically.

Second, populism has been approached as a *political strategy*. Kurt Weyland (2001: 14–16) argues for a redefinition of populism 'in political-organizational terms' as 'a political strategy through which a personalistic leader seeks or exercises government power based on direct, unmediated, uninstitutionalized support from large numbers of mostly unorganized followers'. According to this definition, political actors need to implement strategies to gain and/or maintain power, and populism is one of those strategies. More recently, Weyland (2017: 80) argued that populism is 'a coherent set of approaches and mechanisms for structuring relations of political participation, support building, and governmental authority', that is, it is an issue of top-down strategic leadership. Also, Robert Barr (2018) and Hans-Georg Betz (2002) argued that populism is a political strategy. According to Betz (2002: 198), rather than an ideology, 'populism is primarily a political strategy, whose political rhetoric is the evocation of latent grievances and the appeal to emotions provoked by them'.[6] The conception that Semiotics has of strategies will be discussed subsequently.

Also stemming from comparative political science, a third relevant account equals populism with 'democratic illiberalism' (Pappas, 2019a). Pappas (2019a: 3), who is less interested in the genus of populism than in operationalizing the concept to conduct empirical research and achieve a theory of populism, argues that 'modern populism – whether seen as a set of ideas, a political leader acting on such ideas, a particular party championing them, or even an entire political system in which significant parties promote its essence – is fundamentally democratic but in opposition to the liberal canon'. This account aims at placing populism within the broader network of political phenomena and it does so by placing it between authoritarianism and liberalism. According to Pappas (2019a: 3), 'remove its democratic ethos and populism will turn into authoritarianism, but reverse its illiberal disposition and whims, and liberal democratic order is likely to be reinstituted'.

2.4 On the compatibility of these accounts

As discussed in the previous pages, throughout the history of populism studies, there have been multiple accounts with regards to what populism is. These accounts depend not only on what trait of this political phenomenon is brought to the fore but also on the disciplinary background of researchers studying it. As Weyland (2001: 1) argues, 'conceptual confusion prevails when different scholars emphasize divergent attributes as defining characteristics of a concept'. It was also argued that these accounts look at different things when dealing with populism: while comparative political scientists might be more interested in achieving a minimal definition that can operationally be used in empirical and comparative studies, discourse-theoretical accounts seem to be keen on finding the defining logic of populist discourse as a social and ideological practice.

Even if there are differences and divergences between these accounts, some commonalities can be found between them. In the first place, ideological, discursive and performative-communicative accounts of populism escape the domain of policy-making, organizational structures and socio-economic causation, which has also been a focus in the study of populism by political scientists. There seems to be something inherent to populism that is related to ideas, language, representation and, more broadly, with sense- and meaning-making.

Mudde (2017) refers to these accounts as *ideational* because they are interested in the *ideas* – in a broad and diffuse sense of the term – of populism and in how these have an impact in the world as ideational entities that shape perceptions and guide action. In this sense, there is *a constructivist premise* inherent to this approach (Searle, 1995; Wendt, 1992). Hawkins and Rovira Kaltwasser (2019) also refer to an ideational approach to encompass those accounts of populism that share their putting of ideas – also in a broad and diffuse sense of the term – at the core of populism and their leaving non-ideational elements aside.

The notion of an ideational account of populism is a positive step in grasping the nature of the political. Ideologies, communicative styles, discourse and discourses, performances, rhetoric and political 'logics' and strategies are all modes of representing the world through the use of language and semiotic resources. Ideologies are not something pre-existent to social – and hence discursive – reality: they are constructed in and shaped by language and, in Freeden's morphological account, depend on a coherent and relatively stable articulation of political concepts.[7] These articulations can only be perceived through the mediation of the discourses and performances produced by political actors. Therefore, examining what populist political actors say and do, and *how* they say and do it, is a crucial part of understanding how ideational elements shape and influence meaning-making within the social realm. Even if they are normally presented as competing accounts, all the accounts on populism are compatible; they just focus on *one* dimension of this multidimensional sociopolitical phenomenon.

Also compatible are non-ideational accounts of populism. Once a specific mode of representation – that is, a combination of ideas, discourses, styles and performances – is established and gains certain consistency within society, it can be used strategically to achieve specific goals within the political field. Once a strategy has proven effective and becomes meaningful for social actors for meaning-making, it can easily become a political movement. In its essence, the logic governing populism does not differ from the logic governing the establishment of discursive *genres*, for example, in television or in the movies. In this sense, populism could be conceived of as 'a kind of mental map through which individuals analyse and comprehend political reality', as proposed by Mudde and Rovira Kaltwasser (2017: 6).

The adjective *ideational* seems legitimate to group accounts of populism that emphasize the *discursive* elements of this political phenomenon – such as ideas, discourses, language use, performances, bodily language, communicative styles and framing – over organizational, structural or economic elements. As is demonstrated in this book, all these accounts can contribute to the semiotic study of populism, that is, the study of populism with a focus on meaning-making and signification. Instead of *ideational*, these accounts would be described in a more pertinent manner if they were labelled *discursive* or *semiotic* accounts. Although ideas are certainly crucial within these accounts, even more prominent are discourses and performances and, with them, meaning-making.

Even if they do not agree on the genus of populism, a majority of the accounts of populism identify a set of elements at its core – a *nucleus* (Rooduijn, 2014). According to Panizza (2005: 1), 'while there is no scholarly agreement on the meaning of populism, it is possible to identify an analytical core around which there is a significant degree of academic consensus'. When examining populism from a semiotic perspective, four aspects seem to be constitutive of that analytical core – a core that is of a purely discursive nature.

The first aspect is the reference to 'the people' in the sense of the Latin word *populus* as a collective identity to be found in the social space and that should be the source of any political legitimacy. As discussed, populism is the *-ism* of the *populus*, that is, 'the people'. Therefore, 'the people' will have a central role within the populist ideology/discourse/style, whatever that signifier might denote. For Müller (2016: 20), 'there can be no populism [...] without someone speaking in the name of the people as a whole'. Confusion on this point has been common mainly due to the following issue: if populism puts forward 'the people' as the source of political legitimacy, how does it differ from democracy and nationalism, which also revolve around 'the people'? As is argued in Chapter 5, there is a specific mode in which populist discourse constructs the social actor of 'the people'.

A second aspect common to the existing accounts is the belief that the collective identity of 'the people' is valorized in positive terms against the corrupt 'elites', which in opposition are valorized negatively. This gives place to the normative proposal regarding that 'popular' or 'general will' should be the principle guiding the structure and management of political issues within a given society. In populist discourse, the positive valorization of 'the people' takes place through an opposition to an 'other' – normally, albeit not exclusively, 'the elite' – that is also constructed in discourse following the logic presented in Chapter 5. It is not enough for the discourse and performances of a political actor, party or movement to revolve around the collective identity of 'the people' to be populist: it also needs to divide the social space in two halves. Scholars seem to agree in that 'the people's other' is the elite, that populism opposes elitism and that both groups are usually depicted as monolithic and homogeneous, that is, without internal differences. The identification of 'the people's other' with the elites is challenged in Chapter 5, where a more encompassing articulation of the collective identity 'not-the-people' is discussed.

Third, there seems to be agreement regarding a relationship between 'the people' and the 'other' presented in discourse as *antagonistic*. This feature will be crucial to identify the Populist Narrative Structure in populist actors' discourses and performances. A discourse revolving around 'the people' is not populist *per se*. Neither is one that speaks of 'the people' as opposed to an 'other'. This book argues that it is a necessary condition for a discourse to be populist to present the social space as fragmented through an irreconcilable gap. This gives place to a relationship of hate – which is constructed in discourse – between 'the people' and an *enemy*. Depending on how the Populist Narrative Structure is combined with specific ideological and political contents and other discourses, the types of populism that will emerge (e.g. right-wing and left-wing populism). Any form of populism will highlight a troublesome relationship between 'the people' and an 'other'.

Finally, there seems to be a partial agreement – not all scholars agree on this point[8] – regarding the crucial role played by populist leaders (and, in particular, charismatic leaders) in performing the Populist Narrative Structure. Fukuyama (2018a) identifies a specific 'style of leadership' as one of the defining features of populism. It includes a cult of personality, charismatic authority and the attempt to develop 'a direct and unmediated relationship with "the people"'. Even if they are not a necessary condition for populism to exist, populist leaders are crucial in bringing the Populist Narrative Structure to life through and in their discourses and performances. These result from a strategic use of semiotic resources such as language, gesture, manners, images, symbols, performative tricks and attitudes towards the political system, among others, to produce meaning within the political field. It is the political leader who shows what 'the people' denotes and who 'the people' are by filling this empty category with specific context-dependent meanings.

This characterization of populism in ideational terms leaves aside other non-ideational components that have been identified as constitutive of populism. For example, Fukuyama (2018a) argues that one of the defining features of populism is the pursuit of 'policies that are popular in the short run but unsustainable in the long run, usually in the realm of social policies'. The author lists price subsidies, generous pension benefits and free medical clinics as examples of these policies. While these non-discursive or non-ideational aspects might be relevant to make sense of populism holistically, they are not relevant for a discursive perspective like the one embraced by Semiotics. For these purposes, it is enough to conceive of populism as a discursive practice consisting of a construction in discourse and through performances of the social actor of 'the people' as opposed to an 'other', depicted as an enemy with whom it coexists in a conflictive and antagonistic relationship. These are the three defining features of the Populist Narrative Structure, as is argued in Chapter 5.

3

Social Semiotics and the Study of 'Meaning in Action'

This book draws on the discipline of 'social Semiotics' to examine populism. This chapter argues what that discipline can add to the efforts of making sense of populism as a social phenomenon based on meaning-making and explains how such an account differs from the existing discourse-theoretical, discourse-analytical, communicational, pragmatic and performative accounts of populism.

Given the multiple and divergent uses of the terms 'Semiotics' and 'social Semiotics' within the social sciences and humanities, it is a good practice to begin any semiotic enquiry by stating in a clear manner what is understood under these two terms. As is demonstrated in this chapter, they refer to different things depending on the research traditions. This book deals with 'Semiotics' as the discipline within the social sciences whose object of study is *semiosis*, a phenomenon also referred to as *meaning-making, sense-making* and *signification*. Even if they both are interested in meaning, Semiotics does not equal Semantics, a branch of linguistics interested in meaning in lexical terms.[1] For Semiotics, both the semantic and the pragmatic dimensions are crucial in the attempts to explain the functioning of meaning- and sense-making (Paolucci, 2021a).

When defined in these terms, Semiotics is an *empirical* social science that works with an anchorage on corpus of analysis. The nature of the texts – in a broad sense, that is, linguistic utterances, written texts, images, audiovisual spots, practices, situations and interactions – depends not only on the branch of the discipline embraced by the research tradition. Over the last three to four decades, semioticians have been attracted by meaning-making linked to practices and interactions. Given that these semiotic objects are dynamic, open and *in vivo*, the concept of *meaning in action* is the manifestation of meaning usually identified as the object of study of social Semiotics.

3.1 Semiotics and the 'semiotic outlook'

The question 'What is Semiotics?' is challenging because its answer requires a thorough examination both in historical and methodological terms. The aim of this section is to present a clear understanding of the *semiotic outlook* (Eco, 1976; Fabbri, 1973) as a specific way of approaching social and cultural phenomena under the assumptions that every sociocultural phenomenon is based on meaning-making and signification and that sense-making is always social because it is based on the production, circulation and consumption of discourses (Verón, 1988).

The *Oxford Advanced English Dictionary* defines *semiotics* as 'the study of signs and symbols and of their meaning and use'.[2] Although this is a simplistic definition unsatisfactory from a theoretical viewpoint, it condenses a common identification of *Semiotics* with the study of signs, symbols and meaning. As any dictionary definition, it serves to have a general and basic idea of what the word refers to in the English language. This definition contains one of the most salient causes of confusion within the academia regarding the nature of this study: the confusion of *semiotics* and *Semiotics*.

In English – as well as in other languages – the noun *semiotics* is used mainly in two different senses, although they are closely related and interdependent. On the one hand, it is used preceded by an article and written with an initial low-cap *s* as a way of referring to *a dimension* of sociocultural phenomena: the one related to signs, meaning, sense and signification. To these manifestations of the semiotic dimension, one could also add the more general concepts of language and discourse since these depend on signs, meaning, sense and signification. This move has caused a considerable theoretical trouble during the twentieth century.

In the title of this book, *The Social Semiotics of Populism*, the noun *semiotics* is used in this first sense: given that populism is a social phenomenon, it will be grounded on meaning-making and, hence, have a constitutive semiotic dimension. Therefore, the purpose of the book is to study, analyse and make sense of that dimension of populism. In this sense, when leaving aside the capitalization of titles that is customary in English publications, the book would be entitled *The social semiotics of populism*. Here, *semiotics* would refer to the dimension of populism revolving around signs, meaning, sense and signification – and, more extensively, to language and discourse. In this case, as a noun that can be preceded by the definite article *the*, *semiotics* refers to a specific dimension of populism, one that has been broadly studied by researchers approaching the phenomenon from a discursive perspective.

When used in this first sense, the type of phenomena to which the word 'semiotics' refers to has been of interest for thinkers since Antiquity (Manetti, 2013) and has been – and still is – an object of study for all social sciences and humanities – even if tangentially – especially after the so-called linguistic turn of the twentieth century. References to *the semiotics of such and such* can be found in the work of philosophers, political theorists and other researchers that do not identify themselves as *semioticians*. Scholars working in the field of the 'sciences of language' (Ducrot & Todorov, 1972) regularly deal with semiotics in this sense. This is the case for discourse analysts (Angenot, 2010; Charaudeau, 2011; 2014; Charaudeau & Maingueneau, 2002; Dagatti, 2012; Maingueneau, 2009; 2017), critical discourse analysts (Fairclough, 1992; Wodak & Meyer, 2001; Wodak & Fairclough, 2013; Catalano & Waugh, 2020) and pragmatists (Verschueren, 2001; 2012; Zienkowski, Östman & Verschueren, 2011; Zienkoswki, 2017), among other researchers usually trained in linguistics. As it is evident, multiple confusions exist within the academia as a result of the use of this general, imprecise and vague sense of the noun *semiotics* as one to refer to almost everything that is related to signs, signification, meaning, language and discourse.

However, a second sense of the noun *semiotics* refers to a specific science, discipline, research field or outlook – discussions on the epistemological status of Semiotics are still ongoing – within the social and human sciences. This discipline has its origins in the late nineteenth century, took the form of a relatively autonomous discipline in the 1960s and made of semiotics its object of study. *Semiotics* – spelled with an initial capital *S* – can be hence defined as *the social science that studies the semiotics of a broad spectrum of phenomena*. In this sense, the title of this book could also be read as *The social Semiotics of populism* given that its content employs the concepts, methods and tools that have been developed during the twentieth century within Semiotics by scholars and researchers that identify themselves as *semioticians*.[3]

In his introduction to Semiotics, Daniel Chandler (2017: 2) writes that semioticians 'study how meanings are made and how reality is represented (and indeed constructed) through signs and sign systems'. Although this statement encompasses in a simple and clear manner what semioticians do, it does not set clear boundaries between their activity and that of discourse analysts, linguists with an interest in pragmatics and discourse, cultural anthropologists or other social scientists. As Eco (1976: 5) argues, there are 'many disciplines other than Semiotics' that have 'already undertaken [. . .] research on subjects that a semiotician cannot but recognize as his own concern'. Chandler (2017: 3) also states bluntly that Semiotics 'is still not widely institutionalized as an academic discipline'. This lack of institutionalization is the result of how the discipline was born and evolved during the twentieth century.[4]

The relationship between *semiotics* and *Semiotics* is not always clear and consensual for those who research in the field. The issue of Semiotics' disciplinary status has been the object of long and complex discussions between semioticians. Is Semiotics a discipline, a science, a viewpoint/outlook, a research field or a theoretical position? Is it a social science or is it rather a humanistic discipline? Is it a descriptive enterprise or does it have a critical-normative goal? Positions vary in answering these questions between attempts for a strong disciplinary delimitation and construction – such as in the work of Algirdas J. Greimas and his followers – and more encompassing conceptions of Semiotics as a general – normally critical – outlook or viewpoint, like that of Chandler (2017: 3), for whom Semiotics is 'a way of looking at the production of meaning from a particular critical perspective'.

In *A Theory of Semiotics*, Umberto Eco (1976: 3) explores 'the theoretical possibility and the social function of a unified approach to every phenomenon of signification and/or communication'. According to the author, such an approach would take 'the form of a *general semiotic theory*, able to explain every case of sign-function in terms of underlying systems of elements mutually correlated by one or more codes'. Eco (1976: 7–8) asks the question of whether Semiotics should be regarded as a field or a discipline and acknowledges the existence of a *semiotic field*. This field is heterogeneous, disparate and manifests itself in 'many and varied forms' with a characteristic disorder. A general semiotic theory should be capable of encompassing that heterogeneity.

As a relatively autonomous science, discipline, research field or outlook, Semiotics finds its roots in the work of Ferdinand de Saussure (Arrivé, 2002; Hénault, 2002) and Charles Sanders Peirce (Santaella, 2002; Tiercelin, 2002). This double paternity is treated as a given in semiotic scholarship. For example, Eco (1976: 14–16) begins his enterprise of building a general semiotic theory by discussing the works of Saussure and Peirce since the Swiss linguist and US philosopher 'foretold the official birth and scientific organization of the discipline' (Eco, 1976: 14).

In the *Cours de linguistique générale*, Ferdinand de Saussure tried to establish linguistics as a positivist science whose object of study would be the *langue*, that is, the dimension of language consisting of the system of signs that individuals use to express ideas (Saussure, 1959: 16). For Saussure, the *langue* is only *one* system of signs, albeit the most relevant for linguistics. He argues that researchers could envisage a *Semiology* [*sémiologie*] as the science whose object of study would be 'the life of signs within society' [*une science qui étudie la vie des signes au sein de la vie sociale*] (Saussure, 1959: 16). This science would be part of social psychology – for Saussure, psychologists study 'the sign-mechanism in the individual' (p. 17) – and would teach us 'what constitute signs' and 'what laws govern them' (p. 16). According to Saussure, linguistics is part of semiology, although this new science did not exist as such at the time Saussure held the lectures that were later published as a book. In John Deely's opinion (2015: 37), the *Cours* 'provided the original focal point for what became for the first time in the twentieth century something like a *general interest* across intellectual culture in the subject of signs'.

Saussure conceptualizes the sign as a relationship between a signifier [*significant*] and a signified [*signifié*]. While the former is empirically perceivable through the senses, the latter is the content expressed by the signifier. In Saussure's view, signifier and signified are linked arbitrarily and coexist as the two sides of a sheet of paper.[5] Some decades later, this duality was re-elaborated by Danish linguistic Louis Hjelmslev (1961), who replaced the terms 'signifier' and 'signified' by *expression* and *content*, respectively. For Semiotics, this substitution proved more useful than Saussure's because it is not limited to natural languages or signs only.[6] Following Hjelmslev's re-elaboration, Eco (1976: 48) defines the sign as 'an element of an *expression plane* conventionally correlated to one (or several) elements of a *content plane*' and proposes to leave aside the concept of *sign* and replace it with that of *sign-function* to render visible the dynamic nature of meaning-making as based on a relationship between these two planes. That is precisely what *semiosis* is about.

More or less concomitantly to the work of Saussure, US philosopher Charles Sanders Peirce was also concerned with signs and meaning as part of his research in logic and epistemology. Peirce identified himself as 'a pioneer, or rather a backwoodsman, in the work of clearing and opening up [. . .] *semiotic*, that is the doctrine of the essential nature and fundamental varieties of possible semiosis' (Peirce, 1931; quoted in Eco, 1976: 15). Peirce defined *semiosis* as 'an action, an influence, which is, or involves, a cooperation of *three* subjects, such as a sign, its object and its interpretant' (Peirce, quoted in Eco: 1976: 15). His theory was influential in the work of Eliseo Verón (1988; 2013), one of the main representatives of social Semiotics in Latin America. Peirce's work is complex and cannot be easily summarized. One of his main contributions to the development of semiotic theory was the classification of signs in three types depending on how they relate to what they refer to: *icons, indexes* and *symbols*. Moreover, by defending a triadic conception of the sign, Peirce opened the field to the importance of the role of interpretation of signs. This idea is crucial in the works of Eco and Verón.

During the twentieth century, Saussure's and Peirce's seminal ideas were embraced and re-elaborated by researchers in the two margins of the Atlantic. In Europe, Louis Hjelmslev (1961), Roland Barthes (1957) and Claude Lévi-Strauss (1958) embraced Saussure's structuralist semiotics; in the United States, Charles Morris (1938; 1964) and Thomas Sebeok (1994) developed Peirce's theory further and founded new research fields based on the examination of meaning-making, such as *Zoosemiotics*. Other researchers – Roman Jakobson (1963), Umberto Eco (1976) and Eliseo Verón (1988) – placed themselves in-between the two approaches and tried to articulate the theories of the two founding fathers of Semiotics.

As discussed previously, Hjelmslev (1961) updated Saussure's distinction between signifier and signified as a distinction between a plane of the expression and one of the content. According to the author, 'there can be no content without an expression, or expressionless content; neither can there be an expression without a content, or content-less expression' (1961: 49).[7] This is an interesting thesis because it points out the necessity of a perceivable trace (on the plane of the expression) to gain access to *semiosis* (the process through which a given content is expressed or through which a given content is associated to an expression by the reader thanks to cultural conventions that shape interpretation).

3.2 Greimas and Eco

In spite of the slow but steady theoretical developments during the first half of the past century, it was during the 1960s and 1970s that semiotics – the general interest in signs, meaning and signification – started taking the form of a Semiotics, that is, the science envisaged by Saussure as a Semiology and by Peirce as a Semiotic. Two names are the unavoidable references in this process of disciplinary consolidation: Algirdas J. Greimas and Umberto Eco. While the former grounded his disciplinary construction on a *structuralist* premise – that is, in the work of Saussure and the interpretations it was object of in structural linguistic and other social sciences – the latter drew inspiration from Peirce's interpretative account. Since the 1980s, it has been common practice to refer to these two theoretical schools as *structural* – also *generative* – and *interpretative* Semiotics due to the main conceptions of meaning-making they put forward (Traini, 2006; Violi, 2017).

Lithuanian-born and Paris-based Algirdas J. Greimas made significant efforts in creating a meta-language that could provide Semiotics with the status of a science. Besides his multiple semiotic studies compiled – among others – in the books *Du sens* (1970) and *Du sens II* (1983), Greimas wrote in collaboration with Joseph Courtés a disciplinary dictionary (Greimas & Courtés, 1982) with the aim of achieving a homogenization and harmonization of the approaches interested in studying meaning through a coherent theory where terms and concepts are interdefined. As the authors write in the Preface to the analytical dictionary, its purpose is to contribute to the 'elaboration of a rigorous conceptual metalanguage which is a necessary preliminary toward the establishment of any language theory as formal language' (Greimas & Courtés, 1982: xii).

Greimas's work has a number of phases depending on what his main focus of interest was. Some of his most well-known tools are the *semiotic square* [*carré sémiotique*], the *narrative scheme* and *débrayage* as a mechanism of enunciation. These will be of use when studying populism from a semiotic perspective. Hence, a brief introduction seems in order.

For Greimas and his followers, 'every discourse is not a macro-sign or an assemblage of signs, but a process of signification supported by enunciation' (Fontanille, 1999: 1, my translation). Reflecting a structuralist premise that draws on the work of Hjelmslev, Greimas assumes that meaning emerges as the result of differences and oppositions and argues that discourses (fictional, but also social) contain a series of levels [*niveaux de signification*] through which meaning is generated. This is where the idea of a *generative* Semiotics originates as the approach that examines how meaning comes into being in texts through a series of semiotic mechanisms, and whose study implies conducting a process of segmentation in a number of levels.

The semiotic square is a tool used to examine and map the more abstract and basic of those levels, usually referred to as the level of the *deep structures* (also of the *basic semantic structures*). According to Chandler (2017: 125), the semiotic square is 'a map of the semantic space within the particular universe of discourse that is under investigation'. As such, it 'represents an implicit conceptual framework' that constitutes the basis of a discourse (Figure 2).

The square contains four positions: A, B, –A and –B. These are occupied by concepts (semantic units) that entertain among them bilateral relationships of contrariety, contradiction and complementarity. For example, A could be occupied by the semantic unit *good*, B with *bad*, –A with *not good* and –B with *not bad*. When examining a particular discourse like that of a specific populist political actor, the semantic universe at the basis of that discourse can be organized in this logical manner, that is, as a network of concepts that relate to each other. As is argued in Chapter 5, populist discourse normally fills the upper positions of the square with the categories of 'the people' and an 'other' – like 'the elite' or 'the establishment' – and assumes a relationship of *contrariety* between them. These two semantic units are the ones that render populist discourse meaningful.[8] As Chandler (2017: 126) proposes, the semiotic square 'highlights "hidden" underlying concepts in a text or practice'.

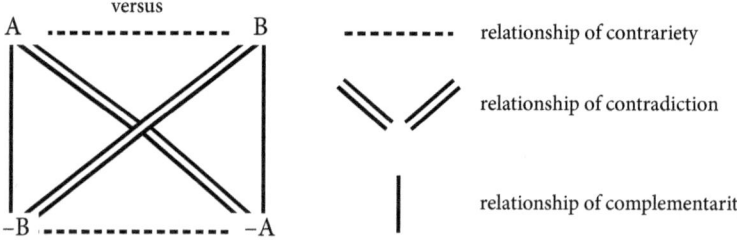

Figure 2 The semiotic square. Source: Own elaboration based on the work of Greimas, Floch and others.

A second major contribution by Greimas to semiotic theory is his model of the narrative scheme (Greimas, 1970; 1986; Courtés, 2007; Hénault, 2012). It stems from Russian folklorist Vladimir Propp's research on the morphology – structure – of Russian fairy tales. According to Greimas's model, every narrative scheme can be examined in terms of a Subject that seeks to possess an Object valuable to it. Therefore, any narrative programme involves the passage from a state of disjunction between the Subject and the Object of Value to one of conjunction. This model does not only imply that there is a sort of 'narrative grammar' that is common to all discourses and texts with a narrative component (Greimas & Ricoeur, 1989; Marrone, 2007; Paolucci, 2012; Pozzato, 2007) but also that the only way to grasp meaning is through its transformation, that is, 'in the passage from one situation to another, from a state to another, and in the relationship between at least two terms' (Fontanille, 1999: 6–7, my translation).

A third relevant contribution by Greimas to semiotic theory is his work on enunciation, which is based on the work of French linguist Émile Benveniste. For Benveniste (1966; 1974), discourses contain traces of the individual who enunciated them. Some of them are of a *deictical* nature – from *deixis* – like those that revolve around the person that enunciates (I), *time* (now) and *space* (here). Although many discourses do not speak of an *I* that is *here* and that enunciates *now*, enunciation is always bounded to a subject who utters a text now in a given space, even if those traces are deleted from the *énoncé*. For Greimas, any narrative study should pay attention at how an empirical enunciator deals with the 'I-here-now' triad and creates alternate universes that modify that specific *deixis* through a process of *débrayage*.

When studying populism from a semiotic perspective, it will be crucial to examine how populist political actors speak about themselves through the use of a self-referential enunciation. But more important will be to examine how they construct in discourse the structure of the social space through an opposition between 'the people' and its 'other'. That discursive construction takes place in narrative terms. For Patrick Charaudeau (2011: 105, my translation), studying populism as a discourse implies that researchers must 'analyze it within the socio-historical context where it appears and within the communicative situation that produces a specific process of enunciation'.

Umberto Eco, for his part, made significant efforts to bridge Peircean and Saussurean Semiotics. In *A Theory of Semiotics*, Eco identifies Semiotics with a theory of culture and argues that it is the discipline 'concerned with everything that can be *taken* as a sign'. In the book, Eco develops a theory of codes and a theory of sign production. Eco believes that 'a sign is everything which can be taken as significantly substituting for something else' (1976: 7) and claims that 'the whole of culture is signification and communication and [. . .] humanity and society exist only when communicative and significative relationships are established' (Eco, 1976: 22). Semiotics aims at grasping and making sense of how these relationships function. Eco's approach is close to Clifford Geertz's (1973) interpretative account of culture, which regards culture as a 'web of significations' that guide human action. Eco's (1976: 22) thesis is that 'the whole of culture *should* be studied as a communicative phenomenon based on signification systems' since it is only 'by studying [culture] in this way [that] certain of its fundamental mechanisms [can] be clarified' (Eco, 1976: 22). As is argued in the following chapter, the political domain clearly reflects this logic. That is why Semiotics cannot be left aside in the attempts of making sense of it. Eco's thesis is that 'in culture every entity can become a semiotic phenomenon. The laws of signification are the laws of culture. For this reason culture allows a continuous process of communicative exchanges, in so far as it subsists as a system of systems of signification. Culture can be studied completely under a semiotic profile' (Eco, 1976: 28).

The generative (Greimas) and interpretative (Eco) semiotic paradigms have been frequently considered as incompatible mainly due to their different theoretical roots (Violi, 2017). However, they share some commonalities that can be regarded as those that define the scope and nature of Semiotics as it is practised nowadays (Broden, 2014; Violi, 2017). In the first place, both paradigms set the focus in *semiosis* – also referred to as *meaning-making, sense-making* or *signification* – and not in signs, sign systems, communication and language as their object of study. The phenomenon of *semiosis* is always social and, therefore, possible only within a sociocultural context. It is cultural convention what renders an occurrence in the plane of the expression meaningful (Eco, 1976; Verón, 1988; Halliday, 1978). Therefore, Semiotics aim at mapping and describing how *semiosis* works in any context through the examination of objects of an heterogeneous nature: language, images, practices, situations, strategic styles and forms of life are only a few objects of interest for semioticians.

Second, semioticians tend to accept a constructivist premise as the point of departure for their studies. Constructivism (Berger & Luckmann, 1966; Searle, 1995; Wendt, 1992) sees social reality as partially constructed through and in language, discourses and social practices, even if its material dimension is indisputable. While Verón (1988: 125, my translation) argued that 'every social functioning has a constitutive signifying dimension', for Chandler (2017: xvi) 'our sign systems (language and other media) play a major part in "the social construction of reality" (or at least "the construction of social reality") and [. . .] realities cannot be separated from the sign systems in which they are experienced.' As argued by Michael Halliday (1978), human experience cannot escape the mediation of signs, meaning-making and, more generally, discourses. Therefore, semioticians tend to reject *essentialist* positions, that is, those that assume that meaning is pre-social or given prior to intersubjective interactions (Violi, 2017).

Third, Semiotics works with *semiosis* as it is encountered in 'signifying conglomerates' that can be empirically perceived (Verón, 1988, my translation). Even if semioticians engage in theoretical digressions, it is not a purely theoretical discipline: it normally works with specific objects of study – linguistic utterances, literary texts, speeches, images, objects, social practices, among many others – that are analysed through Semiotics' toolbox to render visible the underlying mechanisms through which they express and produce meaning. That is why semioticians have dealt with such a broad spectrum of phenomena, ranging from culinary practices to the ways in which individuals (re)present themselves on social media platforms. In any case, semioticians normally anchor their arguments in a *corpus* that they gather and delimit in the stage of constructing their objects of study and analysis. It is based on that *corpus* that their conclusions regarding meaning-making and signification will be valid. In this sense, Semiotics is 'a scientific rather than a philosophical project', as argued by Anne Hénault (2012: 10, my translation).

Over the decades, semioticians have discussed about the nature, methods and theoretical framework of the discipline. A first relevant discussion revolves around the conception of the sign and of *semiosis* as involving two or three elements. While for Saussure – and the structural Semiotics that developed based on his work, including that of Greimas – *semiosis* is a dual phenomenon that links a signifier (expression) and a signified (content), other approaches prefer Peirce's triadic approach to explain how culturally guided interpretations are crucial in meaning-making. Verón's (1988) book *La semiosis social*, which delineates a social Semiotics based on the study of social discourses, begins with a discussion of the opposition between dualistic and triadic conceptions of the sign. In this book, the focus is set in the dualistic conception, that is, the one that fixes its attention in the relationship between the plane of the content and the plane of the expression. Nevertheless, this does not exclude references to the triadic interpretative approach when appropriate, which is an approach more interested in the circulation of discourses between the moment of their production and that of their reception (Verón, 1988).

Second, there is a disciplinary divergence regarding the emergence of the interest for signs and *semiosis*: while for Saussure the focus is set on language, Peirce is more interested in understanding the cognitive dimension of *semiosis*. During the 1990s, Semiotics experienced a sort of 'perceptual turn' and semioticians started paying more and more attention to *semiosis* as an experience that produces cognitive and affective effects. This is how a 'Semiotics of passions' was born (Greimas & Fontanille, 1991; Pezzini, 1991). Populism is a discursive practice used strategically to produce both cognitive and emotional effects of sense. Therefore, while discourse-analytical approaches might be more interested in studying how populist political actors use language and other linguistic resources to produce meaning, Semiotics considers language *only one* of the multiple signifying systems they use to have a cognitive and emotional impact in their audience.

Finally, the disciplinary purpose of Semiotics is still a matter of discussion among semioticians. For some researchers – including Greimas – Semiotics is first and foremost a descriptive, scientific and objective enterprise aimed at explaining the functioning of *semiosis* and meaning through the use of rigorous methods. As such, it should follow the principles of positivist science. For others, Semiotics has an inescapable critical aim and is hence a discipline with a normative and transformative purpose. The first studies that employed a semiotic methodology – Roland Barthes's *Mythologies* (1957) or Eco's *Apocalittici e integrati* (1964) – intended at rendering visible the influence of ideology and hegemony in mass culture. A semiotic approach to populism could aim at both things: on the one hand, at mapping, describing and understanding its meaning-making logic and, on the other hand, at rendering visible its discursive strategies with the purpose of deconstructing them.

3.3 Social Semiotics and the study of 'meaning in action'

Social Semiotics is the branch or subfield of Semiotics that studies 'meaning in action', that is, 'the social practices used for managing meaning', in Anna Maria Lorusso's

(2015: 2) words. Here, social Semiotics is regarded as the part of general Semiotics interested in studying *semiosis*, meaning-making and signification as dynamic phenomena that take place *in vivo*, through the mediation of discourses and that emerge in the interactions between social actors (Landowski, 2014; Verón, 1988).

However, *social Semiotics* also refers in scholarship to other recent developments within linguistics and discourse studies, two fields that have also broadened their scope to include in their analyses other elements than merely linguistic utterances (van Leeuwen, 2005; Hodge & Kress, 1988). As it happens with general Semiotics, social Semiotics developed concomitantly in different academic circles, normally as an extension of the historical interest of Semiotics for texts (in particular, texts of linguistic nature). As a consequence, different types of social Semiotics coexist which originate from different research traditions and that employ different concepts, working methods and tools: as an example, while the French *sociosémiotique* practised by Eric Landowski and his followers is anchored mainly in Greimas's work, the English-speaking social Semiotics is anchored in linguistics – in particular in Halliday's (1978) work – and discourse studies.

The label '*social* Semiotics' might seem redundant because, as argued earlier, *semiosis* can only occur within the social domain (Eco, 1976; Marrone, 2001; Verón, 1988). The same argument applies to the idea of a '*cultural* Semiotics' (Lorusso, 2015), a label frequently used to refer to meaning-making in dynamic, open and *in vivo* contexts and situations.[9] According to Lorusso (2015: 4), 'after the first-order analysis, it is essential to continue in the direction of meaning in action.' For reasons of simplicity, in this book, social and cultural Semiotics will be regarded as a unique research field within general Semiotics.

Since Saussure, linguists tended to focus their research in studying language as a sign system. Therefore, they normally embraced synchronic and formalistic approaches to the *langue* through a focus on the phonetic, morphologic, syntactic and semantic levels of language, and left aside its use for communication and meaning-making (Fairclough, 1989: 6). In the middle of the twentieth century, a number of linguists developed the sub-branch called *Sociolinguistics*, which had a specific interest in studying variation in the use of language as a way of expressing meanings that are not linguistic but *social*. William Labov (1972) studied how variations in pronunciation by a community can express identity and motivational preferences besides socio-economic belonging. For Sociolinguistics, language is not only a sign system that must be described and made sense of: it is first and foremost a means of expression of particular cultural and emotional contents that are relevant from a linguistic but particularly from a semiotic perspective. This premise is also crucial in the work of Halliday (1978).

For social and cultural Semiotics, meaning-making is an active and open process; that is, it is in permanent development and new events can affect the attribution of meaning to past situations. As Lorusso (2015: 6) proposes, 'culture is a profoundly malleable and relative entity, whose meaning changes depending on the subject that observes and inter-defines it.' Recently, semioticians have shown interest in developing semiotic approaches to make sense of situations that can be quite ephemeral, but nevertheless meaningful. The basic assumption of social Semiotics follows Saussure's and Hjelmslev's structural conception of meaning and consists in that *semiosis* 'lives through relationships and differences' (Lorusso, 2015: 6). Social Semiotics examines how this occurs in close cooperation with anthropology, social psychology and other social sciences.

When mapping the development of social Semiotics, three corners of the world must be mentioned: Europe (with a focus on France and Italy), Latin America and Australia. If social and cultural Semiotics are conceived of as a unified research field, the Baltic region of Europe is also crucial in this disciplinary development.

3.3.1 French *sociosémiotique*

Although the idea of a Socio-semiotics (*sociosémiotique*) was introduced by Greimas, it was developed by some of his former collaborators from the Paris school (Pozzato, 1994). Greimas and Courtés (1982: 302–4) included the entry *Socio-semiotics* in their *Dictionnaire* to refer to a discipline that would encompass the study of non-linguistic signifying practices, such as 'behaviour regarding clothing, cooking, habitat, etc.' with the aim of contributing to Semiotics goal of grasping 'the universality of culture' and 'cultural specificities'. Just as Sociolinguistics examined the meanings expressed by language variation, Greimas and Courtés (1982: 303) saw in Socio-semiotics the study of 'the vast domain of social connotations'.[10]

Since the 1990s, Greimas's collaborators have made significant contributions to create a social Semiotics in line with his conception of Semiotics capable of explaining *any* signifying phenomenon. Hence, they tried to make of Semiotics a 'science of culture' rather than only a 'science of language'. The works of Jean-Marie Floch (1986; 1990; 1995; 2002), Eric Landowski (1997; 2004; 2014) and Jacques Fontanille (2008; 2011; 2015) were crucial in the incursion of Semiotics into the sociocultural domain beyond its usual objects of study. These three authors aimed at making of Semiotics an all-encompassing discipline capable of making sense of *the whole of human experience* in descriptive and explanatory terms (Demuru, 2019). Therefore, they and other members of the Paris school have focused on non-traditional objects of study such as practices, objects, passions, architecture and other sociocultural phenomena.

Since they worked directly with Greimas in the 'Paris school', the influence of the master is clearly visible not only in the complexity of the theoretical and conceptual tools employed by these researchers but also in the density of the prose. This has made their work not always accessible for readers that are not familiar with Greimas's basic vocabulary. As Chandler (2017: xv) argues, it is common that some readers get frustrated by books on Semiotics that seem 'confusing, dull, and deeply obscure, as if designed to keep out those who are not already "members of the club"'.

Jean-Marie Floch studied a broad spectrum of social phenomena such as branding and visual identities (Floch, 1995), photography (Floch, 1986) and strategic marketing (Floch, 1990). Floch is mostly known for his semiotic study of the trajectories that users make when using the Parisian metro and short-distance train lines. Observing and interviewing the users of the metro, Floch came up with a typology that uses Greimas's semiotic square to classify users in four types according to the use they make of the metro and the metro stations. In his case studies, Floch presents in accessible terms Greimas's complex theoretical apparatus. Moreover, he was a pioneer in using the methodology of Semiotics to study practices, opening the field to a Semiotics of the social. In opposition to texts – which present a high degree of closeness –, practices are ongoing, dynamic, changing and do not have a fixed closure apart from the segmentation that researchers might do for methodological purposes (Floch, 1990; Fontanille, 2008; Dondero, 2017; Demuru; 2017).

Floch (1990: 4, my translation) defines Semiotics through its object of study: 'languages – all languages – and signifying practices, which are essentially social practices'. For the author, 'signs are not themselves Semiotics' object of study: they are the surface units through which one aims at discovering the game of underlying signification' (Floch, 1990: 5, my translation). Floch is also known for bringing into Semiotics the concept of *bricolage* – taken from the work of structural anthropologist Claude Lévi-Strauss – as a way to refer to the semiotic practice of creating new meanings by employing already existing materials and resources.

Besides Floch, if there is a salient name in the development of French social Semiotics – certainly in France but also in other European academic circles and in Latin America – that is Eric Landowski. Landowski's three major books (1989; 1997; 2004) share the same subtitle: *Essais de socio-sémiotique* [Essays in Socio-semiotics]. In these books – and in myriad articles – Landowski has made significant efforts to shape the *sociosémiotique* envisaged by Greimas by examining *interactions* between social actors in multiple social contexts and fields, including the political (Landowski, 1984; 1985; 1997; 2005a; 2013; 2017; 2018; 2019; 2020). Landowski proposed a semiotic square that maps four general types of interactions that can be identified as underlying any social exchange: manipulation [*manipulation*], programming [*programmation*], adjustment [*ajustement*] and accident [*accident/assentiment*] (Figure 3). This square has been extensively used by semioticians to make sense of different social phenomena such as conversation (Pessoa de Barros, 2017) and cultural styles (Demuru, 2015). We will come back to this semiotic square in our discussion of the meaning-making dynamics that characterize populism, a subject that Landowski has also addressed in his recent work (Landowski, 2018; 2020).

A third crucial researcher in French post-Greimas social Semiotics is Jacques Fontanille. Fontanille worked extensively to make of Greimas's Semiotics a theory useful to explain the whole of culture and human experience. To start with, he co-wrote with

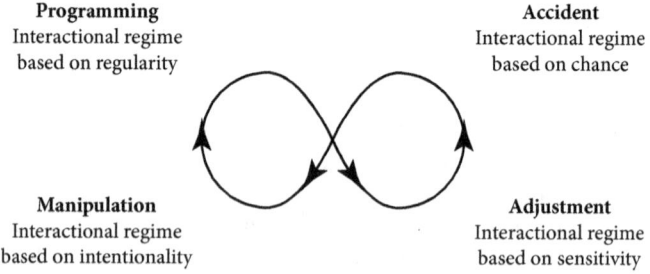

Figure 3 Landowski's interactional regimes. Source: Own elaboration based on Landowski (2005: 72), with permission from Presses Universitaires de Limoges.

Greimas *Sémiotique des passions* (1991), a book that presents a semiotic framework for the study of the emotional dimension of *semiosis*. With the purpose of founding a Semiotics capable of encompassing the whole human experience, in *Pratiques sémiotiques* (2008) Fontanille proposed that the study of meaning and signification should overcome the usual focus on signs and texts – the customary objects of study of Semiotics – and embrace also objects, practices, strategies and 'forms of life'.

The concept of 'forms of life' [*formes de vie*], also announced by Greimas, is currently an active research subject since it might allow to map cultural differences and commonalities by examining the basic units of meaning that individuals use to act in the world (Fontanille, 2015; Perusset, 2020; Fontanille & Perusset, 2021; Landowski, 2012). According to French social Semiotics, 'forms of life' are coherent sets of doing things (strategies, practices, using objects, producing texts and signs) that underlie and guide action. Fontanille's account constitutes a milestone in the development of methodological and conceptual tools that allow Semiotics to make sense of signifying systems other than natural and visual language, with a focus not only in textual artefacts but also in practices.[11]

Although contemporary French semioticians have shown a common interest in expanding semiotic research beyond language and texts of a linguistic nature, it would not be accurate to speak of a unified French *sociosémiotique*: rather, it could be argued that Floch, Landowski, Fontanille and others share a vision of Semiotics as a science of culture rather than only a science of language. However, every researcher works within their own theoretical and methodological framework – for example, Landowski's *sociosémiotique* is in practice almost purely a Semiotics of interactions.

3.3.2 Semiotics in Italy

Under the influence of Greimas's and Eco's semiotic accounts, over the last three to four decades, Italian researchers have used the concepts, methods and tools of Semiotics to study sociocultural phenomena such as collective and individual traumatic experiences (Violi, 2014; Lorusso, 2015), conflict (Demaria, 2006; Mazzucchelli, 2010), memory (Violi, 2014; Demaria, 2012), space (Giannitrapani, 2013), tourism (Brucculeri, 2009; Giannitrapani, 2009), political discourse (Cosenza, 2018) and everyday life practices, like gastronomy and food (Marrone, 2016; 2022; Mangano, 2022), among multiple other objects of study that fall beyond the scope of traditional text-focused Semiotics (Marrone, 2001; Marrone & Migliore, 2022; Marsciani, 2007).[12] Italy has been a hotspot of applied social and cultural Semiotics (Ventura Bordenca, 2022; Sorrentino, 2022), even if semioticians do not always use these labels to refer to their work and prefer to use that of Semiotics. Italian semioticians have also been extremely productive within the 'traditional' branches of Semiotics such as visual Semiotics and Semiotics of photography.[13]

Italian scholars usually work by delimiting and analysing specific *corpus* to grasp how and through which procedures they are meaningful. In studying trauma and conflict, research usually examines monuments, sites of memory and practices of remembrance, among other articulations in the plane of the expression, because all these empirically perceivable events are manifestations of the sociocultural organization of discourse in the dimension of the 'deep structures' (Violi, 2014; 2019; Bellentani & Panico, 2016).

In this use of semiotic theory to study sociocultural phenomena, the interdisciplinary dialogue that is constitutive of social Semiotics has been implemented in a fruitful manner: Italy is perhaps the country where semiotic theory became more proficient in collaborating with other disciplines without being trapped in its own jargon and theoretical complexity. The research field of ethnosemiotics (Marsciani, 2007; Lancioni & Marsciani, 2007; Mazzarino, 2022) is a good example of this collaboration.

Apart from Eco, another crucial Italian researcher was Paolo Fabbri, who not only tried to strengthen semiotic theory by insisting on the relevance of narrativity and the affective dimension in meaning-making (Fabbri, 1998) but also studied political discourse and was keen on developing a 'marked', theoretically consistent and empirically informed type of Semiotics (Fabbri, 2021). More recently, Claudio Paolucci – a former student of Umberto Eco and by drawing on Peircean interpretative Semiotics – became a central figure in the development of *cognitive* Semiotics (Lobaccaro, 2022) through the study of the 'principle of narrativity' and the concept of *persona* in enunciation (Paolucci, 2012; 2020; 2021b).[14]

3.3.3 Social Semiotics in English

In Australia, the so-called Sydney group – also 'Sydney Semiotics Circle' – developed a social Semiotics based on the work of linguist Michael Halliday (1978) and influenced by the developments within discourse studies, which started being *critical* by examining the relationship between discourse, ideology and power. Halliday studied language from a functional perspective and with a particular interest in how it plays a crucial modelling role in the process of socialization. Based on his general approach that conceives of 'language as social semiotics', since the late 1980s the label *social Semiotics* has been used by scholars like Theo van Leeuwen (2005), Robert Hodge and Gunther Kress (1988) to refer to a more encompassing linguistics that takes into account also non-linguistic aspects of discourse.

For Hodge and Kress (1988: viii), 'meaning is produced and reproduced under specific social conditions, through specific material forms and agencies. It exists in relationship to concrete subjects and objects, and is inexplicable except in terms of this set of relationships.' This premise is the reason why they use the adjective *social* to modify the noun *Semiotics:* they define Semiotics as 'the general study of *semiosis,* that is, the processes and effects of the production and reproduction, reception and circulation of meaning in all forms' (Hodge & Kress, 1988: 261). The authors' theory departs from two basic premises: on the one hand, 'the primacy of the social dimension in understanding language structures and processes' and, on the other hand, that meaning 'resides so strongly and pervasively in other systems of meaning,' including 'visual, aural, behavioural and other codes,' and not only in verbal language (Hodge & Kress, 1988: vii). The authors argue in favour of 'the need for linguistics and the study of verbal language to be thoroughly assimilated into a general theory of the social processes through which meaning is constituted and has its effects' (Hodge & Kress, 1988: viii).

For Theo van Leeuwen (2005: 1), social Semiotics is 'a form of enquiry' that must be applied 'to specific instances and specific problems' and that 'always requires immersing oneself not just in semiotic concepts and methods as such but also in some other field'. In the glossary included in *Introducing Social Semiotics*, van Leeuwen (2005:

285) defines Semiotics as 'the study of semiotic resources and their uses', a definition that matches the conception of social Semiotics embraced in this book, as it presents commonalities with every other socio-semiotic account. According to van Leeuwen (2005: 270), Hodge and Kress wrote 'the book that put social semiotics on the map.' This statement might be true for English-speaking academic circles, but it is not for other circles: Greimas had already announced a social Semiotics and, in the 1980s, Landowski (1984) was already working in developing the field.[15]

In their enterprise, these three researchers made of the category of *multimodality* one central in approaching meaning-making as an articulation of semiotic resources of different nature. According to Hestbaek Andersen et al. (2015: 143), Kress and van Leeuwen 'have been in the lead of developing the field of multimodal research based on Halliday's understanding of how the social underpins all kinds of meaning making'. As such, English-speaking social Semiotics has been of interest for linguists because it provides them with conceptual tools that allow to transcend the examination of language in grammatical and pragmatic terms and to extend it to more complex modes in which natural languages function in the world.

Besides the work of these three scholars and others interested in multimodality (Kress, 2010; Kress & van Leeuwen, 2001; Machin, 2007; Ledin & Machin, 2020; van Leeuwen, 2021) and in the role of *semiosis* in the learning process (Hodge, 2014; Kress, 2001), Semiotics has also been influential in Canada, where scholars have used semiotic theory to analyse sociocultural phenomena, such as *emojis* (Danesi, 2016), love (Danesi, 2019), and the circus (Bouissac, 2020), among other phenomena that have 'meaning in action' at their core.

3.3.4 Latin American social Semiotics

Social Semiotics has also been of interest for researchers in Latin America, particularly Brazil and Argentina, two countries where Semiotics was introduced relatively early (Barros, 2012). In Brazil, and under the direct influence of Landowski, the *Centro de Pesquisas Sociossemióticas* [Centre of Socio-Semiotic Research] of the Pontifícia Universidade Católica of São Paulo is a major centre for social Semiotics, as evidenced in its vast bibliographical production on subjects of a sociocultural nature, such as practices (de Oliveira, 2013) and interactions (de Oliveira, 2004). The works of these researchers usually follow Greimas and the post-Greimas French semiotic tradition (Gonçalves & Martynuk, 2021).

Eliseo Verón was an Argentine-born and Paris-based scholar whose work has been extremely influential in Argentina and in Spanish-speaking Latin America. Verón developed a theory of *semiosis* as social discursivity that tried to overcome the Saussure-Peirce divide between dual and triadic conceptions of the sign. According to the author, every social practice has a significant dimension, and meaning is always anchored in the social. Therefore, social Semiotics can only consist in 'a theory of production of social discourses' since it is 'in *semiosis* that the reality of the social is constructed' (Verón, 1988: 124–6, my translation).

While Verón was active researching multiple subjects, he is nowadays mostly remembered by his contributions to three topics: (1) his theory of social discourses and, in particular, his thesis that studying them requires focusing on the gap that is produced between their production and their recognition (Verón, 1988); (2) his studies of the political domain, of which he conceived as a *polemic* discursive field (1987; 1989); and (3) his conceptualization of mediatization – of politics, and also as an anthropological process that characterizes human evolution (Verón, 1994; 1997; 1998). These three items are useful for our semiotic study of populism and are discussed with more detail in the following chapter.

3.3.5 Juri Lotman and the Tartu-Moscow school

When dealing with social Semiotics, the question usually arises regarding what the differences with cultural Semiotics – also referred to as *Semiotics of culture* (Lorusso, 2015; Lancioni, 2015) – are. The question could by answered by referring to the history of the two research fields: while *social* Semiotics is linked to the French tradition, *cultural* Semiotics is based on Juri Lotman's work and that of the members of the 'Tartu-Moscow school' of Semiotics. In any case, multiple commonalities are evidenced between the two research strands, such as the centrality of the sociocultural dimension in meaning-making and the aim of understanding how culture and human experience are meaningful. Therefore, it is pertinent to treat social and cultural Semiotics as being part of a same overarching theoretical project: the study of sociocultural phenomena as grounded on sense, meaning-making and signification.

If this postulate is accepted, then the work of Juri Lotman is central to a sociocultural Semiotics (Lotman, 1990; 2005; 2009). In parallel to Greimas and influenced by French structuralism – but also by Russian scholarship on discourse and literature – Lotman aimed at building a semiotic theory capable of grasping, describing and explaining the totality of culture. According to Laura Gherlone (2020: 4), 'the ultimate goal was to elaborate, through an exact, interdisciplinary and objective method, [. . .] an all-encompassing science of language: semiotics'. Lotman wrote extensively on cultural issues and introduced relevant concepts and analytical categories such as that of the *semiosphere*, which will be of use when studying populism from a semiotic perspective. For Lotman, culture is based on the prevalence of memory through its presence as texts that circulate within the semiosphere and that are carriers of meaning.

Lotman made of *text* a central category of analysis and approached culture as a semiosphere, that is, as a delimited space with a semiotic core and the respective boundaries within which the production, circulation and consumption of meaning is possible. Because it is a delimited space, the semiosphere has a periphery where interesting and productive phenomena of exchange and translation occur. For Lotman (1990), language is the primary modelling system and it is based on it that the cultural world takes its form as a secondary modelling system. This premise is aligned Eco's proposal in *A Theory of Semiotics*, with Halliday's in *Language as Social Semiotics* and with Saussure's conception of *Semiology*.

Although he is the most salient scholar, Lotman did not work alone. The expression 'Tartu-Moscow school' is usually employed to refer to Baltic Semiotics influenced by Lotman, not only of his contemporary collaborators but also in current scholarship – mainly in Estonian universities – embracing his views on culture and meaning-making (Tamm & Torop, 2022; Madisson & Ventsel, 2020; Ventsel, 2011). Lotman and his colleagues founded the very first semiotic journal of the world: *Trudy po znakovym sistemam* (Gherlone, 2020).

As Semiotics consolidated as a relatively autonomous discipline – or research field – within the social sciences with *semiosis* as its object of study, researchers understood that a dialogue with other sciences and disciplines was necessary to grasp the dynamics of meaning-making at the heart of human experience. As demonstrated here, this theoretical and methodological interest occurred in parallel in different academic circles around the world. Nevertheless, the theoretical and epistemological commonalities between French, Italian, English-speaking, Latin American and Baltic social Semiotics are many. First and foremost, Semiotics stopped being considered a mere science of language and the text (Rastier, 2001) and started being conceived of as a science capable of studying the complex and dynamic mechanisms of culture and society. In 2023, social Semiotics still needs to delimit its scope and boundaries by encompassing the developments experienced by all these research circles. This book is a step in that direction.

3.4 Studying populism from a socio-semiotic perspective

As demonstrated in the previous chapter, the contributions to the debate on populism during the last two decades are numerous. Therefore, any new contribution must justify its relevance for the debate. Why is it pertinent and relevant to approach populism from a semiotic perspective? As a political phenomenon that occurs in the public sphere of various societies, populism has a constitutive discursive dimension. Since politics is a social activity based on intersubjective interactions that revolve around persuasion, meaning-making is crucial in producing effects of sense to persuade the electorate to support the projects of populist political actors, parties and movements. To achieve the adherence of the electorate, populist political actors develop and use discursive strategies that imply practices of discursive articulation of semiotic resources of diverse nature, such as language use, non-verbal communication, visual and audiovisual products, attitudes towards opponents and the political system and other resources that contribute to meaning-making.

As discussed, scholars working in the field of populism studies have already theorized extensively the discursive dimension of populism. In doing so, they have normally embraced Laclau and Mouffe's discourse theory. Therefore, with the exception of a few journal articles – two salient examples are a dedicated *dossier* in the French journal *Actes Sémiotiques,* from 2018, and a full issue of the Latin American journal *DeSignis,* from 2019, together with some articles dispersed in other journals – the discursive approaches to populism have not used tools, concepts, categories and models from Semiotics. In other words, although the semiotics of populism have been studied in existing scholarship – although they do not say it, Laclau and Mouffe's approach to the political and to populism is highly semiotic, as is argued in the next chapter – there has not been an examination of populism from Semiotics, that is, by employing its theoretical, conceptual and methodological apparatus. This is the gap in research that this book aims at filling with the purpose of enriching the discourse-oriented accounts of populism by adding the perspective of a discipline with a solid history within the social sciences. In this sense, the project of a 'social Semiotics of populism' aims at introducing into populism studies a viewpoint that can replace Laclau and Mouffe's discourse theory as the hegemonic perspective to study the political field.

Studying populism from a Semiotic perspective implies not only using the discipline's terminology and methods but also looking at dimensions of reality that transcend language use: while existing discursive, linguistic or pragmatic accounts of populism usually examine what populist political actors say and do *with language* orally in speeches and declarations, on social media, in their manifestos and, eventually, books, an approach to populism from social Semiotics will examine how they produce meaning more generally, not only in their use of language but also of other semiotic resources like attire, music, gestures and attitudes towards opponents and the political system.

In this sense, a proper social Semiotics of populism implies working with a broad and heterogeneous corpus, ranging from textual productions to performances and including the sense of closeness that is constructed in the populist leader's performances in rallies and other face-to-face events. Of particular interest for social Semiotics will also be how populist political actors construct in their public discourses and performances a specific view of the social space. Grasping populist meaning-making is an ambitious quest that requires the cooperation with other social sciences – particularly, ethnography – capable of describing and capturing meaning in action, *in vivo*, as it develops. This book is, therefore, only a first step in that direction by focusing on how populist discourse is meaningful discourse, that is, one that over the years became a type of discourse socioculturally codified with a proper name.

How do populist political actors articulate their discourses and performances? Is there a shared narrative configuration evidenced in those discourses and performances? Which 'deep structures' can be found as the basis of those discourses and performances? How do populist political actors bring the populist world view to life? How are 'the people' imagined, represented and referred to in discourse? Which features are presented as constitutive of 'the people'? Which other collective identities are present in populist discourse? How do political actors articulate populism with other political contents and discourses? How is the relationship between the populist leader and the audience built? These are some of the questions that social Semiotics will look at when studying populism.

Over the last decades, discourse analysts – including Critical Discourse Analysis (CDA) researchers – studied populism with great interest (Wodak, 2015; Wodak, KhosraviNik, & Mral, 2013; Charaudeau, 2011).[16] The socio-semiotic approach to populism shares several commonalities with those studies and also differs in some aspects. The first aspect is that language – the main object of interest for linguistics and discourse studies – is considered *only one* signifying system among others in populist meaning-making. The second is that the main object of interest for social Semiotics is set on *semiosis* and meaning-making as the results of specific *practices* of a discursive – and hence social – nature. These practices occur within the political field and, as such, are codified in culture. Therefore, Semiotics will certainly examine the plane of the expression and also the plane of the content with the purpose of rendering visible what is the internal structure of populist discourse. Moreover, while CDA is troubled by how language and discourse express power inequalities, this is an aspect usually left aside by semioticians, who tend to operate mainly in descriptive terms. In the fourth place, studying 'meaning in action' implies dealing not only with texts – in the traditional sense, that is, as speeches, posts on social media, advertisements – but also with *situations* that are ongoing and hence do not have a closure that allows considering them as delimited units of analysis (in semiotic terms: 'texts'). Finally, populist meaning-making will be studied with the concepts, categories and methods developed within Semiotics and not by recurring to the work of philosophers like Foucault or Derrida, as is a common practice for CDA. This disciplinary focus should also strengthen Semiotics status through the application of its theoretical apparatus to the study of a specific phenomenon.

Laclau and Mouffe's discourse-theoretical account on the political and on populism – the standard scholarship with a discursive perspective within populism studies – also deals with discourse and meaning. However, it differs from a semiotic account in multiple aspects. To begin with, their discourse theory and their theory of populism[17] have a strong ontological component that seeks to explain the grounds of the social. This type of study is not of interest for Semiotics, an empirical discipline interested in studying how *semiosis*, meaning- and sense-making are *evidenced* in specific texts, objects and practices. In opposition to discourse-theoretical accounts of populism, semioticians are not interested in grasping the essence and nature of the social realm (Laclau, 1991; 1994) but begin their analysis working with concrete configurations of meaning such as speeches, advertisements, audiovisual spots, social media posts, gestures and use of the body for meaning-making purposes, attire, attitudes and the creation of situations in face-to-face and online interactions, among other objects of study. The purpose is to understand how these configurations are meaningful by tapping into contents already existing in culture.

According to Chandler (2017: 126), 'identifying the primary concepts in relation to the thematic or narrative structure of the material being examined and selecting the particular words to be used to refer to them is the initial analytical task' of Semiotics. This is one of the main contributions that Semiotics can do to scholarship on populism, as is demonstrated in Chapters 6, 7 and 8. Working within Laclauian discourse theory, Panizza (2005: 20) argues that 'as in any other political narrative, the narrative of populism articulates a variety of myths, symbols, ideological themes and rational arguments, telling its audience where the people come from, how to make sense of their present condition, and offering a path towards a better future.' Semiotics will shed light on populist political actors' meaning-making strategies by examining the narrative configurations they employ by drawing on Greimas's narrative scheme, semiotic square and theory of enunciation, by studying the interactional strategies developed by them drawing on Landowski's model, by scrutinizing their discourses and performances with the help of Verón's analytical categories, by examining multimodal strategies of meaning-making and by using Lotman's category of the *semiosphere* to understand how the empty units of 'the people' and the 'other' are filled with content, among other inputs. Moreover, the semiotic study of populism will strengthen the ideational account of populism by demonstrating how political ideologies, discursive logics, communicative styles, performances, cognitive frames and political strategies are all part of meaning-making within the political.

As discussed in Chapter 2, in the 1960s, Minogue (1969: 197) stressed the importance of identifying the *structure of feelings* that convinces and moves individuals to take action in the name of something greater than themselves. Minogue argued that for that purpose, scholars must consider the statements and actions that mobilize individuals. According to Minogue, in doing so a distinction needs to be established between the *rhetoric* used by the members of a movement, 'which may be randomly plagiarized from anywhere according to the needs of the moment', and the *ideology* which expresses the deeper currents of the movement (Minogue, 1969: 198). This intuitive distinction between the form and the content to be found in the first notable book published on populism already evidences the need of a semiotic approach to make sense of it.

In her first analyses of populism, Mouffe (2005b: 55) saw one of the causes for the growth of right-wing populism in Europe in 'the incapacity of traditional parties to provide distinctive forms of identifications around possible alternatives'. According to Mouffe (2005b: 55), 'right-wing populist parties are often the only ones that attempt to mobilize passions and create collective forms of identifications.' The semiotic imprint of this argument is salient: populist political actors not only appeal to the electorate by employing discursive strategies aimed at producing an effect of sense related to identity and belonging, but they also actively seek to activate passions – Wodak (2015) speaks of a *politics of fear* to refer to one of the main strategies employed by right-wing populist actors – and propose new alternative political scenarios. This is nothing else than a discursive strategy aimed at reshaping the political imaginary through an activation of the emotions of the electorate (Moreno Barreneche, 2019a).

Collective identities are crucial in the discursive articulations of populist political actors. Besides the narrative dimension and that of enunciation, a semiotic approach to populism will examine how populist discourse constructs the political field through the employment of semiotic resources that express collective social identities. The constructivist premise of Semiotics does not take identities for granted.[18] If identities are not anything given or determined by social structure, then they are constructed (even if partially) in discourse. However, to argue that identities are constructed discursively does not imply that they are *only* discourse: it would be a theoretical challenge to argue that identities are purely fictional and cultural and that they do not have any type of material anchorage. As shown in the next two chapters, social Semiotics has the potential to explain how that construction occurs.

The social Semiotics of populism could then be summarized as an enquiry that will examine the discursive practices and strategies used by political actors labelled as *populist* to produce effects of sense in their audiences. Due to the nature of populism, this enquiry will necessarily deal with the construction of collective social identities in political discourse.

4

Politics as a 'Contest over Meaning'

Social life is structured in multiple spheres or fields organized around specific discursive practices. The educational, the religious and the private are all social spheres that are culturally coded. The political is one of those spheres. This chapter looks at the dynamics governing that sphere, which is one related to how individuals conduct their lives together and manage power relations in the public sphere (Landowski, 2019; Peñamarín, 2020; Charaudeau, 2014; Dagatti & Velázquez García-Talavera, 2020). As is argued in the following, the political field – as any other social field – has an inherent semiotic nature because it is based on the production and circulation of discourses that it can be a meaningful social field. Therefore, social life is structured in different *semiospheres*.

Examining the political from a semiotic perspective certainly implies dealing with language and how it is used strategically. Discourse analysts Isabella and Norman Fairclough (2012: 1) argue that 'politics is most fundamentally about making choices about how to act in response to circumstances and goals, it is about choosing *policies*, and such choices and the actions which follow from them are based upon practical argumentation'. While discourse analysts might be particularly interested in examining how language is used for argumentative purposes, semioticians will focus on meaning-making and signification. This does not mean that semioticians regard the political as being about *semiosis* only: there are certainly material and policy issues that affect people's life in multiple ways that are constitutive of the political. Nevertheless, as every other social phenomenon, politics is a meaningful social activity due to its anchorage on social discourses.

The semiotic nature of the political has multiple expressions. One of them – one that is crucial for any study of populism – is to be found in political actors' discursive construction of collective identities. Another is the 'contest over meaning' inherently linked to the dynamics of the competition for power that takes place within the political semiosphere. The political is hence an appropriate object of study for Semiotics not only in a general manner as a specific field of the social life based on *semiosis* but also in its multiple forms and manifestations across geography and history. Populism is one of those forms.

4.1 The conflictive nature of the political

Multiple theories exist in the history of thought about politics and the political field. The topic can be found already in Antiquity, for example, in the works of Plato and Aristotle. Besides its long history, conceptions of politics and the political vary depending on the theoretical background of the scholars that have dealt with these objects of study. To map the various existing conceptions of politics and the political, one productive analytical distinction is that which opposes a *consensus-based* type of politics to a *conflict-based* type of politics (Mouffe, 2005a; 2013).[1]

While the former argues – based on a liberal, rational and individualistic tradition of thought – that politics is about compromises, negotiations and finding agreements between parties and groups with different interests, the latter highlights the inescapable polemic and adversarial nature of this social field that cannot be overcome through partial agreements. In semiotic terms, while consensus implies conjunction, identity and compatibility between political actors, conflict implies disjunction, incompatibility and difference (Landowski, 1976).

A compromise with any of these positions is not necessary for the purposes of this book. Politics can be easily conceived as an adversarial activity – different projects and world views compete in accessing power to manage and set the course of the common life of a community – that needs of agreements to achieve something at the policy level. This is particularly the case in coalition governments and when a country's parliament is fragmented in various political groups: only through consensus and agreements the political sphere can function and achieve something.[2]

However, as demonstrated in this chapter, scholars who have approached the political field from a discursive and/or semiotic perspective (Mouffe, 2005a; Verón, 1987; 1998; Laclau, 2005a; 2005b; Landowski, 2019; 2020; Fabbri & Marcarino, 1985; Demuru & Albertini, 2009; de Oliveira, 2021) have normally emphasized the conflictive, polemic and adversarial nature of this social field. These scholars are usually interested in political discourse rather than in policy outputs. For them, politics implies an adversarial logic that takes the form of a 'contest over meaning'. This is the case because one of the key mechanisms that define the political field consists in creating collective identities in discourse. These cultural artefacts serve to facilitate individuals' making sense of the social space in the form of a social categorization based on a sense of belonging to a group. As these artefacts are created culturally through the use of language and other semiotic resources, their meaning can only emerge through an opposition to other identities that coexist with them in the social space. This gives place to the logic of antagonism in the form of a competition between 'us' and 'them'. This logic has been highlighted by political theorists, discourse analysts and semioticians that have studied the political.

In a book that aims at building bridges between Semiotics and political theory through the study of populism, a good starting point to examine the conception of the political as a conflictive social field is the work of Chantal Mouffe. This is the case because her work combines a political with a discursive perspective.[3] Moreover, her work with Ernesto Laclau is the most common reference in populism scholarship, even if it is only to take distance from their assumptions and normative stance.

In *Agonistics*, Mouffe (2013: xi) argues that 'society is permeated by contingency and any order is of an hegemonic nature, i.e., it is always the expression of power relations'. This statement does not seem to allow the subscription to a consensus-based type of politics, since it poses that there is always a group that holds power and imposes its world view through hegemonic discourse. Mouffe (2013: xi) believes that, in this context, 'the search for a consensus without exclusion and the hope for a perfectly reconciled and harmonious society have to be abandoned'. This is the case because liberal consensus-oriented approaches overestimate rationalism and individualism and take for granted 'the availability of a universal consensus based on reason' (Mouffe, 2013: 3).

To elaborate her proposal, Mouffe establishes a distinction between *the political* and *politics*. These labels refer to two different dimensions of the social practice of managing power relations in the public sphere: while *politics* refers to 'the ensemble of practices, discourses and institutions that seek to establish a certain order and to organize human coexistence' (Mouffe, 2013: xii), *the political* is related to the ontological dimension of politics, which for Mouffe consists in an inescapable antagonism that can 'take many forms and can emerge in diverse social relations' (Mouffe, 2013: 2) and which informs the social practice of politics. The distinction serves to render visible that 'proper political questions always involve decisions that require making a choice between conflicting alternatives' (Mouffe, 2013: 3).

Mouffe's distinction is useful to understand that the management of power relations in the public sphere has different dimensions: one more pragmatic and the other more ontological. Politics is the manifestation of the political. Since she is a political theorist, Mouffe's work normally focuses in understanding the discursive mechanisms through which antagonism emerges and occurs as the engine of political life. It is in this point that the semiotic approach differs from Mouffe's discourse-theoretical one: instead of focusing only on issues of a philosophical nature, it works with a strong empirical anchorage, that is, looking at the dynamics that govern *politics* as a perceivable expression of *the political*. Speeches, tweets, public performances, communicative styles and other texts will serve as the entry point for semioticians to understand the configuration that the political has in a given society.

Mouffe (2005b: 55) argues that the conflictive nature of the political implies that politics 'always consists in the creation of an "us" versus a "them" [and] implies the creation of collective identities'. Elsewhere she wrote that 'the political is from the outset concerned with collective forms of identification, since in this field we are always dealing with the formation of "us" as opposed to "them"' (Mouffe, 2013: 4). This conception of the political – which will be approached from a semiotic perspective in the following sections of this chapter – is crucial for a semiotic study of the political, and in particular of populism. For Mouffe (2005b: 55), populism 'provides collective forms of identification around "the people"'; that is, it is about constructing in discourse and through the employment of multiple semiotic resources of *social categories* with which people are expected to identify and mobilize politically. Therefore, as argued by Panizza (2005: 28), conflict is constitutive of the political because 'it is through antagonism that political identities are constituted, and radical alternatives to the existing order can be imagined'.

Mouffe bases her conception of the political in the work of Carl Schmitt. For Schmitt, the political is defined by a *relationship* between those one can consider friends [*Freunde*] and those considered enemies [*Feinde*]. According to Schmitt (1932: 25, my translation), 'every religious, moral, economic, ethnic or other opposition transforms itself in a political one when it is strong enough as to effectively group individuals in friends and enemies'. This is how in Schmitt's account, the social becomes political. Dividing the social space in groups is at the core of his proposal.

Mouffe elaborates on Schmitt's distinction and argues that the inescapable conflictive nature of the political can take two forms: it can either be antagonistic or agonistic. While *antagonism* consists in conceiving the rival as an *enemy* – as argued by Schmitt – the *agonistic* model implies conceiving the rival as an *adversary* with whom the 'we' is in a legitimate struggle over the management of power. Mouffe subscribes to the second account and her theoretical efforts aim at providing 'the institutions which will permit conflicts to take an "agonistic" form, where the opponents are not enemies but adversaries among whom exists a conflictual consensus' (Mouffe, 2013: xii). Instead of a war that implies annihilating an enemy, politics would be more like a *game*, where rival teams compete legitimately to achieve victory.

One of the most interesting aspects of Mouffe's account of the political is the idea of an increasing moralization of the political struggle, which facilitates the supremacy of antagonism over agonism (Mouffe, 2005b: 57). Moralization refers to a discursive phenomenon through which the 'other' is not only identified as different from Us: it is also valorized in negative terms. For Mouffe (2005b: 58), 'frontiers between us and them are constantly drawn, but nowadays they are drawn in moral categories, between "good" and "evil"'. According to Panizza (2005: 23), 'moral divides [. . .] disqualify political adversaries, without leaving room for legitimate dissent'. In the case of populism, 'against the corruption of politics, populism offers a promise of emancipation after a journey of sacrifice' (Panizza, 2005: 23). In brief, according to Mouffe (2005b: 59), 'when the opponent is defined in moral terms, it can only be envisaged as an enemy, not as an adversary. With the "evil them" no agonistic debate is possible'.

Like semioticians and discourse analysts, Mouffe (2005b: 55) acknowledges the centrality of discursive elements as constitutive of the political field and argues that 'when democratic politics has lost its capacity to shape the discussion about how we should organize our common life, [. . .] the conditions are ripe for talented demagogues to articulate popular frustration'. She adds that 'it is the lack of an effective democratic debate about possible alternatives that has led in many countries to the success of political parties claiming to the "voice of the people"' (Mouffe, 2005b: 51). As it can be seen, for Mouffe, populism would be the result of the dynamics inherent to the political: when a public sphere does not count with alternative political imaginaries that are plausible, some political actors might try to take advantage and come up with new ones.

To sum up, in Mouffe's conception of the political there is an inescapable adversarial logic. This logic can take different forms, depending on how the 'other' is conceived – as an enemy or as a legitimate adversary. For Mouffe, when politics has taken a direction in which the deep discussions of society do not occur as they should, political actors can capitalize on the existing frustration and start implementing discursive strategies to transform relationships that should be agonistic into antagonistic. Similarly, Eirikur Bergmann (2020: 7) sees in populist politics 'an ongoing move away from merely seeing political opponents as adversaries who are competing within a level playing field and according to shared rules. Instead, opponents are increasingly being turned into enemies'. In Mouffe's account, even if the dimension of politics can give place to agonistic interactions, the ontological level of the political is defined by an inescapable antagonism.

4.2 The political as a discursive field

Politics and the political have been objects of interest and study for scholars from different research traditions within the social sciences and humanities such as political theory, political science, discourse analysis and Semiotics, among others.[4] As a result, multiple approaches coexist that not always enter in a fruitful dialogue, even if their commonalities are salient.

4.2.1 Laclau and Mouffe's discourse theory

One of the most salient discursive accounts of the political is the one presented by Ernesto Laclau and Chantal Mouffe in their 1985 book *Hegemony and Socialist Strategy* (2001). Despite the normative political position that the authors make manifest in that book – they aim at overcoming Marxism to give the Left a new strength with the inputs of Gramscian theory and poststructuralist thought – the discourse theory they put forward in the chapter 'Beyond the Positivity of the Social: Antagonisms and Hegemony' is a good starting point to approach the political field from a perspective interested in discourse and meaning-making. Besides, studies on populism with a focus on discourse normally embrace Laclau and Mouffe's discourse theory. Examining its foundations will serve to render visible the commonalities it has with Eliseo Verón's social semiotic account based on the study of discourses.

One of the central concepts in Laclau and Mouffe's discourse theory is that of *articulation*, which is conceived of as a *practice* that combines already existing discursive elements to produce new meanings. According to the authors, *articulation* refers to 'any practice establishing a relation among elements such that their identity is modified as a result of the articulatory practice'. In semiotic terms, it consists in doing something new or original with existing semiotic resources, like a *bricolage*.

Laclau and Mouffe (2001: 91) define *discourse* as 'the structured totality resulting from the articulatory practice'. If one speaks of *populist discourse*, what is meant with this expression is *a type of articulatory practice* carried out by social actors identified as 'populist' that produces a specific 'structured totality'. Laclau and Mouffe's conception of discourse – which they only introduce in a general fashion and do not fully develop in their book – is more in line with the notion of 'discursive formations', that is, relatively stable and coherent systems (synchronic totalities) that can be evidenced in a given moment of time and accessed through texts such as speeches, news articles and so forth (Angenot, 2010; Fairclough, 1992).

These discursive formations are not cast in stone. Rather, they are recognized by following a method of 'regularity in dispersion': 'it is sufficient that certain regularities establish differential positions for us to be able to speak of a discursive formation' (Laclau and Mouffe, 2001: 95). A discursive formation is hence an analytical construction that analysts do inductively by identifying an 'absent structure' (Eco, 1968) as underlying different discursive practices and events. As is argued in the following, this is precisely what occurs with populist discourse: a specific articulatory practice that has been used by multiple political actors around the world and in different historic moments is regarded as a discursive formation with particular features. The noun *populism* is used to refer to that discursive formation. The following chapter examines the narrative structure of that discursive formation.

Laclau and Mouffe's discourse theory draws on the work of Saussure, for whom meaning emerges through relational differences – oppositions – between the terms that are part of a given signifying system in a given moment of time. Within Semiotics, this idea was further elaborated by Hjelmslev, embraced by Eco, assumed by Greimas and nowadays is considered to be part of Semiotics' constructivist premise. It is also an idea accepted by Laclau and Mouffe in their conception of the political as defined by a struggle over hegemony. They conceive of a discourse as 'a differential and structured system of positions' (Laclau and Mouffe, 2001: 95).

Within Semiotics, the assumption is that 'semiosis [. . .] lives through relationships and differences' (Lorusso, 2015: 6). For Lorusso, the specificity of the semiotic outlook is that it can 'capture and analyze the network of relationships and differences in which meaning is given'. This is the case because 'culture and meaning tend to organize themselves in a structural, differential, contrastive and stratified way' (Lorusso, 2015: 18). Saussure's theses about value and meaning being grounded on oppositions was re-elaborated by Hjelmslev, who used the example presented in Figure 4 to show how different linguistic communities refer to portions of the plan of the content with different words following a segmentation of reality. Figure 4 shows how Danish has only two words to refer to that to which German and French refer with three words, although their segmentation of *wood* and *forest* is different.

That meaning is relational and based on differences and oppositions means that it is only through the existence of *an 'other'* that meaning can emerge. For Eco (1976: 73), 'a cultural unit [. . .] is defined inasmuch as it is *placed* in a system of other cultural units which are opposed to it and circumscribe it'. This premise – inherited from structuralist linguistics – is one of Semiotics' main tenets. It can not only explain Mouffe's conception of the political but be also the foundation of a *Semiotics of the*

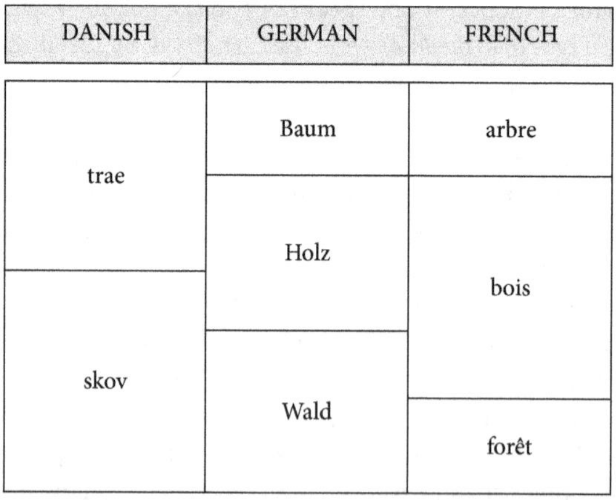

DANISH	GERMAN	FRENCH
trae	Baum	arbre
	Holz	bois
skov	Wald	
		forêt

Figure 4 Meaning as a cultural unit. Source: Own elaboration based on the work of Hjelmslev and Eco.

political, particularly useful for the purpose of examining the construction of collective identities in discourse, as is discussed in Section 4.3.

Although Laclau and Mouffe use Saussure's model of the sign and his theory of value, they criticize him for having assumed that, in a given moment of time, linguistic systems are *closed*. For the authors – it is here where the poststructuralist nature of their theory is visible – the total closure of the system is impossible and new meanings are (or try to be) introduced as a result of the political struggle (cf. Laclau, 1991). When a new element enters into the system, it affects the meaning of the elements that are already part of it.[5] The 'contest over meaning' that defines the political sphere aims at establishing a particular *hegemony*, that is, the supremacy of one discursive formation over others. This is where Laclau and Mouffe's theory becomes heavily poststructuralist, ontological and philosophical, and stops being of interest for semioticians. It is also here that the label of *political theorists* is justified to describe their positioning within the academia.

Laclau and Mouffe's theory of discourse shares multiple similarities with Verón's conception of social – and political – discourses in his quest of founding a social Semiotics grounded in the study of the production, circulation and recognition of social discourses. As Laclau and Mouffe argue, the distinction between discursive and non-discursive practices is not accurate because every sign, object or practice gains its meaning from the specific discursive context in which it is embedded. It is *through the mediation of* discourses that objects come into being and gain meaning:

> a) every object is constituted as an object of discourse, insofar as no object is given outside every discursive condition of emerge; and b) [. . .] any distinction between what are usually called the linguistic and behavioural aspects of social practice, is either an incorrect distinction or ought to find its place as a differentiation within the social production of meaning, which is structured under the form of discursive totalities. (Laclau & Mouffe, 2001: 93)

Laclau and Mouffe do not argue that every social practice is discursive in the sense of a mental and linguistic activity, as opposed to material and physical facts. To illustrate how discourses impregnate and make social meanings possible, the authors use the following example:

> An earthquake or the falling of a brick is an event that certainly exists, in the sense that it occurs here and now, independently of my will. But whether their specificity as objects is constructed in terms of 'natural phenomena' or 'expressions of the wrath of God', depends upon the structuring of a discursive field. What is denied is not that such objects exist externally to thought, but the rather different assertion that they could constitute themselves as object outside any discursive condition of emergence. (Laclau & Mouffe, 2001: 94)

Discourses are *symbolic structures of differences* that nevertheless have a material dimension. They are not only speech, words and linguistic utterances. The selection of attire for a specific social situation – a wedding, a funeral, a formal dinner, an informal barbeque – also reflects this mechanism: depending on the meaning that an individual associates to a given social situation based on his/her knowledge of the social world –

that is, the competent knowledge of a discursive formation that is culturally codified – the type of clothes s/he will wear. The meaning of the practice of wearing specific attire depends on social discourses that invest that practice – and the attire – with meaning.[6] This example evidences how the non-material – the discursive – dimension has an impact into the material dimension.

When introducing the theory of their masters, David Howarth and Yannis Stavrakakis (2000: 2) – two referents of the Essex school of discourse analysis – argue that 'discourse theory assumes that all objects and actions are meaningful, and that their meaning is conferred by historically specific systems of rules'. The authors conceive of a discourse as 'a social and political construction that establishes a system of relations between different objects and practices, while providing (subject) positions with which social agents can identify' (Howarth & Stavrakakis, 2000: 3).

To sum up, for Laclau and Mouffe (2001: 95) 'the practice of articulation, as fixation/dislocation of a system of differences, cannot consist of purely linguistic phenomena; but must instead pierce the entire material density of the multifarious institutions, rituals and practices through which a discursive formation is structured'. Semioticians could easily subscribe to this premise. Actually, the theoretical assumptions presented in the last couple of paragraphs are the ones underlying semiotic research as well. It is surprising that the Essex school did not look for more insights into semiotic theory to develop their own approach to the political. Even if Laclau and Mouffe ground their conception of the functioning of the political on a dynamic that is clearly and evidently semiotic in its nature, they leave Semiotics out of the picture: the book does not include any references to Eco, Greimas, Hjelmslev, Peirce, Lotman or any other semiotician apart from Saussure.[7]

The discourse theory presented in *Hegemony and Socialist Strategy* constitutes the theoretical basis for Laclau's study of populism in *On Populist Reason* (2005a). There, the author defines *discourse* as 'any complex of elements in which relations play the constitutive role' and argues that 'whatever centrality an element acquires, it has to be explained by the play of differences as such' (Laclau, 2005a: 68–9). This theory will be discussed in Chapter 5.

4.2.2 Semiotic accounts of the political

Laclau and Mouffe's discourse theory shares a number of commonalities with Verón's social semiotic account. Like Laclau, Verón was born and raised in Argentina and influenced by the country's politics. In *La semiosis social*, Verón (1988: 125, my translation) argues that the theory of social discourses he puts forward is 'a set of hypotheses about the modes in which *social semiosis* functions'. The hypotheses underlying this theory are two:

a) Any production of sense is necessarily social: a signifying process cannot be satisfactorily described or explained without explaining its social productive conditions;
b) every social phenomenon is in one of its constitutive dimensions a process of sense-making, whatever the level of analysis might be. (Verón, 1988: 125, my translation)

Verón claims that it is through the analysis of specific material traces that these productive social dynamics can be accessed and that 'by studying products, we aim at processes' (1988: 124, my translation).[8] This premise will be central to the study of populism from a semiotic perspective, as is demonstrated in Chapters 6, 7 and 8. The assumption is that through examining concrete manifestations of meaning that occur at the level of politics, researchers can have access to the *populist discursive formation*, that is, a discourse (in Laclau and Mouffe's sense) that is at the basis of concrete discursive and performative events and manifestations that shape a society's political space.

The specificity of a Semiotics of the political would, therefore, rely in studying *semiosis*, meaning-making and signification based not principally on logical or theoretical deductions – as Laclau, Mouffe and their followers tend to do, even if in their analyses they frequently consider case studies (Howarth, Norval, & Stavrakakis, 2000; Howarth & Torfing, 2005) – but on the empirical scrutiny of concrete configurations of meaning, such as speeches, social media posts, communicative styles and strategies, interactions in face to face and in online events and other signifying practices, among many other articulations of the dimension of the expression that carry meanings (Landowski, 2019). It is in this aspect that the work of discourse analysts will be of help for semioticians, as is demonstrated in Chapters 6, 7 and 8.

Verón studied with great interest the political field, which he also conceived of as inherently adversarial, a trait that is based on the fact that it is in the political field that social identities are managed in the long term (Verón, 1989: 140). For Verón, the political field takes the form of a *struggle between enunciators*. This is a thesis that makes of political enunciation an activity that is inherently *polemic*, that is, 'inseparable of the construction of an *adversary*' (Verón, 1987: 16, my translation). From a semiotic perspective, this mechanism is at the heart of the 'contest over meaning' that occurs in the level of politics as the manifestation of Laclau and Mouffe's 'contest over hegemony' occurring at the level of the political. The level of politics is constituted by *discursive games* between political actors based on a 'theory of articulation of differences' (Verón, 1989: 141, my translation).

In the previous chapter, it was argued that an examination of populism from a semiotic perspective will be interested in studying *enunciation*, that is, the production of discourses and performances in the form of concrete *texts* – in a broad sense – through the manipulation of semiotic resources. For Verón (1987), in the political field enunciation normally implies three addressees: (1) the *pro-addressee* [*prodestinatario*]; (2) the *counter-addressee* [*contradestinatario*] and (3) the *para-addressee* [*para-destinatario*]. The *pro-addressee* consists of those individuals that are imagined as part of the collective identity anchored around the 'we' that a political enunciator uses in his/her utterances. The *counter-addressee* is the collective identity that groups all those that are imagined as the 'other', that is, the adversary or the enemy, depending on the type of logic – agonistic or antagonistic – underlying the conception of the social that political actors present, as evidenced and registered in their discourses and performances. Finally, there is the group of those who are neither imagined as being part of the 'we' nor of the 'they', but that nevertheless are part of the political field and are expected to take a political stand (e.g. in an election). For Verón, this *para-addressee* must be persuaded through political discourse.[9]

According to Verón (1989: 139, my translation), 'every act of discourse within mass communication media constructs an enunciator and an addressee, and proposes a relationship between them'. The analytical category of *collective* [*colectivo*] is central in Verón's thought. Collectives are imaginary entities that correspond to the 'deep structures' of meaning that can be identified by examining specific political discourses, as is argued in the next section and demonstrated in Chapters 6, 7 and 8. For Verón (1989: 139, my translation), 'all communication interpellates the individual as a "knot" of belonging' and 'every act of mediatised discourse proposes a modelling of social identities'. Therefore, identity and alterity become central to make sense of the political (Fatala, 2013).

In a similar line to Verón's argument, Paolo Fabbri (2019) saw in collective identities the constitutive language game within the political. Collective identities are expressed in the first person of plural – 'we' – and are always opposed to a (plural) 'you' and a 'they'. For Fabbri, the meaning of the verb *to believe* changes depending on the pronoun it is used with: while 'we believe' expresses certainty, 'you believe' expresses doubt and 'they believe' means that 'they' are wrong (Fabbri, 2019). Fabbri conceives of political discourse not as *representative* discourse, but as *field* discourse [*discorso di campo*], that is, one aimed at attracting, persuading and convincing, and not only a means to reproduce and represent reality (Fabbri & Marcarino, 1985). That is why he believes that traditional linguistic analyses – lexical, syntactic – do not suffice to make sense of the political. Like Verón, Fabbri claims that one of the key dimensions of analysis is that of enunciation. Also embracing a structuralist premise, Fabbri argues that political discourse 'could be defined structurally based on positions and differences' (Fabbri & Marcarino, 1985, my translation).

Fabbri believes that political discourse does not work exclusively anchored in the concept of truthfulness, but that it has also a *modal* component of *making-look-true*. This occurs in the form of a proposal of meaning that enunciators make to persuade their addressees, together with an interpretation by the addressee of that proposal of meaning that will conduct to its acceptance or not. For Fabbri, political discourse is a *contractual* type of discourse grounded in the social representations that enunciators construct in their discourses and performances. In this sense, political discourse implies a (semiotic) *manipulation* by the enunciator of semiotic resources in the public sphere to create a proposal of meaning – equivalent to Minogue's *structure of feeling* mentioned in a previous chapter – to make their addressees believe, feel and/or do something related to the management of power within society. In semiotic terms, there is a manipulation of semiotic resources aimed at manipulating perceptions, impressions and attitudes. Therefore, the concept of veridiction gains relevance (Alonso Aldama, 2018; Charaudeau, 2020).

The concept of *manipulation* is central in Greimas's theory. In the *Dictionnaire*, Greimas and Courtés (1982: 184) define *manipulation* as 'an action of humans over other humans with the goal of having them carry out a given program'. Manipulation is about *making* others *do* [*faire faire*]. This analytical category is also central in Landowski's (2019) approach to the political: in fact, it is one of the four types of interactions that are part of the author's socio-semiotic framework, together with programming [*programmation*], adjustment [*ajustement*] and accident [*accident/assentiment*]. For the author, (democratic) politics consists in trying to persuade – manipulate, in semiotic terms – the electorate as a means to achieve agreements between subjects.

In his social Semiotics of the political based on the study of interactions, Landwoski (2019) distinguishes between *la politique* and *le politique* as concepts that are equivalent to Mouffe's *politics* and *the political*, respectively. Landowski proposes that Semiotics' method to grasp political meaning-making consists in studying *political communication*, which occurs at the level of politics. According to Landowski (2019), political communication is *strategic* communication aimed at persuading the electorate. In our present time, this type of communication is normally the result of a collaboration of political actors with media and public relations experts, who develop discursive and performative strategies to produce specific effects of sense in the electorate.[10] It is only through examining this level that the dynamics of the political can be accessed.

For Landowski, political communication is the institutionalization of the political. As such, it is coded in concrete discursive and rhetorical games and practices that have a manipulative goal. For Landowski, semioticians' goal consists in accessing the deep structures that underlie the *relations of sense* [*rapports de sens*] between social actors revolving around power relations and the management of public life. In short, a Semiotics of the political is a constitutive part of social Semiotics and can be conceived of as the study of how power relations are structured based on a particular syntax (Landowski, 2019).

Landowski (2020) uses his model of four types of interaction to propose a semiotic square that includes four general political regimes: totalitarianism, absolutism, representative democracy and direct democracy/populist demagoguery (Figure 5). In totalitarian political systems, such as communist and fascist regimes, society is structured around rigid principles that orient social interactions through strictly planned programmes aimed at producing regularities by reducing individual agency.

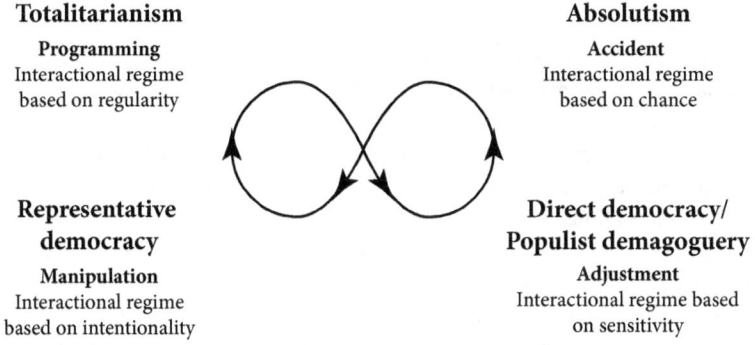

Figure 5 Types of political regimes. Source: Own elaboration based on Landowski (2019: 20), with permission from *Rivista Italiana di Filosofia del Linguaggio*.

In semiotic terms, totalitarianism is a political regime based on the interactional regime of *programming*: nothing is left up to randomness.

Second, absolutist regimes such as European monarchies from the post-Medieval age depend on the ruler's will and desires. That is why Landowski sees accident as the underlying interactional regime: it is hard to predict what an absolute ruler might want. Therefore, citizens must be ready to assent to whatever the ruler arbitrarily wants. For Landowski (2020), this interactional logic explains political actors like Donald Trump, Boris Johnson and Jair Bolsonaro: although they have been democratically elected, it is not clear what they might come up with, and societies must adapt to their unpredictable occurrences.

Representative democracy and direct democracy/populist demagoguery oppose totalitarianism and absolutism in that they are *democratic* regimes (Landowski, 2020). According to Landowski, nowadays even dictators call themselves *democrats*. The author argues that representative democracy is the political system that exemplifies perfectly the semiotic regime of manipulation, that is, the use of semiotic strategies in the public sphere to make individuals believe, feel and do things that are politically relevant. As the author argues, populist political actors are enemies of this logic and defend its opposite: a *direct* democracy without the mediation of political representation. By doing this, at first sight they seem to be embracing the interactional principle of adjustment, since the political leader needs to listen to the *demos* and act following their will. However, this is the case only in appearance, that is, in how populist political actors articulate their role in populist discourse.

The regime of adjustment implies a capacity of reading situations *in vivo*, of feeling in *aesthesic* terms what is going on as and while things develop, and being able to adapt to those developments.[11] According to Landowski, a political regime based on the principle of adjustment implies an interaction between equals (as in cooperative co-sharing economy). Populist political actors use a semiotic strategy articulated as follows: although they actually use a discursive strategy aimed at a manipulation – since they are part of representative democratic systems – in their discourses and performances they frame their action as a strategy of adjustment by posing as part of 'the people', that is, as members of the collective body of society (Kharbouch, 2018). However, they probably know that, if elected, they will be in charge of nothing close to a direct democracy. Directness and non-representativeness will be performed discursively but will not be an actual fact. In Landowski's social Semiotics, interactions and relations between social actors are constitutive of the social domain.

Influenced by Lotman's cultural semiotics, Peeter Selg and Andreas Ventsel (2020) draw on relational sociology to build bridges between Juri Lotman's cultural semiotics and Laclau and Mouffe's discourse theory. Their goal is to build an analytical method that draws on relational thought – that is, the strand of sociological research that assumes that relations are constitutive of the social and its objects (Moreno Barreneche, 2020b) – to capture 'the constitution of power, governance and democracy within and through communication' (Selg & Ventsel, 2020: 2). According to the authors, the categories of *power*, *governance* and *democracy* have a 'discursive and communicative core' (Selg & Ventsel, 2020: 6) and this claims for a semiotic approach interested in meaning-making within the political. For the authors, the political has a constitutive *public* dimension and political actors seek to achieve public relevance. Selg and Ventsel develop a Semiotics of the political that is inherently *relational* since meaning depends on a system of relations for its existence. According to the authors, 'this system of relations is a phenomenon that is a dynamic unfolding process whose constituent elements cannot be grasped separately from the flows within which they are embedded and vice versa' (Selg & Ventsel, 2020: 2). This statement reflects social Semiotics main theoretical tenet.

Selg and Ventsel's account is an interesting attempt to bridge political theory, Semiotics and relational sociology. It is also based on the assumption that meaning and value are relational. Their assumption that relations are constitutive of the social is a good starting point for the understanding of the political field from a semiotic perspective. Their project is particularly relevant to introduce the semiotic tradition into the discourse-theoretical research tradition based on the Essex school which, as discussed, is normally the starting point for any discursive account of populism. Therefore, identifying the commonalities between discourse theory and Lotman's cultural Semiotics is a matter of understanding how the two theoretical frameworks can fit together. As Selg and Ventsel (2020: 7) propose, 'despite different theoretical vocabulary, the core categories of the Essex school (discourse, logic of difference/equivalence, empty signifiers, nodal points, articulation, naming, hegemony, constitutive antagonism) and those of the Tartu-Moscow School (semiosphere, discrete/continuous coding, center/periphery, translation, naming, dominant metalanguage, untranslatability, boundary) are pointing to the same underlying conceptual logic'. The same can be argued when taking other semiotic traditions into consideration.

Finally, also the English-speaking research tradition acknowledges the centrality of meaning-making in the political domain. Hodge and Kress (1988: vii), for example, argue that 'society is typically constituted by structures and relations of power, exercised or resisted; it is characterized by conflict as well as cohesion, so that the structures of meaning at all levels, from dominant ideological forms to local acts of meaning will show traces of contradiction, ambiguity, polysemy in various proportions, by various means'. This assumption also explains the project of Critical Discourse Analysis, which is aimed at dismantling those structures and relations of power through the analysis of discourses as carriers of ideology.

As demonstrated in this section, the discursive dimension of politics has been of interest for discourse-theoretical researchers, semioticians and discourse analysts. The insistence in comparing the first of these two strands of research lies on the fact that within scholarship on populism, the approach presented by Laclau and Mouffe in the 1980s and extended until the present is usually the starting point for discursive approaches to populism. However, as argued earlier, Laclau, Mouffe and the Essex school do not engage with Semiotics besides the use of some of Saussure's principles as the grounds of their discourse theory.

Concomitantly to the development of Laclau and Mouffe's theory, and sharing the premises that pose that (1) discourse is a necessary condition for meaning to emerge, (2) meaning is always relational, (3) collective identities are central in political discourse and (4) enunciation is crucial to identify those collective identities, Verón developed a social Semiotics that has commonalities with their account. Moreover, other semioticians like Fabbri, Landowski, Selg, Ventsel and others have also approached politics and the political focusing on its semiotic and discursive dimension. Although this does not mean that politics is only made of discourse and discourses, approaching the political as a field of the social that is governed by particular discursive and meaning-making mechanisms, dynamics and strategies is fundamental to properly grasp this social field.

4.3 Collective identities in political discourse[12]

This section discusses the role that collective identities play in the political sphere and introduces an original framework for their study through the identification of five semiotic mechanisms: (1) segmentation; (2) generalization; (3) actorialization; (4) axiologization and (5) figurativization.

4.3.1 Identities as semiotic artefacts

Identity has been the subject of various and long-standing discussions in the social sciences and humanities. It has been a topic of interest for social psychologists (Burke & Stets, 2009; Tajfel, 1982), sociologists (Eisenstadt, 1998; Berger, 1966; Goffman, 1956; Somers, 1994), anthropologists (Lévi-Strauss, 2010), philosophers (Appiah, 2018; Ricoeur, 1990), political theorists (Fukuyama, 2018b; Laclau, 1994; Malasevic, 2006), sociolinguists (Bucholtz & Hall, 2005) and cultural studies' scholars (Hall & Du Gay, 2011). While some researchers have proposed to avoid using the concept due to the confusions it generates (Brubaker & Cooper, 2000), others have tried to deconstruct identities and challenge extended conceptions that take them for granted and consider them factual givens (Appiah, 2018).

Identity is one of the concepts included in Greimas and Courtés (1982: 148) *Dictionnaire*. The authors claim that 'the concept of identity, an undefinable one, is opposed to that of alterity (as "same" to "other") which cannot be defined either. Yet, this pair is interdefinable by a relation of reciprocal presupposition, and is indispensable for founding the elementary structure of signification'. According to the authors, 'identity serves to designate the features or the set of features [. . .] that two or more objects have in common'. Within the semiotic framework presented in this book, *identity* is an analytical category used to refer to articulated and more or less coherent sets of discourses, narratives, social imaginaries, signs, texts, objects and practices, among other signifying elements, that can be conceived of as those elements that individuals have in common and that allow grouping them in encompassing cultural units. Identities are hence cultural units of meaning that serve the purpose of simplifying, ordering and mapping the complex and diverse social space. As units of meaning that are codified and embedded in culture, identities are artefacts of a semiotic nature.

Individuals do not *have* or *possess* identities: they *identify* with specific cultural 'packages' that exist as codified units of meaning in the cultures they were socialized in.

Identities are available to individuals as specific contents of the cultural semiospheres they are embedded in: they are nothing else than elements that subjects can make sense of because they are necessarily embedded in the 'webs of signification' of culture (Geertz, 1973). Greimas and Courtés (1982: 148) regard identification as 'a metalinguistic operation which requires, beforehand, a semic or phemic analysis', that is, a scrutiny of the traits that define a given identity. Moreover, they claim that 'far from being a first approach to the semiotic material, identification is one operation among others in the construction of the semiotic object'. Therefore, identification occurs *through* processes of meaning-making and signification.

Identities are cultural artefacts of a discursive nature that become meaningful following the logic of meaning-making explained earlier: through oppositions with other identities (Arfuch, 2005; Escudero Chauvel, 2005; Fatala, 2013). They are not 'essences' or 'things' that people possess, but units of meaning segmented culturally through language and in discourse that serve the purpose of personal identification and that facilitate a cognitive simplification of reality.[13] They are used to make sense of the social realm through an opposition to other identities: it makes sense speaking of a national identity X – in the sense of an articulated set of discursive elements that are used by members from both the in- and the out-group to make sense of a dimension of their existence – because other national identities coexist with it as different national identities (not-X).

Social psychologist Henri Tajfel (1982) argued that identities have a *cognitive*, an *evaluative* and an *affective* component. They are not only cognitive artefacts used to make sense of the world in rational terms but also trigger passions, emotions and attitudes towards the in- and out-groups. Also Mouffe (2005a) believes that emotion is central in understanding political identities.

There are differences between *personal* and *collective* identities. While the former are anchored in individuals with a material existence outside discourse, the latter are more complex to handle from a semiotic perspective because they are usually an 'effect of sense' that does not always have a referential correlate. Even if specific traits can be *indexical signs* of a collective identity, every collective identity is constructed through the intervention of some semiotic mechanisms (see 4.3.2). This issue will be crucial in the analysis of the collective identity 'the people' in the next chapter.

Collective identities are central for individuals to make sense of the social realm, including the political. Mouffe (2013: 5) argues that

> once we understand that every identity is relational and that the affirmation of a difference is a precondition for the existence of any identity – i.e., the perception of something 'other' which constitutes its 'exterior' – we can understand why politics, which always deals with collective identities, is about the constitution of a 'we' which requires as its very condition of possibility the demarcation of a 'they'.

For Mouffe (2005b: 51), 'the refusal to acknowledge the political in its antagonistic dimension, and the concomitant incapacity to grasp the central role of passions in the constitution of collective identities, are [. . .] at the root of political theory's failure to come to terms with the phenomenon of populism'. Carlos Meléndez and Rovira Kaltwasser (2017: 521) see political identities as one crucial aspect in understanding populism. In particular, they underline the relevance of the existence of an *antiestablishment* political identity within a given political context for populism to emerge because 'populism seeks to alter the existing electoral choices by breaking the electorate's ties of loyalty to established political parties'. For the authors, an *antiestablishment political identity* has 'a generalized feeling and belief that *all* mainstream political parties are untrustworthy'. They argue that when the electorate finds those parties appealing or convincing in terms of identity, there is little room for populism to emerge. Their thesis is hence that 'only when voters systematically reject all mainstream existing parties and are ready to transform this rejection into a new political identity, there is fertile soil for the rise of populist forces' (Meléndez & Rovira Kaltwasser, 2017: 521).

Populism is indeed a political phenomenon articulated around the construction of collective political identities in discourse, together with the establishment of an antagonistic relationship between them in narrative terms. According to Panizza (2017), populism is a *mode of identification* that aims at constructing a single, homogeneous and uniform identity – 'the people' – through a dichotomization of the social space. As is argued in the next chapter, the Populist Narrative Structure is the narrative articulation of that conflictive relationship between two collective identities (one of them being 'the people'). Therefore, populism is a discourse characterized by the segmentation and mapping it does of the social space in a particular way and by how political actors use it to mobilize people to act according to that mapping.

Panizza (2005: 6) uses the example of the 9/11 aftermath in the United States to illustrate how collective identities work. According to the author, US society is characterized by a 'web of differences' in the form of racial, class, gender, religious and other differences anchored in specific markers of identity, such as skin colour, creed and ethnicity (Appiah, 2018). After the 9/11 attacks, those differences were put on hold and people started feeling *American*. This was the case because the 'we' had been attacked by an external 'other'. Although that 'we' existed beforehand, the identification of *being American* gained weight in that particular context: according to Panizza (2005: 6), in that context, *being American* meant being part of 'a single people threatened [...] by a violent external enemy'. For the author, 'the attack itself was a material event that only acquired its meaning by being placed within a certain discursive framework in which the relation of antagonism was constituted' (Panizza, 2005: 6).

4.3.2 Mechanisms for the construction of collective identities in discourse

Given that collective identities are discursive artefacts, they can be handled as texts. And if they can be handled as texts, their meaningfulness can be studied by examining the process through which they are constructed in discourse using Greimas's levels of generation of meaning, as discussed in Chapter 3. Following Greimas's model, this process starts with the recognition of the deep semantic structures that organize the social realm. In our case, those structures would be the different identities found in a given discourse. The process continues by examining how these deep structures are referred to and represented in discursive configurations such as speeches, images, manifestos, advertisements and other texts. The process of discursive construction of collective identities occurs by employing five mechanisms: (1) segmentation; (2) generalization; (3) actorialization; (4) axiologization and (5) figurativization.

4.3.2.1 Segmentation

The mechanism of *segmentation* refers to how social reality – the social continuum – is divided and how social space is organized *in groups*. When discussing Hjelmslev's comparison between Danish, German and French, it was demonstrated how different linguistic communities segment the plane of the content differently. The mechanism of segmentation is also visible in naming colours: the light continuum is cut into different sections and different words are used to refer to segmented portions of that continuum. Why does Italian distinguish between *blu* and *azzurro* and Spanish between *azul* and *celeste*, while English uses an adjective to distinguish *blue* from *light blue*?

The same mechanism applies to the segmentation of the social space into collective identities, which are smaller meaningful units defined through oppositions. Segmentation is hence an operation that categorizes the world and human experience (Greimas and Courtés, 1982: 271): the different collective identities that exist within a society as codified in culture are the *units* that result from the operation of categorization, that is, of *division* of the social space. Segmentation consists in setting boundaries and frontiers between units that are regarded as different according to one or more parameters or traits.[14]

Once the social continuum has been segmented into different units – here is where the groups of 'we' and 'they' emerge, following Mouffe's conception of the political – these 'empty spaces' within the grid of meaning need to be filled with specific content. When dealing with *national* identities, it is known that the world is conventionally segmented into nation-states. As a result, people tend to be classified based on their national belonging. For many Europeans, establishing a difference between Uruguay and Paraguay represents a challenge since, for them, these might be only 'empty spaces'. For individuals born and raised in Argentina or in Brazil, Uruguay and Paraguay are probably not 'empty spaces' within the grid of national identities: in their everyday life, they are exposed to discourses, contacts and other interactions that fill them with specific meanings.

What is interesting from a semiotic perspective is that this segmentation occurs by assuming that collective identities possess specific *cores*. In the case of national identities, the core consists in the assumption of a special relationship of the group with 'the nation', whatever that noun might mean. In the case of religious identities, the core consists of a series of supernatural beliefs. In the case of gender identities, there is a relationship with the body and its social interpretation at the core of the multiple collective identities. For Appiah (2018: 26), 'the colour of hair and skin and other aspects of physical appearance play a role in determining what sorts of people are grouped together'. Core and boundaries are the defining semiotic features of collective identities as discursive configurations that serve the purpose of making sense of social reality in cognitive and emotional terms.

4.3.2.2 Generalization

Once a collective political identity has been delimited by identifying a defining core and some boundaries, it must be filled with content. But identities must also be easy to grasp so that they serve the purpose of simplifying social reality for cognitive purposes. This is where generalization – which is also a process of homogenization – takes place: based on the core that defines the identity, a set of traits and features is imagined and discursively used to define it as applicable to *every* member of the group.

Greimas and Courtés (1982: 128) define *generalization* as 'the procedure by which the properties or determinations recognized in a limited number of entities are attributed to a whole class'. This semiotic mechanism is almost a given in any type of act of grouping elements into encompassing categories. As such, it is at the basis of the construction of social representations, imaginaries and stereotypes: when saying that 'Germans are so and so' and that 'Brazilians do this and that', a process of generalization occurs. While this operation serves the purpose of simplifying social reality, it does not respect the diversity, heterogeneity and complexity of the social.

It is in this sense that collective identities – including political identities – can be conceived from a semiotic perspective as *forms of life* [*formes de vie*] (Fontanille, 2008; 2015; Perusset, 2020). Forms of life are nothing else that discursive and imaginary generalizations constructed upon induction and a comparison of individual practices. If one visits Vienna and sees that it is common for Viennese people to eat *Schnitzel* and have *Kaffee und Kuchen* in the early afternoon, then an equivalence will be established based on a mechanism of induction between 'being Viennese' and 'eating such and such' or 'doing this and that'. Moreover, statements of a general and universal scope such as 'the Viennese eat such and such' will emerge.[15] This is a process of generalization that does not reflect the diversity of how the Viennese people are and what they do. In spite of how it betrays social heterogeneity, the mechanism of generalization serves to the cognitive process of simplifying social reality and making it easier to grasp.

4.3.2.3 Actorialization

After a collective identity has been segmented as a cultural unit of meaning and some generic statements have been identified to fill that 'empty space' with a basic meaning, the process of discursive creation of those units in the plane of the expression begins. The first step in that process is one of *actorialization*. Together with temporalization and spasialization, actorialization is one of the three components of discursivization (Greimas & Courtés, 1982).

As Greimas and Courtés (1982: 8) argue, actorialization 'aims at establishing the actors of the discourse by uniting different elements of the semantic and syntactic components'. Actorialization usually implies the creation of a narrative plot that establishes relationships between collective identities and that fills them with some basic contents that will be expressed in the plane of the expression through specific semiotic configurations such as names, logotypes, flags, songs, manifests, advertisements, colours, practices, rituals and many other semiotic resources. These resources are used to bring into being the political collective identity that has been segmented and delimited in the plane of the content as an identity that is distinct from others.

This first step in the process of making collective identities *perceptible* helps the identification of individuals with them based on the recognition of the equivalence and/or coincidence of their political interests, values, preferences and demands with those that are discursively placed within the core of the different units of meaning – the political identities – that constitute the political sphere. The semiotic work that political candidates and parties do (naming, logotype, advertisements, rallies, etc.) is instrumental to this end: to fill the 'empty spaces' of the political grid – once it has been segmented – with specific contents that individuals can relate to.

It is in the process of actorialization that narrative structures become visible. For Semiotics, the configuration of perception is mediated by a principle of narrativity (Paolucci, 2012; Greimas & Ricoeur, 1989; Marrone, 2007; Pozzato, 2007). This implies that making sense of the social realty is bound to stories and storytelling (Bruner, 2002; Cosenza, 2018; Salmon, 2008). When bringing a collective identity to life in the discursive level, stories will be told not only regarding the past of the collective but also regarding the basic dynamics of confrontation with the 'other'. This operation reflects the 'we'-versus-'they' narrative scheme discussed before.

4.3.2.4 *Axiologization*

The mechanism of axiologization consists in investing a portion of the semantic universe with value. Anne Hénault (2012: 275) defines this mechanism as 'the static valorization of a given universe of discourse'. According to Greimas and Courtés (1982), semantic units within a given discourse can be axiologized in positive or negative terms, depending on the value system – axiology – that is used. Normally, the *euphoric* (positive) axiologization equals the moral dimension of Good, while the *dysphoric* (negative) axiologization equals the moral dimension of Bad. This is why Greimas and Courtés (1982) name this operation *moralization*.

Axiologization occurs mainly in the form of an attribution of *connotative marks* to the actors involved in the narrative plot. These marks are culturally loaded with positive and negative meanings. According to Mouffe, moralization is one of the most salient features of the political in our contemporary age: as the author argues, 'the we/they, instead of being defined with political categories, is now established in moral terms', that is, as a struggle between Good and Evil (Mouffe, 2005a: 5). These two units of meaning are *contingent* because they are the product of a social construction throughout history.

4.3.2.5 *Figurativization*

The last mechanism involved in the discursive construction of collective identities is *figurativization*, that is, the rendering them *tangible* through specific semiotic articulations that can be *empirically perceived*. For Greimas (1984), discourses can be abstract or figurative depending on how they operate at the discursive level. The objects of study that are of interest for social Semiotics will normally produce meaning in a figurative manner, because the discourse needs to be perceived by individuals to act in the world. For Greimas and Courtés (1982: 118), 'almost all texts called literary and historical belong to the class of figurative discourse'.

In politics, it is in the mechanism of figurativization that *performances* come into play (Moffitt, 2016; Ostiguy, Panizza, & Moffitt, 2021). The semantic units segmented when dividing the social space are accessible only though specific configurations of meaning that are *concrete*, that is, figurative (as opposed to abstract). That is why collective identities might differ from a social context to the other, even if they are based on the same abstract unit of meaning in the dimension of the deep structures.

As is argued and demonstrated in the following chapter, this is what occurs with 'the people', a semantic unit that reflects a collective identity and that is enacted and filled with specific contents depending on the context where it is used. That is why 'the peoples' of different political actors around the world differ. Nevertheless, these are reducible to the same semantic unit in the plane of the deep structures: a collective identity defined by a semiotic core, with boundaries and opposed to an 'other'. The following chapter examines how 'the people', its 'other' and the relationship between them are constructed in populist discourse following these five semiotic mechanisms.

4.4 Politics as a 'contest over meaning'

This chapter puts forward two theses regarding the political: (1) that collective identities are central in the articulation of political discourse and (2) that politics can be conceived of as a contest over meaning. These theses are functional to the semiotic study of populism as the discursive practice of using the Populist Narrative Structure as the ground for meaning-making. While the previous section argued how collective identities come into being through five semiotic mechanisms, this section focuses on explaining the thesis of politics as a 'contest over meaning'.

Before liberal representative democracies became the norm for the articulation of the political sphere of societies around the world, the public management of power relations was based on coercion and violence: *hard* power – physical violence, punishments, war – was the norm. Within democratic societies, power is rather *soft*: it is about persuading and convincing the electorate to gain their support. Power within democracies is about manipulating – in semiotic terms – beliefs, emotions and actions, as was argued in the previous section. That is why politics is structured around an inescapable need for political actors, parties and movements to propose *specific projects and world views* and convince members of society to support them, both by the recourse to rational arguments and other discursive strategies aimed at having an impact on values and emotions (Charaudeau, 2011; 2014).

Within pluralist liberal democracies, politics implies hence the competition of projects and world views. The competition can take place at the level of ideologies – liberalism, socialism, conservatism, Right, Left and so on – but it can also revolve around specific policy issues, such as building a road or closing a country's borders due to a health emergency. It could also be argued that every decision regarding the common life of a group will give place to divergent opinions and positions, and that democratic politics is about finding consensus between the conflictive views, even if it is partial and temporary.

In semiotic terms, the political can be conceived – following Greimas's narrative scheme – as a field in which Subjects struggle over the possession of an Object of Value. This is the thesis put forward by Landowski in an article from 1976 entitled '*La mise en scène des sujets de pouvoir*'. Landowski argues that political Subjects are defined not in philosophical, psychological or sociological terms but rather based on the relationship that they have with a specific Object of Value. To illustrate this idea, Landowski uses the example of the sentence 'The government wants to build a road through the city' and argues that, in it, *the government* becomes a Subject thanks to its capacity to relate to a desired Object – the construction of the road – its capacity to do so – expressed in the verb *to want* – and an anti-Subject, that is, those that will oppose this desire. According to Landowski (1976: 78), the three defining features of any political discourse are: (1) the attribution of a will to do something, (2) the constitution of Objects of Value and (3) the instauration of Subjects.

This very basic premise – which capitalizes on Greimas's semiotic theory and points out to the *narrative* configuration of the political (Alonso Aldama, 2014) – will serve to approach the phenomenon of populism from a semiotic perspective. Simply put, it is through the employment of semiotic resources that political actors try to impose their world views and make them prevail. As De Cleen (2017: 343) argues, political projects 'produce a structure of meaning through the articulation of existing discursive elements'. This mechanism can take different forms and can occur in different arenas, ranging from traditional political sites as the parliament and the media to the use of public space, like in the case of activism (Zienkowski, 2017).

The semiotic conception of politics espoused here as a contest over meaning that occurs in the form of the production of discourses and performances is not far from Laclau and Mouffe's conception of the political as a 'struggle for hegemony'. However, for a semiotic approach, it does not seem necessary to introduce the (Marxist) premises and assumptions that the concept of *hegemony* has as it was used by Antonio Gramsci, let alone the psychoanalytical premises based on the work of Lacan and other poststructuralist premises embraced by Laclau and Mouffe. On the contrary, it might be a safer theoretical move to work with the category of *meaning* to cover the semantic field of what Laclau and Mouffe call *hegemony*. While for political theorists like them, the latter might be central due to their interest in grasping the nature and ontology of the political, for semioticians the focus of interest is the former, as they aim at describing meaning-making and signification in the level of politics.

This chapter approached the political field from a semiotic perspective. Although some of their assumptions are shared, such an approach differs from Laclau and Mouffe's discourse-theoretical account, which is the standard in populism studies. Moreover, in contrast to the work of discourse analysts, semioticians are not satisfied with mapping political discourse as it is expressed in words and other linguistic utterances: besides examining these and other resources that contribute to a multimodal – or syncretic – type of meaning-making, they will also be interested in having access to how the *plane of the content* is structured and organized in semantic units by examining which actors, values, relationships and narratives are constructed in discourse, together with how these are meaningful. The theoretical building is now set to begin with the semiotic examination of populism.

5

'The People' and Its 'Other(s)'

The previous four chapters set the scene for a semiotic study of populism. This chapter focuses on examining the structure of populist discourse by using the concepts, methods and tools from Semiotics. As argued before, every social phenomenon has a discursive dimension. This does not imply, however, that all social phenomena are *only* discursive, that is, that they do not have a material anchorage. The notion of a *discursive-material knot* proposed by Nico Carpentier (2017) is useful to understand social Semiotics' work with meaning as produced in the interplay between discursive and material aspects. Semiotics' constructivist premise is not a radical one: it is rather moderate and acknowledges the material basis of every discursive phenomenon. To begin with, meaning and discourse can only be accessed through configurations of meaning that have a material dimension and that can be conceived of as *texts* (Verón, 1988; Landowski, 2014; Floch, 1990; Marrone, 2001; Ventura Bordenca, 2022).

Dealing with populism from a semiotic perspective implies dealing with how meaning-making and signification occur in the phenomena labelled as 'populist'. Following the approach to the political presented in the previous chapter, the social Semiotics of populism will look at how a specific configuration of the social[1] is constructed recurring to the collective identities of 'the people' and an 'other', which are set into an antagonistic relationship with each other. In this sense, the purpose of this and the following chapters is essentially descriptive: they aim at rendering visible how populist discourse produces meaning and serves to make sense of political reality.

The focus on *semiosis* and meaning-making implies that populism will not be approached here as a whole, that is, as a political activity that mobilizes the electorate and that eventually takes political actors to power, who put forward and implement specific policies. Rather, the focus is set in one of its dimensions (the one that has been more interesting for those who have studied populism). As argued in Chapter 3, the semiotic approach serves to make compatible the conceptions of populism as an ideology, a discourse, a communicative style, a performance and a frame: all these analytical categories imply dealing with meaning-making through the mediation of cognitive and narrative structures that serve to map social reality. Moreover, all these accounts seem to agree on a core of populism constituted by (1) a distinction between 'the people' and 'the elite' and (2) a relationship of antagonism between them, among other items that might vary from researcher to researcher.

The first section of this chapter studies how populist discourse divides the social realm in two major groups and establishes an antagonistic relationship between them.

Laclau (2005a: 81) claims that in populist discourse 'a frontier of exclusion divides society in two camps'. Hence, discourse is used to produce effects of *sense* that produce effects of *reality* because they revolve around *the structure of the social*. After studying this process of discursive construction of the social, the focus of the chapter shifts to the category of 'the people'. Due to the common assumptions shared by the discourse-theoretical approach and Semiotics, the discussion of Laclau's (2005a; 2005b) theory of populism will serve to visualize how 'the people' becomes a meaningful unit within political discourse to the point of providing a specific political movement, ideology or discourse with a semiotic core that grants it the privilege of being named with a 'proper name' ended in *-ism*. In this sense, if environmentalism's Object of Value is 'the environment' and nationalism's, 'the nation', then populism's Object of Value is 'the people'. The last section of the chapter deals with 'the people's other', which usually coincides with 'the elites' but can take different forms due to a series of semiotic mechanisms that are discussed next.

5.1 The populist dichotomization of society

As discussed in Chapter 2, one of the points upon which scholars of populism seem to agree regarding the nature of the phenomenon is that populist political actors tend to present society as divided in two homogeneous groups. The logics governing this mechanism have been explained in the previous chapter. It should be added that, from the perspective of Semiotics, the use of binary formulas that divide the social space in an oversimplified manner seems to be one of the defining features of the political in our present time. Giovanna Cosenza (2018) calls this phenomenon *the binary scheme*.

In other words, the phenomenon of dividing in discourse the social space in two groups is not exclusive of populist discourse. Nowadays, in an era of growing mediatization of politics (Verón, 1998; Mazzoleni & Schulz, 1999), online networked political participation (Theocharis, 2015), filter bubbles (Pariser, 2012) and other phenomena that foster a type of affective political polarization (Iyengar, Sood, & Lelkes, 2012; Moreno Barreneche, 2020d), more and more political spheres (at the national, subnational and supranational level) are experiencing this semiotic logic. In this sense, when a politician speaks of 'us' and 'them', the underlying logic is Cosenza's binary scheme.[2]

In populist discourse, the binary scheme takes the form of an opposition between a collective social actor referred to as 'the people' and its alleged opponent. In affirmative terms, populism revolves around a 'people'. But its 'other' is segmented originally in logical terms as 'not-the-people'. If this logical opposition is taken to a semiotic square, the following scheme results at the level of deep structures (Figure 6).

This logical opposition is the basis of populist discourse. The assumed premise of populist discourse is that the social space is divided between those individuals who belong to the category of 'the people' and those who do not. However, to affirm the exclusion of those that do not belong to 'the people' in negative terms – that is, by using the particle *not* – is not productive in discursive terms. Therefore, what in Figure 6 is represented with an X needs to be filled with *positive content*, so that an 'other'

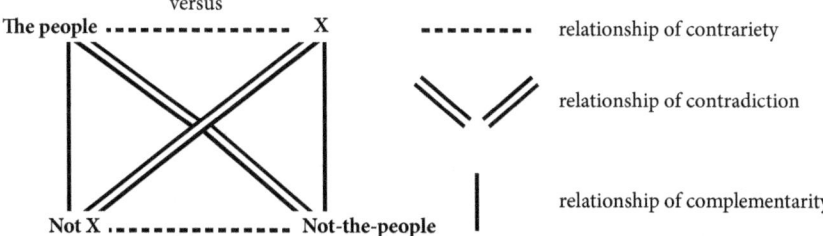

Figure 6 The populist dichotomization of the social space.

can be made sense of by the audience in positive terms, recognized as an enemy and axiologized negatively.

Although research on populism has insisted that 'the people's other' are the elites (Mudde, 2004; Müller, 2016), this dichotomy oversimplifies the mapping of social space proposed by populist discourse (at least in the actual use of the term 'populism'). In the original historical manifestations of populism and in its current left-wing variant, 'the elite' and its variations – 'the establishment', 'the oligarchy' and so on – are an appropriate and sufficient 'other'. This is the case since, in its original historical sense, populist politics is an *inclusionary* type of politics aiming at broadening political participation to sections of society usually marginalized (Tarragoni, 2021). However, from the moment the noun *populism* started being used to refer also to right-wing political movements, and particularly when a public figure like Donald Trump is labelled 'a populist', this explanation is not any longer satisfactory. What sense does it make to state that Donald Trump is part of 'the people' if he is a representative of the purest form of the US elites? Clearly something occurred that allows an evident member of the group 'the elite' to be considered a representative of 'the people'.

A possible explanation of this dynamic can be based on a displacement of one of the features of original populist political movements – from the nineteenth and twentieth centuries – now used to also make sense of phenomena that do not match their inclusionary, left-wing characteristics. This displacement took place at the level of the discursive strategies and is well captured by Laclau (2005b: 33) when he writes that 'a movement is not populist because in its politics or ideology it presents actual *contents* identifiable as populistic, but because it shows a particular *logic of articulation* of those contents – whatever those contents are'. In other words, the noun *populism* and the adjective *populist* are nowadays used to refer to a discursive dimension of political movements, actors and parties that has something in common with the discursive dimension of the original forms of populism. That would be the reason why the concept of *populism* is currently used to make sense of these contemporary political phenomena as well, even if they do not seem populist in the original sense of the word.

This strategic discursive dimension is a particular logic of discursive articulation that consists in recurring to a basic *narrative structure*. This is what this book calls the *Populist Narrative Structure*. *The Populist Narrative Structure relates two collective identities in an antagonistic manner and fills them with context-relevant contents through the use of semiotic resources.*[3] As Laclau argues, populism is characterized by the form its discourse takes, and not necessarily by the specific contents it is filled with.[4] This might explain why so many political actors, movements and parties around the world have been recently labelled as *populist*.

The collective identities embedded in the Populist Narrative Structure are not pre-existent to that narrative emplotment: they are constructed in discourse *through* the antagonistic relationship that is established between them. 'The people' becomes 'the people' *relationally*, that is, through an opposition to the semantic unit 'not-the-people', and 'the people's other' obtains its meaning as a collective identity thanks to the (discursive) existence of 'the people'.

Independently of how these collective identities segmented in the dimension of the deep structures are brought to life through actorialization and figurativization, what does not let room for discussion is that populist discourse establishes differences, that is, it builds a gap between portions of society, one of the being 'the people'. According to Panizza (2005: 28), 'the divide between the people and its "other" defines the political nature of populism'. The first conclusion is, then, that populism segments meaningful units within the social space to make sense of it and that this segmentation is based on a binary scheme that oversimplifies the complexity of social reality by identifying two collective identities. These identities match the 'we' and the 'they' studied in Chapter 4.

As discussed in that chapter, relationships of rivalry can be interpreted in different ways. When an opponent is seen as a legitimate competitor in the quest for an Object of Value (power, being in charge of a country's government, a trophy in a sports competition, etc.), there is an agonistic mode of relating to it: the 'other' needs to be defeated but not necessarily annihilated. This is what normally happens in sports and musical competitions. However, antagonism makes of the 'other' not a legitimate rival but *an enemy*. Therefore, discursive strategies will be employed to reinforce the identity of the 'other' as one that is dangerous and that represents a threat to Us. Therefore, segmentation and generalization lead to a negative axiologization.

In an essay entitled 'Inventing the Enemy', Eco (2012) reviews how the social role of 'the enemy' has been imagined and represented throughout history. Eco argues that the existence of something perceived as an enemy is fundamental to construct the idea of a 'we' and argues that 'having an enemy is important not only to define our identity, but also to provide us with an obstacle against which to measure our system of values' (Eco, 2012: 2). Antagonistic relationships could be seen as drawing on this mechanism of demonization of the 'other' as a way of reinforcing the idea of a 'we' that needs to stay together.[5] That is why the author believes that 'the figure of the enemy cannot be abolished from the processes of civilization' (Eco, 2012: 17).

Two aspects are involved in the process of 'invention' of the enemy. On the one hand, there is an identification of an 'other' as an enemy that represents a threat to the 'we'. This enemy can be another social agent and also a natural phenomenon, such as a virus (Moreno Barreneche, 2020e). On the other hand, there is a semiotic process that invests that enemy with negative value: the enemy is not only an 'other' that competes with Us; it is dangerous, ugly and evil – a monster that needs to be destroyed for Us to survive.

The Populist Narrative Structure includes an 'other' that is depicted as a threat to the well-being and the interests of 'the people'. How that 'other' is invested with meaning as an enemy varies from one cultural context to another, as does the specific actorialization and figurativization that the 'other' takes in positive terms. However, what is maintained in every occurrence of populism throughout different political contexts is the *dynamic of othering* – that is, of establishing boundaries between 'us' and 'them' – and of culturalizing the 'other' with traits and features that justify conceiving it as an enemy.

According to Panizza (2005: 3), 'an anti-status quo dimension is essential to populism, as the full constitution of popular identities necessitates the political defeat of "the *other*" that is deemed to oppress or exploit the people and therefore to impede its full presence'. That is why populist political actors tend to take their discourses to *a moral level*. For Panizza (2005: 22–3) 'in order to talk politics while denouncing it as a dirty game, the populist leader often substitutes political discourse for the discourse of morals, and uses universal abstractions to contrast the high moral grounding of his/her message with the corruption and betrayal of the political establishment'.

Populist discourse's division of the social space in two semantic units that correspond to social groups seems to serve two purposes. On the one hand, it fosters the creation of an enemy in the social imaginary, so that the electorate can feel threatened and its identification with the collective identity of 'the people' can be activated. On the other hand, it reproduces the conflictive nature of politics as an activity in which Subjects compete with each other to obtain their Object of Value, thus making of a state of agreement – or conjunction – something impossible to achieve. As Pappas (2019a: 45) argues, in contrast to liberals – who seek to achieve consensus within pluralism – populist actors see 'political adversity as an intrinsic characteristic of politics, which thus makes them more appreciative of polarizing confrontation than consensus-seeking and political compromise within the constitutional framework'.

If a given society (e.g. of a country X) is regarded as a totality (a circle), then populist discourse is defined through the rupture it proposes of the totality of the social space by establishing boundaries between two groups. This boundary- or frontier-setting mechanism is part of the process of segmentation introduced in the previous chapter: the social space is segmented through the use of cultural units to make sense of it. Its continuity is broken and some criteria are used to conduct a segmentation of that totality into smaller meaningful units. Once the gap has been established and 'the people' has an enemy in positive terms – that is, not any longer as the empty and void semantic unit of 'not-the-people' but as a positive content – the mechanisms of generalization, actorialization, axiologization and figurativization occur for both actors. This logic is represented in Figure 7.

The Populist Narrative Structure is an 'absent structure' to be found in Mouffe's level of *the political*. However, semioticians gain access to the logics of this dichotomization of society through what populist political actors say, write and do, that is, by examining the logics of *politics* and political communication. See, for example, this excerpt from a speech by Donald Trump during a rally in 2016:

> My opponent asks her supporters to recite a three word loyalty pledge. It reads 'I'm with her'. I choose to recite a different pledge. My pledge reads 'I'm with you, the American people'. I am your voice [. . .], I am with you, I will fight for you, and I

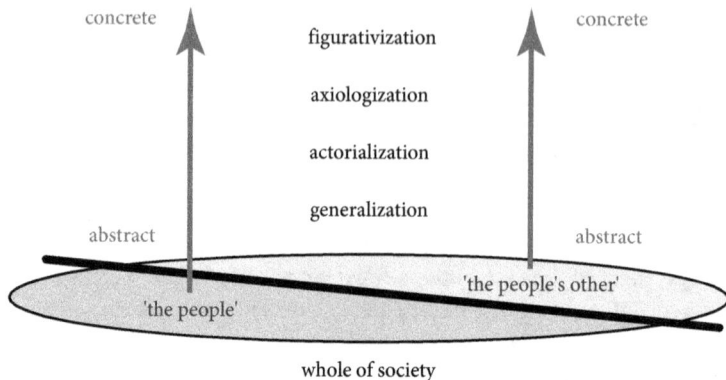

Figure 7 The semiotic construction of 'the people' and its 'other' in populist discourse.

will win for you [...] We will make America great again. God bless you and good night. I love you![6]

At first sight, the reference to Hillary Clinton in terms of 'my opponent' seems to reflect an agonistic relationship with the adversary since she is conceived as a legitimate opponent, and not as an enemy. However, when Trump refers – as he usually did – to his opponent as 'crooked Hilary' and says of her that she is 'dishonest', agonism becomes antagonism, not only because of the impoliteness these adjectives express but also because these references axiologize the opponent in moral terms. The transformation of agonism into antagonism can be evidenced in specific occurrences in the plane of the expression, such as impoliteness towards the 'other', together with the words – adjectives, nicknames, and so forth – chosen to refer to them.

Axiologization would, therefore, be a consequence of populist dichotomization of society and its assumption of an antagonistic relationship between 'the people' and its 'other'. Mudde (2004) sees in moral axiologization a constitutive feature of the populist 'thin-centred' ideology. For Mudde (2004: 543), populism is 'an ideology that considers society to be ultimately separated into two homogeneous and antagonistic groups, "the pure people" versus "the corrupt elite", and which argues that politics should be an expression of the *volonté générale* (general will) of the people'. While Mudde's definition of populism does not shed much light on 'the people', it qualifies it in moral terms: 'the people' are *pure*, while their rival – that is, the second collective identity to be found in the social space after it has been divided – is *corrupt*. For Mudde (2004: 544)

> populism is moralistic rather than programmatic. Essential to the discourse of the populist is the normative distinction between 'the elite' and 'the people', not the empirical difference in behaviour or attitudes. Populism presents a Manichean outlook, in which there are only friends and foes. Opponents are not just people with different priorities and values, they are evil! Consequently, compromise is impossible, as it 'corrupts' the purity.

In semiotic terms, although axiologization can indeed occur in moral terms, this does not seem to be a necessary condition for populism to occur. In populist discourse, 'the people' will always be axiologized in positive terms against an 'other' that is an enemy but not necessarily as *pure* or *good*.

To sum up, if there is something that can be said of populist discourse to begin with, that would be that (1) it simplifies the social space by dividing it into two semantic units that correspond to social groups; and (2) it axiologizes each of these in opposed terms so that the relationship between them cannot be one of consensus but must be antagonistic; that is, it looks like a war. Consequently, the electorate is expected to react to this social contingency by *taking sides* after identifying with one of those social groups, as evidenced in Trump's except. This is the reason why scholars (Mudde, 2004; Müller, 2016) have argued that one of the opposite concepts of populism is *pluralism*: contrary to what occurs with pluralism, in populist discourse the 'other' cannot be accepted as a contender with a valid voice in the political contest over meaning.

The dichotomization of the social space does not need to be an intended or conscious process. Not every political actor that encourages or assumes polarization is aware of what they are doing: many of them just act guided by their world views or social intuitions as granted by the common sense that prevails in their political contexts. This means that the dichotomization of society can also be a constitutive feature of social imaginaries related to the political and not necessarily an active political strategy. Social imaginaries are also social discourses and, as such, have an impact on what individuals do. Their study poses interesting methodological challenges for semioticians regarding how they can be accessed through discourse.

5.2 The discursive construction of 'the people'

The previous section argued how populist discourse divides the social space in two semantic units that correspond to two collective identities: 'the people' and its rival. This rival is defined in logical terms as 'not-the-people' and serves two purposes: on the one hand, it is the semantic unit opposed to which 'the people' becomes meaningful in populist discourse; on the other hand, it fulfils the role of the enemy against which the collective identity 'the people' will compete in the political contest over meaning in antagonistic terms. As is argued in this section, populist political actors use the category 'the people' due to its *vagueness* and *ambiguity*, as these serve the purpose of creating a *logic of equivalence* to make sense of and to justify the dichotomization of society presented in the previous section.

5.2.1 The semantics of 'the people'

Understanding this aspect of populist discourse requires paying attention to the semantics of the concept 'people'. According to Pappas (2019a: 82), while democracy is based on an inclusive conception of 'the people' as a whole – that is, as the *demos* – 'quite different is the idea of the people in the populist mind, in which the people is always a part of society in constant conflict with other parts of society'. There are semantic challenges related to the noun 'people' that have not helped conceptual clarification around populism. Let us examine them with more detail.

As argued in Chapter 1, the noun *populism* originates in the Latin word *populus*, which was used to refer to a particular social group in Roman society: the plebeians. While that word somehow remained in the vocabulary of Romanic languages – Spanish: *pueblo*; Italian: *popolo*; French: *peuple*; Portuguese: *povo* – non-Romanic languages had to find equivalent words to make sense of populism as 'the *-ism* of the *populus*'. While in German, the Subject of *Populismus* is *das Volk*, in English it is 'the people'.

One first issue at stake in dealing with 'the people' as a term used to denote something is that, as pointed out in Chapter 4, what in English is covered by the word 'people' is covered in other languages by multiple signifiers. If one looks up the Spanish noun *pueblo* [one of the possible translations of *people*] in the Dictionary of the Spanish Royal Academy, two of the proposed meanings are 'group of people of a place, region or country' [*conjunto de personas de un lugar, región o país*] and 'common and modest people of a population' [*gente común y humilde de una población*]. In Spanish, the noun *pueblo* covers (at least) two different units of meaning: 'the people' as a group tied to a particular geographical reality and 'the people' as the popular classes of society, that is, the plebeians.

However, the English word 'people' can also be translated into Spanish as *gente*, which means 'a plurality of individuals'. In English, besides the noun *people*, *la gente* could be also translated as *the crowd*. Since Spanish was his mother tongue, it does not come as a surprise that Laclau begins *On Populist Reason* examining psychological theories of the crowd. Nevertheless, speaking of 'the people' as a multiplicity of individuals in the sense of a crowd is quite different than speaking of 'the people' as the legitimate subject of democracy – as when territorial sovereignty is claimed in the name of the people of a country – and it is certainly something different than speaking of 'the people' in the sense of the popular, plebeian, 'lower' sections of society.

Margaret Canovan (1984: 315) identified the problems linked to 'the people' early enough in the scholarly debate on populism. She argued that it is a vague noun that refers to at least three different things: (1) 'the people' as nation, (2) 'the people' as underdogs and (3) 'people' as everyman, that is, as a collection of individual human beings.[7] Canovan argues that these three different meanings that 'the people' might take in different contexts are somehow equivalent to the subjects of the three main political ideologies: conservatism, socialism and liberalism.

According to Canovan (1984: 315), in conservatism 'the people' designates 'a corporate whole that encompasses all living members, but that also reaches back into the past and stretches out to the future'. This conception of 'the people' as nation implies that this collection of individuals is not random but articulated, organic and corporate. Second, when used as in the sense of 'the people' as underdogs, the noun does not refer to the totality of a community but 'to a particular section of the nation' (Canovan, 1984: 315). In socialist discourse, this subgroup has traditionally been linked to the working classes. Finally, Canovan argues that liberals tend to conceive of 'the people' as a collection of individual human beings. Therefore, even if *people* is a collective noun, in English it requires a plural verb (*people are* and not *people is*), something that also happens in German (*die Leute sind*) but not in Spanish (*la gente es*).

For Canovan (1984: 317), *the people* 'can refer either to the whole political community or to a sub-community of the lower classes within it; furthermore it need not refer to any community at all, but can mean individual human beings in aggregate'. As discussed before, these three meanings are possible in English when using the noun *the people*, but they are not covered by its equivalents in Romanic languages (*pueblo, peuple, popolo, povo*) or in German (*Volk*). Canovan's third sense of 'the people' is not encompassed by these nouns in those languages: they can only refer to her proposal's 'people as nation' and 'people as underdogs'.

The adjective *popular* (Bourdieu, 1983) is also illustrative of the semantic challenges of dealing with the concept of 'the people'. To say that something is *popular* can mean different things: it can be (1) related to the popular classes (some practices, traditions, customs and rituals are 'popular' in this first sense); (2) related to the members of a given political unit or community (such as a 'popular' vote in national elections), (3) something that is successful in commercial terms (a musical or movie genre that is 'popular' is one that is appreciated by the masses) and so on.[8]

As it is evident, speaking of *the people* is not deprived of semantic challenges. Pierre Bourdieu (1987) argues that *the people* [*le peuple*] is an ambiguous term with multiple meanings, and so does Canovan (1984). This semantic indeterminacy is useful in politics because political actors can play with the ambiguities and vagueness of the term to generate broad meanings that can attract different portions of the electorate. For Canovan (1984: 317), 'these ambiguities enable the language of 'people' to form a kind of lingua franca which can be spoken by conservatives, socialists and liberals alike' and are, therefore, ideal for catch-all politics. When Donald Trump pronounced the utterance 'my pledge reads "I'm with you, the American people"', it is not clear which 'people' he is referring to only by examining the word 'people'. Is it the totality of the American citizenry? Is it the American people in the sense of the US popular classes? How are these popular classes characterized? As will be argued in Chapters 7 and 8, the ambiguities linked to the concept of 'the people' allow populism to be found both in the left and right sides of the political spectrum.

For Laclau (2005a; 2005b), *the people* is an *empty signifier*, that is, a signifier that has 'no fixed referent or essential meaning' (Panizza, 2005: 5). Laclau's analytical category of *empty signifiers* is complex and loaded with ontological assumptions (Laclau, 1991). Nevertheless, from a semiotic perspective, the concept can be used to refer to a unit – in this case, a word – taken from the lexical repertory of a given language that is used to convey meaning but whose interpretation is not univocal. If someone were tasked with filling a boat with 'the people' to abandon a country because a flood is about to hit it, it is not clear where one should start looking for individuals.[9] Benjamin Arditi (2005: 82) argues that there is a 'vagueness' in the contours of 'the people' that is 'convenient' and 'deliberate', for it enables the blurring of its contours sufficiently enough as to 'encompass anyone with grievance structured around a perceived exclusion from a public domain of interaction and decision hegemonised by economic, political or cultural elites'. In this sense, the semantic unit 'the people' becomes a semiotic resource used as part of a discursive strategy grounded on vagueness and indeterminacy (Sedda & Demuru, 2018a: 5).

The lack of a univocal signified or a concrete reference does not mean that the signifier *the people* does not have a meaning. Any competent user of a language can understand the word. Nevertheless, in each political context in which it is used, the signifier's meaning 'is constituted by the very process of naming', as Panizza (2005: 9) argues. This is what the category of *empty signifier* points out to: the word exists but its meaning is not cast in stone and fixed in a univocal way. The reference of the signifier will depend on the context of use. As Panizza (2005: 16) points out, while in the United States the prototypical representative of 'the people' is 'the ordinary (white) working man', in apartheid South Africa it was 'the disenfranchised black majority'. What remains unchanged is the semantic unit that segments a 'people' by populating its semiotic core with some defining traits and by setting some boundaries with other semantic units.

This is a premise shared by discourse-theoretical and performative accounts of populism. For Mouffe (2018: 62), 'the "people" is not an empirical referent but a discursive political construction' that 'does not exist previously to its performative articulation and cannot be apprehended through sociological categories'. Arditi (2005: 81–2), for his part, argues that 'populism has [. . .] been rather hazy about who the people are, conceiving them variously as the dispossessed, the hard-working middle classes, the burdened tax-payers, the "common man", the moral majority, and so on'. Panizza (2005: 9) is right in arguing that while 'the people' is an empty signifier that has no fixed signified, 'it always evokes the traces of a certain content shaped by language and history', as was discussed in Chapter 3 when introducing Eco's theory of Semiotics. This makes of the sociocultural context a central variable in filling the empty signifier 'the people' with particular meaning.

In semiotic terms, what is at stake in the process of filling the empty signifier with content is the passage from the abstract and conceptual level of the 'deep structures' (plane of the content) to that of discursive figurativization through the mechanisms of generalization, actorialization and axiologization of 'the people' (plane of the expression): while 'the people' is presented as a key unitary actor – a semantic unit – in the narrative structure that serves to make sense of the political, *who* the members of that group are and *how* they look like will depend on context-specific meanings. This seems to be Mudde's (2017: 52) intuition when arguing that 'if populists want to become politically relevant, they will have to define the people in terms of some of the key features of the self-identification of the targeted community'. This is a *strategic* semiotic practice based on meaning-making through the use of semiotic resources whose contents are dependent on the 'webs of signification' of a given culture (Geertz, 1973; Eco, 1976): while in some political contexts waving the national flag might be central into the construction of 'the people', in other contexts it might be more relevant to speak a dialect rather than the standard variety of the official language. In any case, what is at stake is how the abstract semantic unit 'the people' is constructed in discourse in figurative terms by tapping on pre-existent cultural and encyclopaedic contents.

5.2.2 The construction of 'the people' in populist discourse

Having dealt with the semantic ambiguity and vagueness of the signifier 'the people', let us now have an examination at how this collective identity is constructed in populist discourse and used to produce meaning within the political field. Laclau's theory of populism as presented in *On Populist Reason* is a good starting point for that because the book's goal is to study 'the nature and logics of the formation of collective identities', as declared by the author in its first sentence (Laclau, 2005a: ix). Namely, the second of the three parts of the book is entitled 'Constructing the People'. Laclau will be the departing point for our semiotic argument because his proposal on this matter is strongly semiotic.

To explain what 'the people' means, Laclau uses the concept of *chain of equivalences* to describe a discursive articulatory practice through which the claims and demands or sections of society that are not addressed by the hegemonic political order start seeing each other as partners in that exclusion. This fosters the impression of being part of the same collective identity: that of the *unheard* or *ignored* by the political order. Due to its ambiguity and vagueness, the empty signifier *the people* serves to refer to the collective identity resulting from that equivalence of smaller or more restricted collective identities. In this process, the new identity is constituted by *naming* it. As Laclau (2005b: 81) claims, 'the people' is 'something less than the totality of the members of the community: it is a partial component which nevertheless aspires to be conceived as the only legitimate totality'.

This seems to be populist political actors' discursive trick: to segment a portion of the social space and elevate it to the role of its totality. In Laclau's terms (2005a: 81), populist discourse is about making 'the people' as the underprivileged or underdog coincide with 'the people' as the *demos*, that is, the subject of democracy. This is why, for Pappas (2019a: 81), the notion of 'the people' in populist discourse 'refers simultaneously to some part (e.g., the lower class in society) and a whole (i.e., the entire society)'. This logic is represented graphically in Figure 8.

Laclau's theory poses that 'the people' originates in the articulation of specific social demands that exist in society and that are brought together to produce a new collective identity. For Pappas (2019a: 79), 'populist parties appeal to, and potentially unify, unspecified social categories, which, now tagged as "the people" acquire new collective identities, group solidarities, and political commitments'.[10] In Panizza's (2005: 10)

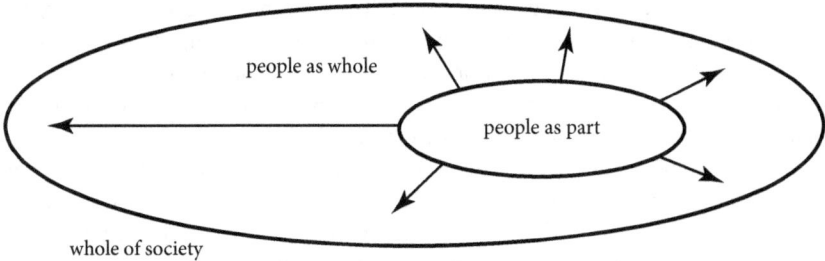

Figure 8 'The people' as part and as a whole of society.

terms, the resulting new popular identity is *a crystallization of discontents*. That is why Laclau's account of populism can be placed in what Paulina Ochoa Espejo (2017) labels *historical* accounts of the people, as opposed to *hypothetical* accounts.

According to Ochoa Espejo (2017: 773), theorists who hold *historical* accounts of 'the people' acknowledge its indeterminacy as a category to make sense of the social, but 'think of it as contingent political movements that surge from demands of actually existing groups of citizens who organize to claim their rights from the state, or to redress wrongs done to the poor, the vulnerable, or the oppressed'. On the contrary, hypothetical accounts hold that 'the people' is an abstract construction that cannot unify *actual* individuals. According to Ochoa Espejo, populist political actors tend to embrace the historical view, while critics of populism subscribe to the hypothetical view.

While Laclau's theory of 'the people' is historical in Ochoa Espejo's terms, Paul Taggart's (2000) concept of *the heartland* serves to illustrate the hypothetical account. Taggart's proposal holds that 'the people' is equalled with an imagined and mythified subgroup of society that is *idealized* as being prototypically representative of the totality. According to Taggart (2000: 95), populism deals implicitly with *the heartland* as a place 'in which, in the populist imagination, a virtuous and unified population resides'. For accounts like these, the empty signifier *the people* does not refer to a social reality – like in Laclau's account – but rather to a *social imaginary*, that is, a set of beliefs shared by a community that ground the functioning of the social (Taylor, 2004; Pereira, 2019).[11]

Against the virtuosity and the idealization of that imagined and hypothetical 'people', social scientists have traditionally dealt with the crowds and the masses as the opposite. As Panizza (2005: 15) argues, in the nineteenth century 'the dividing line between this dangerous and unpredictable mob and the men of good standing was often construed as the divide between civilization and barbarism'. Laclau's discussion of Le Bon, Tarde, McDougall and Freud in *On Populist Reason* goes in this direction. According to Panizza (2005: 15), after the instauration of liberal democracies in Europe, an inversion occurred in the culturally coded axiologization underlying 'the people', who stopped being imagined as barbarian and became the main subject of politics. This is how 'the sovereignty of the people' became a mantra in democratic politics (Panizza, 2005: 15).

When analysing what the signifier *the people* refers to when used by politicians, it is also interesting to study which synonyms are used to refer to that social group. Are utterances such as *the Americans* and *the American worker* equivalent to *the American people* when uttered by Donald Trump? What happens when *the people* is replaced by a reference to the country – America – not in the political-administrative sense but as a nation, like in the slogan 'Make America great again'? Is *the people* equivalent to *the population* or *citizenry*? What relationships of synonymy can be found within a given political context? And in a political actor's discourse?

These questions evidence the challenges of relating 'the people' to 'the nation' and, hence, populism and nationalism (De Cleen, 2017; De Cleen & Stavrakakis, 2017). These questions are examined with more detail in Chapter 7, but one could join Mudde (2004: 549) in arguing that 'the step from "the nation" to "the people" is easily taken, and the distinction between the two is often far from clear'. Here, it might be useful to mention the operation of semiotic equivalence identified by Ochoa Espejo (2017: 774): 'when politically mobilized individuals realize that their group is indeterminate, there is a tendency in political movements to look for a substantive ground of popular unity in the form of a politicized national, religious, ethnic, or racial identity', giving place to forms of nativism.[12]

To sum up, independently of how the concept of 'the people' is used by political actors in different political contexts, this vague and ambiguous semantic category does not help in making sense of social reality in referential terms. However, it seems to serve the cognitive function of constructing a Subject following Greimas's narrative scheme (Landowski, 1976). *Even if it is not clear what the sign* the people *means or refers to when used in discourse, it makes sense to consider its meaning as a collective identity that struggles for some political gains – the Object of Value – and that, to do so, needs to compete in the political sphere against an 'other' that is defined logically as 'not-the-people'*. This is how populism emerges as a distinctive word to refer to 'the *-ism* of "the people"'. It is a cognitive frame used to make sense of social reality by using a specific structure with a narrative form. This is also how *populism* and *populist* became all-encompassing words, (wrongly) used in our present time to refer to any actor, party, movement or government that speaks of and/or in the name of 'the people' as opposed to an 'other'.

The discursive logic governing populism as a social practice does not differ from the logic governing other contemporary political phenomena such as nationalism and feminism: What is 'a nation'? Who are part of it and who are not? Which individuals and collective identities does the subject 'the feminine' – at the lexical basis of the word 'feminism' – encompass in a world of fluid gender identities? Although these political movements can be easily defined in logical terms as the quest of a specific Subject for a conjunction with an Object of Value – where the Subject is the one that gives the movement a proper name in the form of an *-ism* – defining in a clear and precise manner the nature of that Subject is not a task free of complications.

Many more interesting things could be said from a semiotic perspective about populist discourse's main Subject. However, that would be unproductive in English due to the broad semantic field covered by the word 'people'. The following example illustrates the challenges that populism poses as a category that aims to be universalized and used to refer to a phenomenon that has manifestations around the globe.

In February 2015, former Uruguayan president José 'Pepe' Mujica left office and held a public farewell speech. The speech began with the words *Querido pueblo*, which in English can be translated as 'Dear people'. However, that English utterance could also be translated into Spanish as *Querida gente*, in the sense of a group of individuals. While choosing the noun *gente* would have been a more inclusive and less politicized option – in Spanish, *the people* can mean 'the people' as nation, 'the people' as underdog or 'the people' as *demos* – Mujica chose to speak to *el pueblo* and make it his addressee by playing strategically with the ambivalence of the term.

'The people' was a central collective identity in his speech, for example, in the following passage: 'Dear people: thank you! Thank you for your hugs, thank you for your criticism, thank you for your love and, above all, thank you for your deep companionship every time I felt alone during my Presidency.'[13] As a key figure of Latin

America's contemporary Left, it is not evident which sense of *pueblo* Mujica used in his speech: interpretations can oscillate between 'the people' as the Uruguayan people (the whole of society), as the plebeian sections of society (part of society) or as the *demos* that elected him into office (part of society that represents the whole of society).[14]

Does Mujica's speech evidence the use of the Populist Narrative Structure just because of his references to 'the people'? Did, therefore, Mujica use populist discourse? As per the argument presented in this chapter, the answer is negative: populist discourse does not only speak of 'the people'; it also renders explicit a distinction between 'the people' and an 'other' that is axiologized in negative moral terms as an enemy. As Oscar Reyes (2005: 105) puts it, 'an appeal to the people is a necessary but not a sufficient condition for populism, which also requires that popular interpellations be presented in the form of antagonism'. This second trait of populist discourse is not present in Mujica's '*Discurso al pueblo*'. Therefore, it would not be appropriate to label it a speech that expresses populist discourse.

5.3 'The people's other'

When political actors speak of 'the people', they use this concept as a semiotic resource to produce meaning within the public sphere by ordering the social space and proposing a structure for it. As argued before, in doing so they use an ambiguous and vague concept that is hard to define in positive terms. To fill the empty signifier *the people* with particular context-dependent meaning, the 'other' becomes crucial in populist discourse: it is only through the establishment of a gap between 'we' and 'they' that 'the people' can be discursively segmented.

Traditionally, scholars who have studied populism have argued that 'the people's other' are 'the elites' (Mudde, 2004; Müller, 2016; De Cleen, 2019) and that *populism* is an opposite concept to *elitism*. De Cleen (2019: 29), for example, defines populism as

> a political logic centred around the nodal points 'the people' and 'the elite', in which the meaning of 'the people' and 'the elite' is constructed through a down/up antagonism between 'the people' as a large powerless group and 'the elite' as a small and illegitimately powerful group. Populism is a claim to represent 'the people' against a (some) illegitimate 'elite', and constructs its political demands as representing the will of 'the people'.

One could agree with this definition when considering the first historical manifestations of populism and even current left-wing populism. Political actors that were and are populist in this original sense tend to consider the down/up element that opposes 'the people' as underdog to powerful 'the elites' as central. However, as argued in the previous section, the use that populist political actors and parties do of this concept is not always limited to 'the people' as underdog (at least in the political events currently referred to as populist). If anti-elitism were to be conceived of in economic terms, it would not be easy to deny that Donald Trump is part of 'the elite' and that his references to 'the people' are nothing else that political demagoguery. This paradoxical situation might be the result of the stretching that the concept of populism has undergone in time.

It was discussed earlier how the Populist Narrative Structure divides the social space in two groups and that one of them is 'the people'. In Chapter 4, it was argued how the identity of that community or group depends on an opposition to an 'other'. In this sense, 'the people' becomes meaningful as a collective identity thanks to an opposition to another collective identity defined in logical terms as 'not-the-people'. A boundary is established in discourse between these two collective identities. To grasp this semiotic mechanism of boundary-setting, delimitation and identification between collective identities, Lotman's cultural semiotics can be of help.

Setting boundaries and figurativizing who belongs to 'the people' and who does not is not an easy task (Ochoa Espejo, 2017). How could one possibly distinguish in the real world who are part of 'the people' and who are not? If 'the people' were to rule, who should be granted with a seat on the decision-making table? As was discussed previously, the answer to this question depends in the first place of which conception of 'the people' is being used by a specific political actor, as it is them who will fill the empty semantic unit 'the people' with specific context-dependent contents that will bring it to life in discourse. As argued, for a cultural unit to be meaningful – as opposed to other units – a segmentation of the semiotic continuum is necessary. This implies setting boundaries between different units of that continuum.

Lotman (1990; 2005) coined the analytical category of the *semiosphere* to make sense of sense- and meaning-making within a culture. Drawing on the concept of the *biosphere*, he conceived of the semiosphere as a space within which the production, circulation and consumption of meaning is possible. For Lotman, the identity of each semiosphere is defined by a set of elements that constitute its semiotic core. Outside that core, but still within the boundaries of the semiosphere, other elements are arranged in a hierarchical order. The closeness of those elements to the core expresses how relevant they are in the definition of the identity of the semiosphere. In Lotman's account, semiospheres are delimited and boundaries serve to distinguish between an inside and an outside of that semiotic space. According to the author, boundaries are peripheral spaces where processes of exchange, filtering and translation occur. Boundaries, therefore, imply 'the division of self from other' (Lotman, 2005: 210).

Collective identities are not alien to the logic of the semiosphere. As cultural artefacts constructed in discourse, they serve to make sense of social reality in cognitive, narrative and emotional terms. Collective identities are units of meaning that a given culture segments and fills with specific meaning according to their world view, history and tradition. That is why collective identities can be conceptually approached as *semiospheres*, that is, as spaces with an outside and an inside that are delimited by a boundary and where signs, texts, objects, practices and other signifying resources are placed in a core that defines the identity of that semiosphere (Montoro & Moreno Barreneche, 2021a). That placement occurs in discourse but also at the level of social imaginaries.

In populist discourse, the process of delimiting 'the people' from its 'other' does not begin by identifying the core attributes of the former but by doing so with regards to the latter: it is through the affirmation of what and how the 'other' is that the semiosphere of 'the people' is filled with meaning. The positively axiologized 'we' becomes meaningful and gains its identity through a distancing from a negatively axiologized 'they'. Even if a characterization of that 'they' does not occur, the mere negative valorization serves to establish a boundary and some moral contents as part of their respective semiotic cores.

Political actors using populist discourse have normally opposed 'the people' to 'the elite'. This is the case because normally 'the people' of populism is 'the people' as underdog, that is, it is opposed to an internal enemy: as Canovan (1984:315) argues, '"the people" are the workers, the laboring class contrasted with the parasitic capitalists'. Nevertheless, when 'the people' is used in its sense of 'the people' as nation, its identity is normally defined by an external 'other' that is not part of the national people (specific examples are discussed in Chapter 7). Once again, the ambiguity and vagueness of 'the people' allow this type of semiotic phenomenon to take place, rendering the definition of what populism is a complex and challenging task. As Arditi (2005: 83) proposes, 'populism must make an effort to configure the identity of the people and to specify the disagreement that pitches them against named adversaries – the elites, the oligarchy, Big Government, or what have you'.

As is visible when analysing populist discourse, 'the people's other' is not only the collective identity 'the elite' but also other formulations that imply a distancing from 'the people'. For Panizza (2005: 9), populism opposes 'the people' to a 'privileged few'. Instead of talking of 'the elites', which might be a tricky concept to use not only due to its vagueness and ambiguity but also to the multiple levels – political, economic, cultural and so on – where there might be elites, the notion of *the privileged few* might be more enlightening when trying to make sense of the standard Populist Narrative Structure.

This is the case because those *few* can be internal – the elites, the oligarchy, the government, the politicians, those who do not want to abandon their privileges and others – like in the case of left-wing populism, or external – immigrants, a foreign state, a foreign threat, multinational companies and organizations, a global elite – like in the case of right-wing populism.[15] As Panizza (2005: 4) argues, 'the people's other' seems to be 'any other group that prevents the people achieving plenitude', irrespective of what its nature might be. That is why the author argues that 'populism depends not only on a sense of internal homogeneity, but also on a constitutive outside – a threatening heterogeneity against which the identity is formed' (Panizza, 2005: 16–17). For Panizza (2005: 17), 'the "other" of populist identities is as diverse as the identity of the people of which it is the outside'.

In semiotic terms, populist political actors need an 'other', imagined and constructed in discourse as homogeneous and inimical, to invest the semantic unit 'the people' with meaning. While the position of the 'other' – that is, the semantic unit 'not-the-people' – can be conflated with the category of 'the elite' – economic, politic, cultural, media, legal (Rooduijn, 2014: 575) – in the attempt to give it a positive content, it can also be filled with myriad other concepts, like 'the system', 'the rich', 'supporters of globalized capitalism', the European Union, 'EU-inspired austerity' and 'mainstream politicians'. According to James Shields (2013: 183), these enemies were common in French right-wing populist Marine Le Pen's and left-wing populist Jean-Luc Mélenchon's discourses in their campaigns to become head of government.

'The People' and Its 'Other(s)'

What matters for 'the people' to become meaningful is that an 'other' exists. That 'other' might be equalled with a unique collective identity like 'the elite' but can also be constructed through a process grounded on a *logic of equivalence*. In their study of left-wing populism through the case of Greek political party SYRIZA, Yannis Savrakakis and Giorgios Katsambekis (2014) argue:

> the 'enemy of the people,' that is the 'proausterity forces,' the 'memorandum,' the 'troika' and so on; in this discourse, all these forces, also organized through an equavalential logic, were presented as distinct but interrelated moments of the 'establishment.' SYRIZA's discourse thus divided the social space into two opposing camps: 'them' (the 'establishment,' the 'elite') and 'us' ('the people'), power and the underdog, the elite and the nonprivileged, those 'up' and the others 'down.' (Stavrakakis & Katsambekis, 2014: 219)

As per the authors' description, SYRIZA seems to have created a 'we' through the discursive articulation of multiple Others depicted as *a single collective identity* – 'the establishment' – following the same logic of equivalence that Laclau identifies for the construction of 'the people'. This logic is represented in Figure 9, where different 'others' are grouped through a logic of equivalence into a single 'people's other'.

Populist political actors, parties and movements know – even if intuitively – that in their discourses and performances they need to privilege 'the people' as the main actor within the political (otherwise they are not being populist in the sense of trying to achieve 'power for the people'). Nevertheless, due to the prevalence of oversimplification and of binary schemes (Cosenza, 2018) in our mediatized and hyperdynamic political spheres, the social space is simplified and depicted in a dichotomous fashion: there is a 'we' and there is a 'they', where the 'we' gains meaning through an opposition to the 'they'.

According to this argument, it could be argued that the difficulty of identifying 'the people's other' is at the basis of the lack of conceptual clarity regarding what populism is. If populism were only a matter of confronting 'the people' versus 'the elite', it would be easy to classify political actors, movements, parties and even governments as populist or not: Do they speak of 'the people'? Do they oppose 'the people' to 'the elite'?

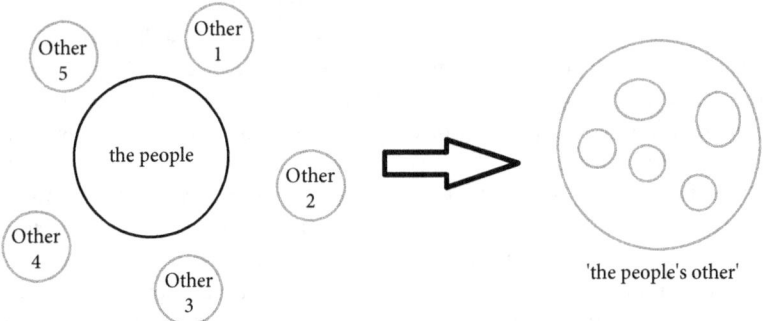

Figure 9 The 'other' as a single collective identity.

Is the relationship between these two collective identities antagonistic? If the answers to the three questions are positive, then it is a case of populism.

However, in our times, due to the lack of a fixed identity to 'the people's other' in the standard Populist Narrative Structure, that collective identity can be filled with different meanings: 'the elites', the 'oligarchy', 'the establishment', 'the plutocracy', 'the rich', 'politicians', 'bureaucrats', 'supporters of capitalist globalization', 'imperialistic attitudes', 'terrorism' and 'supranational organizations' like the EU, among many others. These 'others' are usually depicted as a minority against the extension of 'the people', axiologized negatively and placed in populist discourse on a level of superiority in the sense of vertical power positions and privileges. As is demonstrated in Chapters 7 and 8, in populist discourse 'the people' is normally a collective identity that has been forgotten, betrayed, displaced or ignored by 'the privileged few', whatever the form is that this 'other' takes in discourse.

As a result of the discursive mechanism that characterizes the construction of 'the people's other', populism can exist on every side of the political spectrum – right and left – depending on how the Populist Narrative Structure is combined with other political contents to produce meaning within the public sphere. The case studies presented in Chapters 7 and 8 will help visualize this dynamic of discursive articulation.

This chapter presented the Populist Narrative Structure as the structure that defines populism as a discursive practice. As argued, it opposes in an antagonistic relationship a political Subject ('the people') to an 'other' ('the people's' anti-Subject) that can take different forms since its identity is defined in negative terms as opposed to 'the people', that is, as 'not-the-people'. The Populist Narrative Structure is nothing else than a narrative structure – in the terms of structural Semiotics – consisting of empty semantic units presented in a particular relationship. As such, it does not fill its two main semantic units with specific contents or meanings: it only delimits them in logical and conceptual terms by establishing a boundary anchored in an idealized, positively axiologized and mythified semiotic core that defines the identity of 'the people' as a collective social actor within the political. Every other category becomes meaningful in populist discourse through an opposition to that process of mythification. In this process, the relationship of antagonism that characterizes the Populist Narrative Structure implies that the 'other', independently of whatever form it might take in specific discourses and performances, is an enemy with whom consensus is not possible. Hence, an inevitable gap exists in the social space, and the populist leader's task will be to ensure that the scale moves in favour of 'the people'.

The semiotic nature of this proposal is salient. As Landowski (1997, my translation) argues, 'for the world to produce meaning and be analyzable as such, we need to see it as an articulated universe, as a system of relationships'. The Populist Narrative Structure does not propose anything else that *a logical relationship* between two terms A – 'the people' – and –A, with whom A has a polemic relationship. –A is transformed in discourse into B following the logic presented in Figure 10.

As pointed out, the Populist Narrative Structure is a mere structural abstraction – equivalent to *a political logic* that can be found in populist discourse, according to Laclau (2005a), De Cleen (2019) and others – that needs to be brought to life – that

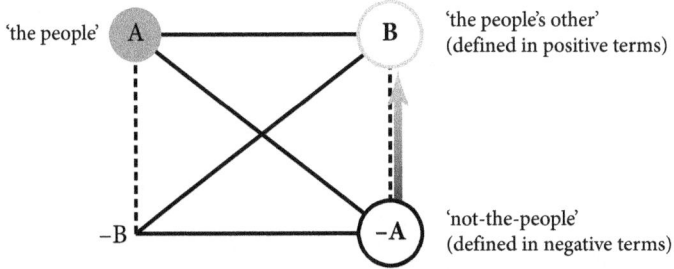

Figure 10 The discursive construction of 'the people's other' in positive terms.

is, performed – by someone so that it can be evidenced in concrete configurations of meaning in order to be meaningful to the electorate. Following Paolucci (2012: 304), 'if we want to study these structures, we must do so on the basis of empirical manifestations (texts), so that we can find there constant forms of structuring of meaning'. In semiotic terms, the Populist Narrative Structure is a *virtual* structure that needs to be *actualized*. As Greimas (1989: 557) argues, 'narrative structures do not exist per se but are a mere moment in the generation of signification. When the subject of enunciation says something, he utters a durative discourse and proceeds by means of figures that are linked up. It is the figures that bear the traces of narrative universals'. In this sense, the populist leader is crucial in the task of figurativizing the Populist Narrative Structure through the use of specific context-dependent and relevant contents, as is argued in the following chapter.

6

The Populist Leader

Academic research, politicians and the media normally link populism to *individuals*: contrary to what occurs with the members of 'the people', populist political actors are specific human beings that can be identified referentially. Donald Trump and Bernie Sanders in the United States; Marine Le Pen and Jean-Luc Mélenchon in France; Beppe Grillo, Matteo Salvini and Silvio Berlusconi in Italy; Nigel Farage and Boris Johnson in the United Kingdom; Geert Wilders in the Netherlands; Evo Morales in Bolivia; Rafael Correa in Ecuador; Pablo Iglesias in Spain; Alexis Tsipras in Greece and myriad other individuals active in the political field are referred to as the specimens of contemporary populist politics.

Before this extensive batch of current populist politicians, Jörg Haider in Austria, Pim Fortuyn in the Netherlands, Jean-Marie Le Pen in France, Hugo Chávez in Venezuela, Alberto Fujimori in Peru, Carlos Menem in Argentina and other individual politicians were also referred to as *populists*. Decades before them, Juan Domingo Perón in Argentina, Getúlio Vargas in Brazil, Lázaro Cárdenas in Mexico and other individuals were the – 'classic' – populist politicians (Hawkins, 2009: 1055). Faced with this lasting mechanism of linking populism to individual political actors, it does not come as a surprise that a strong, personalistic and charismatic leadership has been frequently identified in populism studies as one of the defining features of populism (Canovan, 1999; Weyland, 2001; 2017; Charaudeau, 2011).

Like it occurs with any semiotic segmentation of a continuum and the grouping of units into encompassing categories, the list of individuals to be included in the category of populist political actors depends on how the labels *populism* and *populist* are defined and conceived of, both in descriptive and normative terms. One of the challenges in doing this is that *populism* is not only used as a concept by scholars and academic researchers to make sense of the dynamics of the political but also as a *signifier* by politicians and the media to produce meaning in specific contexts (De Cleen, Glynos & Mondon, 2018). This peculiar situation might explain why over the decades, so many politicians have been referred to and studied as examples of populism.[1]

If populism is defined as a discursive practice characterized by the use of a specific narrative structure, then enunciation is a necessary condition for populism to be apprehended. This means that there can be occurrences of the abstract notion of populism only if *someone* produces texts, discourses and other acts of enunciation that express or reflect the Populist Narrative Structure as the underlying principle guiding meaning-making. There will be no occurrence of populism if the Populist Narrative

Structure cannot be evidenced in the utterances of political actors, independently of the nature of these utterances (verbal, gestural, attitudinal, connotative, etc.).

This is the reason why for social Semiotics, communication science and other disciplines that work with discourse, individual politicians are key figures in *performing* populism, that is, in doing things with language, gestures, their bodies, their attire, on social media that can be recognized as discursive articulations in the plane of the expression that reflect the Populist Narrative Structure as the semiotic principle guiding their meaning-making. It is them who bring the Populist Narrative Structure to life by filling its empty spaces – 'the people' versus the 'other' – with context-dependent contents. Moreover, it is them who will model who and how 'the people' are and explain in narrative terms who the 'other' is and why it is an enemy to 'the people'. In this sense, although populism has an inescapable performative aspect, it is not limited *only* to its performative aspect or to a specific communicative style.

Semioticians (Landowski, 2018; Cervelli, 2018; Sedda & Demuru, 2018a; Demuru, 2021a; Addis, 2020; Fontanille, 2020), communication scientists (Aalberg et al., 2017) discourse analysts (Hidalgo-Tenorio, Benítez-Castro & De Cesare, 2019; Macaulay, 2019; Zienkowski & Breeze, 2019) and discourse-theory scholars (Mouffe, 2005b; Stavrakakis, 2005) have been particularly attracted to study the discourses and practices of populist leaders around the world. Their research outputs are fundamental in Semiotics' attempt to grasp and describe how populist political actors produce meaning by employing a broad array of semiotic resources.

This chapter approaches the figure of the populist leader by examining the role it plays in enunciating texts based on the Populist Narrative Structure. Casullo (2019: 70) proposes that the leading characters of what she calls *the populist myth* are three: a hero ('the people'), a villain (the 'other') and the populist leader. As argued, the leader will be crucial in bringing the *populist myth* – another way of naming the Populist Narrative Structure – to life by rendering its abstract and empty categories *figurative* through a modelling of 'the people', the 'other' and his/her specific role in that political struggle. The first section of the chapter discusses the role of the leader in politics and its relevance from a semiotic perspective. The second section examines the role of the populist leader with a focus on the semiotic resources they might use in meaning-making. The final three sections discuss the cases of Donald Trump, Matteo Salvini and Hugo Chávez.

6.1 The role of the leader in politics

The argument presented in the two previous chapters is of a relatively abstract nature. Concepts such as *the political*, *collective identities*, a *contest over meaning*, *empty signifiers*, *deep structures*, *semantic units*, and *logics of equivalence*, among many others, were used to make sense of how populist discourse produces specific 'reality effects' based on sense and meaning to appeal to the electorate. This is a crucial object of study for social Semiotics as the discipline interested in grasping and understanding how specific discursive practices render the social world meaningful to individuals to the point of having an impact in what they do: who they vote for, what kind of political beliefs they develop and hold, how they feel *vis-à-vis* their political opponents and so on.

Semiotics' disciplinary goal does not differ from that of discourse theorists like Laclau and Mouffe. Nevertheless, the conclusions drawn by semioticians are based not in purely rational and logical deductions – as discourse-theorist tend to do, even if they work with case studies to illustrate the theory – but in the analysis of specific configurations of meaning that can be read as *texts* (Floch, 1990). Critical Discourse Analysis proceeds in the same manner, although its focus is slightly oriented towards the analysis of linguistic utterances and of discourses that are based on natural language rather than on other elements of capital relevance in the attempt of grasping meaning-making holistically, such as the uses that political leaders do of their bodies (attire, gestures, postures, use of the hands, etc.) or the type of images they post on social media.[2]

Within the political field, multiple and diverse figurative configurations of meaning serve to gain access to the processes of segmentation, generalization, actorialization and axiologization taking place in the plane of the content that individuals use to map and make sense of their social and political environment. When abstract categories such as 'the people' are brought to life in concrete manifestations that can be perceived through the senses, then figurativization – the rendering of discourse tangible and perceivable – occurs. The abstract semantic unit 'the nation' can be rendered tangible – figurative – through a name, a set of key symbols such as the flag (Ortner, 1973), texts such as anthems and a constitution, and the identification of specific practices and traditions (Hobsbawm & Ranger, 1987) as being central to that identity (i.e. as being placed within its semiotic core). A political party can use a name, a logo, a specific colour palette and a number of practices and rituals to identify itself as a distinct semantic unit competing in the political contest over meaning against other parties.

In the process of rendering abstract categories – a nation, a political party or any other *collective*, in Verón's terminology – tangible, the role of individual politicians is crucial. In the first place, it is them who will produce texts and discourses – that is, manifestations in the plane of the expression – that grant semioticians and discourse analysts access to the world views underpinning what they say and do – in the plane of the content. Second, due to their visible position within the public sphere in which they are active, these individuals usually receive the media coverage that is necessary to be seen and heard in a state of (hyper)mediatized politics. That is how their discourses and performances travel from one arena (like a rally) to another (the press, social media platforms, etc.). Third, they are the ones who have a legitimate voice to anchor discourses to specific contexts and tie them to a *here and now* (in oral speeches and public appearances and also through the use of social media posts, press releases, interviews, etc.). Last but not least, it is them who, following Verón's logic of discursive construction of collectives in and through enunciation, model who the 'we' and who the 'they' are. Shortly, political actors' utterances and performances are an invaluable source for semiotic analysis.

Moreover, it is the leader who, through a strategic use of semiotic resources, creates specific *situations*, that is, temporary spheres of circulation of meaning between them and their electorates that can be read and made sense of in semiotic terms through the examination of how meaning is produced, circulates and how it is consumed by those who participate in it. A political rally, for example, is a prototypical example of a situation that can be read from a semiotic perspective.[3] The same occurs with the live transmission on streaming of an event through Facebook or Instagram.

When studying the performative dimension of political actors and leaders, Semiotics will be interested in *enunciation* (Benveniste, 1966; 1974). By examining specific texts – words, speeches, attitudes, tweets, social media posts and so on – that function as *traces* of populism, semioticians aim at unveiling the meanings that underlie the act of enunciation. Enunciation can be of a linguistic and also of a non-linguistic nature. Political leaders do not only use words – written or spoken – to produce meaning. They also recur to other semiotic resources such as their bodies, gestures, the tone of voice, the posture, specific discursive strategies, attitudes towards other social actors and the system, and social media posts, among others, for meaning- and sense-making. All these resources can be manipulated and combined to produce specific meanings within the political. Therefore, as researchers in the field of pragmatics and microsociology have argued, meaning-making is not only based on the use and exchange of words but also in other resources used for the purpose of impression management (Goffman, 1956). Therefore, social Semiotics becomes interdisciplinary and closer to sociology, anthropology and pragmatics.

In contemporary democratic politics, every political candidate needs to produce meanings to appeal to and persuade the electorate since power positions are accessed through elections. Even if these efforts are certainly based on reason and arguments (Fairclough & Fairclough, 2012), they are also grounded on an *emotional* dimension linked to identity and belonging which, as discussed in Chapter 4, defines the political as a discursive field. Not all political decisions are made based on the rationality and solidity of an argument: other aspects such as affect, identification, fear and other aesthesic elements[4] also play a role here. In politics, meaning is experienced not only when reading political programmes or party manifestos, not even when listening to speeches pronounced by political leaders: also, interactions with the leader and other actors, both offline and online, are crucial in this sense.

In his attempts to consolidate Semiotics as a *sociosémiotique* capable of making sense of the human experience as a whole, Landowski (1997; 2004) proposed a model to approach the interactions that are established between individuals in different contexts. As argued in Chapter 4, political regimes reflect different types of interactional regimes. Hence, the relationship between the political leader – a dictator, an absolute monarch, an elected head of state and others – and his/her constituents will depend on the links of meaning [*rapports de sens*] that are constructed between social actors. That is why social Semiotics sees in *intersubjectivity* a key notion to approach meaning-making: it is in this space of indeterminacy between the perceptions and the sense constructed by social actors where meaning is produced and negotiated.

6.2 The populist leader: A semiotic discussion

Scholars studying populism have pointed out the role of the leader as one of the defining features of populism. According to Weyland (2001: 14), populism 'emerges when a personalistic leader seeks or exercises government power based on direct, unmediated, uninstitutionalised support from large numbers of mostly unorganised followers'. For Pappas (2019a: 80), 'it is only possible to make sense of populism's collective action problem if leadership is brought to the center stage'. Canovan (1999) believes that a charismatic leader embodying redemption, provocation and antagonism is one of the core traits of populism. More recently, Weyland (2017: 50) argued that 'while charisma is not a definitional characteristic of populism, it can solidify the quasi-direct relationship of personalistic leader and supporters that constitutes the core of populism'.

The relevance given to leadership within populism studies is justified: *someone* needs to name and construct 'the people' and its 'other' in discourse for these empty categories to have a discursive existence. If populism is defined as the discursive practice based on the use of the Populist Narrative Structure to produce meaning within the political, then Semiotics will be interested in examining how political actors use this narrative structure and bring it to life by filling it with specific contents. In semiotic terms, the question is how a virtual, empty and formal narrative structure is *actualized*, that is, brought to life by an enunciator in a specific way so that it can have an impact – cognitive and emotional – in other individuals.

This question does not imply studying only how populist political actors use existing context-dependent contents to bring the Populist Narrative Structure to life. Neither does it imply taking only into consideration language and the words they utter. Since sense and meaning depend on the perceptive system of individuals, semiotic resources of different nature play a crucial role in shaping them in cognitive and emotional terms. Populist political actors develop and implement discursive and performative strategies that imply using these resources in the production of meaning. Hence, examining populist leaders' meaning-making is a multimodal or syncretic enterprise, that is, one that looks at how meaning emerges at the crossroads of the use of multiple semiotic modes (linguistic, visual, proxemic, etc.).

In a brief passage of *On Populist Reason*, Laclau (2005a: 41–5) discusses the role of the leader as it was conceived by French sociologist and social psychologist Gabriel Tarde. His discussion does not take place through the lenses of discourse theory but is rather based on an organizational and psychological perspective. Panizza (2005), for his part, recognizes the relevance of leadership in populist meaning-making as the point of identification between the discursively constructed 'people' and their representative. For him, 'the figure of the leader functions as a signifier to which a multiplicity of meanings can be attributed' (Panizza, 2005: 19). Moreover, he adds that 'the ultimate impact of the leader's appeal depends on the particular story that he/she relates or embodies, and the audience's reception to the story' (Panizza, 2005: 20).

More recently, scholars who conceive of populism as a performance have proposed that populism is *a style of communication* (Moffitt & Tormey, 2014; Moffitt, 2016; Jagers & Walgrave, 2007; Ostiguy, Panizza & Moffitt, 2021; Ekström & Morton, 2017; Ekström, Patrona & Thornborrow, 2018; Wodak, 2015). Here, the role of political actors is crucial because it is their performances that allow the identification of populism. Jagers and Walgrave (2007: 322) see populism as a style or technique of self-presentation that refers to the people and that pretends to speak in their name exhibiting 'a conspicuous exhibition of closeness to (ordinary) citizens'. For Moffitt and Tormey (2014: 387), populism is a political style, where *style* refers to 'the repertoires of performance that are used to create political relations'. The authors identify four styles: populist, technocratic, authoritarian and post-representative. Moffitt (2016: 38) defines a political style as 'the repertoires of embodied, symbolically mediated performance made to audiences that are used to navigate the fields of power that comprise the political, stretching from the domain of government through to everyday life'. The performative account argues that populist leaders *create realities*, such as the sense of a crisis of breakdown (Moffitt & Tormey, 2014; Moffitt, 2016). Therefore, these accounts are close to Semiotics, although they might lack conceptual refinement in distinguishing between *content* and *performance*, or between *style* and *cognitive frame*.[5]

In enacting populism, political actors are crucial because, in many cases, they pose and function as *examples* of who and how 'the people' are (Landowski, 2018; Arditi, 2005). For Arditi (2005: 83), 'the leader appears to be a symbolic device. As the presumed incarnation of the popular will, or as a trustee of the people, his (or her) role is to simplify the issues and to disambiguate the identity of the populist camp'. This mechanism implies producing an effect of sense that is anchored in eliminating the gap of representation between the politician and the electorate. Identification takes place by playing with the interplay between the leader as a symbol and an index of 'the people': while populist leaders present themselves as *indexes* – 'I am one of you' – they are actually *symbols*, that is, signs that are not linked to what they stand for but that play with connotations to create an illusion of indexicality. As Lowndes (2005: 146) argues, the populist leader claims 'an immediate identification between themselves and those they represent' with the aim of producing 'a transparency of representation'. That is why Panizza (2017) sees in *identification* the core of populism.

When studying how populist political actors communicate and perform, Semiotics does not aim at coming up with a universal law regarding how this phenomenon takes place in *any* possible context. It rather seeks to map the different strategies that populist political actors employ to produce meaning in their interactions with the electorate by using the Populist Narrative Structure. For this purpose, the work of discourse analysts and communication scholars is precious since it provides semioticians with empirical data on populist actors' meaning-making.

Recently, semioticians have examined populist meaning-making from different perspectives, ranging from more theoretical discussions to empirical studies. Franciscu Sedda and Paolo Demuru (2018a) identify five traits that define how populism is enacted by political actors: (1) vagueness, (2) implosion, (3) the use of the body, (4) aesthesia and (5) negativity. Focusing on studying Italian populist politician Umberto Bossi and his party Lega Nord, Pierluigi Cervelli (2018) argues that populist political actors produce effects of sense by using language and bodily semiotic resources: not only is it frequent for populist political actors to use dialects, slang and informal registers – particularly in spaces that are invested with formality, such as the parliament or official ceremonies – in their utterances, but they also use the body strategically, for example, through the attire they choose (like wearing or not a suit or a tie to attend a parliamentary session).

Besides language, the body is a key dimension of politics, and in particular of populist politics. The identification of the relevance of the body within populist scholarship (Diehl, 2017; Casullo, 2020; Cervelli, 2018; Landowski, 2018; Demuru & Pimenta Rodrigues, 2021) coincides with the attention that semioticians have given to the bodily dimension in meaning-making (Fontanille, 2011). For Fontanille (2011: 5, my translation), 'the intervention of the body in semiotic theory signalises the search [...] for an evident alternative to Semiotics' original logicism and invites to deal with the theoretical and methodological problems from a phenomenological angle, in relation to the sensitive experience and to practices that involve the body of the operator'.

The phenomenological focus – how meaning and sense are perceived, felt and experienced through the senses and the body – is crucial in the French tradition of social Semiotics, as pointed out by Greimas already in *Sémantique structurale,* a book from 1966. Inspired by the work of Maurice Merleau-Ponty, French semioticians assume that individuals access meaning through their senses in a process that leaves cognitive, sensorial and affective tracks. It is due to this phenomenological focus that the analytical category of *aesthesia* became so central in post-Greimas social Semiotics.

The body can also be used strategically as a means for meaning-making. By using the body as a strategic resource in meaning-making, populist politicians produce specific meanings to present themselves in the public sphere as part of 'the people' in an indexical manner. Paula Diehl (2017: 361) argues that the body is one of the most effective instruments in political representation since it provides 'the physical support for political performances'. Diehl believes that 'it is impossible to dissociate political messages from the bodies of the actors who express them'. This is the case not only because the body articulates the sounds that are expressed orally – where the tone of voice, intonation and rhythm of speaking also contribute to meaning-making – but also because it is by using the body that the meanings that produce the effect of sense of belonging to the abstract category of 'the people' can be articulated: the populist leader will produce meaning by *mirroring* 'the people' (Diehl, 2017), or at least the conception he/she has of it. As Diehl (2017: 366–7) argues:

> In the context of western societies, the codes for body staging in politics suggest professionalization and a certain distance between the office holder and the voter. Political representatives demonstrate institutional attitudes and professionality by dressing up, moderating their words and using restrained body language. Political actors who follow populist logic do exactly the contrary: they embrace an anti-institutional and anti-elite attitude and stress the gap between the people and the elite by presenting their bodies with attributes of blue-collar or folkish qualities. In so doing, they claim to be like the people and not like the elite.

The body, then, serves as a semiotic resource that populist political actors use to bring the Populist Narrative Structure to life in a performative sense. Populist political actors articulate their performances within the political sphere to characterize and construct 'the people' by tapping on the meanings they recognize as relevant within their sociocultural contexts. By not respecting the formal dress code conventionally given to specific situations, by accompanying an improper, colloquial or provocative use of language with bodily gestures, by blurring the line that separates private from public life – for example, by showing their bodies while on the beach – among other strategies that imply the use or display of the body, populist political actors can *model* how 'the people' are and justify why they are part of that group. According to Panizza (2005: 20), 'people identify with a leader chiefly through the stories he or she relates not only with words but, more broadly, by the use of symbols, including the leader's own body and personal life'. However, the author claims that 'the physical presence of the leader does not necessarily make populist discourse less ambiguous or less open to conflicting interpretations' (Panizza, 2005: 20).

Another relevant means of meaning-making that political actors use are social media channels like Facebook, Twitter, Instagram and TikTok. Populist political actors use these channels not only to deliver their political messages – for example, in a tweet – but also to perform their role as populist leaders by showing how normal, authentic, popular or humble they are (Demuru, 2021a). Moreover, with the use of some social media features – Instagram's stories, Facebook's live streaming – they can create the illusion of togetherness that Landowski (2018) identifies as a prototypical type of interaction in populist discourse: by creating an aesthesic reality effect of being part of the same collective identity, populist leaders actually interact with the electorate in a manipulative way to make them feel, believe and want specific things. Sharing a deictic content on social media that affirms the 'I-here-now' triad produces an effect of sense of closeness between the leader and the audience. As semioticians have argued, there seems to be a close link between contemporary populism and internet-based media, such as digital social media platforms (Sedda & Demuru, 2018b; 2019) and the web (Escudero Chauvel, 2019) due to the effects of sense they facilitate.

In their attempts to make sense of populist discourse, semioticians examine numerous dimensions that serve populist political actors to produce meaning through the use of the Populist Narrative Structure. Some of these are the use of language – messages, words, use of dialects, linguistic variation according to context, formality or not; the use of the body – gestures, posture, proxemics, attire, hairstyle, performance when on stage, attitudes as expressed in bodily events; the use of social media channels – topics of their posts, style of messages, types of images posted, social media features used and the definition of *situations* based on the creation of the illusion of an intimate link between them and their audiences. The following three sections discuss how Donald Trump, Matteo Salvini and Hugo Chávez – three political actors frequently labelled as populist – bring the Populist Narrative Structure to life through the use of some of the semiotic resources discussed here.

6.3 Donald Trump

Donald Trump is a paradigmatic example of the irruption into politics of an outsider candidate whose discourses and performances challenge 'politics as usual' by recurring to the Populist Narrative Structure. Since his incursion into politics, Trump was a challenge to the concept of populism as it was traditionally conceived in the United States.

In the United States, populism was traditionally a left-wing, inclusive and even socialist movement that aimed at challenging the economic and political elites, together with other power structures considered unfair. This was the 'political ideology' of the People's Party, although its focus was set on the agrarian sector of US-American society. When Donald Trump burst into US politics to compete in the 2016 presidential election as a candidate for the Republican Party, he was scrutinized through the lens of the concept of populism as it was being used in Europe since the 2000s to make sense of right-wing phenomena. Therefore, Trump quickly became another occurrence of populism at the global level in a country where it did not make much sense to speak of someone like him as being a populist.

One of the many curiosities of Trump's case is that, if there is someone who does not fit the imaginary and homogenous 'people' in any of its alleged meanings – as discussed in Chapter 5 – that is him, a multimillionaire tycoon that seems more to be part of the 1 per cent that exploits the 99 per cent rather than the opposite (Macaulay, 2019: 165). How can there be populism when the populist leader is one of the clearest examples of the country's economic elites? If populism is defined as the use of a specific narrative structure, the biographical background of who uses it is irrelevant. In other words, there can be populism even if the leader is evidently not a commoner or a plebeian.

Trump's discourse and performances evidence a clear case of populism as defined in this book. As evidenced in the excerpt of one of his speeches discussed in a previous chapter, Trump makes of 'the American people' the addressee of his discourse. Moreover, the slogan of his 2016 presidential campaign was 'Make America great again'. Besides, one of the most salient of his political promises was to build a wall to avoid Mexican migrants to enter illegally the United States as a means to protect 'the Americans'.

As is argued in Chapter 7, Trump embraced an exclusionary, right-wing ideology that had a populist component. In other words, Trump framed the right-wing political contents he embraced through the use of the Populist Narrative Structure. Due to his right-wing political positioning – and as evidenced in his permanent reference to 'America' and 'the American people', that is, two collective identities where the *national* component is salient – he used to fill the empty space 'the people' with a national content: the Subject of Trump's politics was not 'We, the people of the United States' but rather 'We, the American people'.

In an analysis of Trump's announcement of his candidacy to run for president, Marcia Macaulay (2019: 172) argues that 'Trump consistently defines and redefines America and specifically "America lost" much along the lines of "paradise lost"'. The author also points out that in that speech – and as begun being characteristic of Trump's discourse since then – 'America' and 'the American people' seem to refer to equivalent entities: there is a conflation of 'the people' and 'the country'. As argued in the previous chapter, different populist actors use different words to refer to the abstract semantic unit 'the people'. The selection of words – which refer to concepts – expresses a *chain of equivalences* that equals different segmentations of society and builds a 'people'.

Macaulay identifies a number of narratives that Trump used in that speech to present his world view to the electorate. One of them is the *absence of victories* that the United States have experienced over recent years, including against 'China' and 'Mexico'. In Trump's discourse, these two countries fulfil the thematic role of 'the people's other' and trigger a discourse of victimhood (Al-Ghazzi, 2021). As Macaulay (2019: 175) claims, for Trump, 'Mexico does not represent a geographical entity or the Mexican people; instead Trump constructs Mexico as a personified political agent that acts for itself against America'. The collective identity 'We, the American people' is defined through the discursive construction of *an external threat* that fills the empty category 'they' and that is actorialized and axiologized in discourse as an enemy.

In one passage of the speech, Trump says, 'they're not sending their best. They are not sending you'. Here, Macaulay (2019: 175) sees that 'the *you* referenced by Trump are technically members of his audience, but more broadly, *you* references and constructs the American "people" and "America" itself'. The 'Mexican other' is demonized by Trump following the mechanisms identified by Eco (2012): Mexico *sends* people who bring drugs and crime with them, who are rapists; in short, who are *bad* (Macaulay, 2019: 175). As Macaulay (2019: 189) points out, in Trump's discourse the verb *to send* is equivalent to a sort of invasion, that is, it indicates that an external enemy is trying to defeat Us. Mexico is, therefore, 'agentivised as an opponent' (Macaulay, 2019: 189).

In the analysed speech, after constructing in discourse the 'we' and the 'they', Trump positions himself as the person who can overcome the situation of disadvantage that the 'we' experiences. This is a typical feature of populist discourse: the leader intervenes in politics to redeem 'the people' (Casullo, 2019). For this purpose, Trump creates a *co-identity* between himself and 'the people' by posing as 'a jobs president', that is, one that can see and implement what is best for 'the American people', who have lost their jobs to external outsourcing (Macaulay, 2019: 178). For Macaulay (2019: 178), since in Trump's discourse he and 'the people' are homogenized, 'the unmet need of himself as President becomes a logical corollary for making America great'.

Trump's discourse reflects the nature of populist discourse as an illusion of co-involvement of the leader as part of the collective identity 'the people'. According to Landowski (2018), populist discourse aims at manipulating the electorate by creating an illusion of togetherness, closeness and sameness. By producing meaning aimed at creating the effect of 'We are one and the same' that implies an aesthesic involvement of the leader in the collective identity of 'the people', what actually occurs is an interaction based on the regime of manipulation, that is, an attempt of making the electorate believe and feel specific things.

Curiously, in Trump's case this occurs even if he is clearly not a prototypical example of 'the people'. On the contrary, he is a clear example of America's 1 per cent. One could argue that this discursive strategy would have not been possible – in the sense of being allowed by the sociocultural encyclopaedia – if populism had not evolved from being a specific left-wing, inclusive ideology to an empty narrative structure that underpins various political discourses around the world and that is brought to life by actors from any side of the political spectrum in diverse political contexts.

In line with Macaulay's argument, Heather McCallum-Bayliss (2019) identifies three concepts as central in Trump's discourse: the nation, the people and the leader. McCallum-Bayliss (2019: 255–6) prefers not to label Trump as a populist but to conclude that he uses *populist tactics* such as posing as '*the voice* of the people', criticizing the political establishment, condemning the American institutions, denigrating opponents and detractors through their delegitimization and the provocation of 'fear and anxiety in "the people"' through the allegation that 'the corrupt elites have *cheated them*', among other discursive strategies that reflect the Populist Narrative Structure as the principle guiding meaning-making.

Trump constitutes a good example of how the Populist Narrative Structure can be performed through the use of semiotic resources of a non-linguistic nature. On the one hand, he permanently fostered antagonisms with his opponents by calling them *crooked*, *dishonest* or *lying*. This constructs a relationship with an enemy rather than with a legitimate opponent that reflects the conflictive relationship between the two semantic units of the Populist Narrative Structure. Moreover, giving nicknames to other political candidates – he referred to Elizabeth Warren as *Pocahontas* – is unacceptable according to the etiquette of political institutions. Although these events are certainly speech acts based on the use of language, their meaning lies at a different level: that of *social relations*. On the other hand, Trump used his social media accounts actively and frequently with a combative attitude: it was not uncommon that some of his tweets were written in all-caps, as if he were shouting (Demuru, 2021a: 511) or ending with emotionally charged expressions such as *Sad!, Bad!* or *Be Honest!* (Gerbaudo, 2018: 746).

Trump also constructed his identification with 'the people' through the creation of situations, as evidenced in the recordings of multiple of his rallies and public appearances prior to and while being president of the United States. He normally used a simple and plain language (Breeze, 2017; Lakoff, 2016a; 2016b; Sclafani, 2018), full of contractions, short sentences and a quite limited repertoire of adjectives such as *good, great, fine, bad* and *wonderful*. Trump's representation of the social realm in discourse was grounded on *oversimplification*, transforming complex issues into things that the common and ordinary 'people' can easily grasp and understand. Trump also preferred conversational mechanisms that are simple to understand and engaging, such as repetitions, questions that need to be answered with 'yes' or 'no' and utterances aimed at producing reactions from the participants in the rallies, such as applauses and boohs.

Finally, he permanently posed as a 'common American citizen' that will not play the political game following its rules, such as when he elaborated on 'being presidential',[6] or in his relationships with representatives from other powers of the United States, like Nancy Pelosi. Nevertheless, while performing as a 'common American citizen', he never left aside his positioning as one of the richest men in the United States. As opposed to other populist actors, he usually wore expensive suits and ties in his public appearances and never quitted showing off his sumptuous lifestyle. While he could have used a semiotic strategy *to look as* part of 'the people', he did not.

In conclusion, Trump's discourse and performances evidence the use of the Populist Narrative Structure as the principle guiding meaning-making. Because it is an *empty* structure that only proposes a relationship between two semantic units, Trump had to fill it with specific content. The contents that Trump used for meaning-making within the political were not only relevant within the US political realm – like the references to American history and the US relationship with countries like Mexico and China – but they also use right-wing, nationalist and even nativist political contents in the discursive articulation, as will be discussed in Chapter 7. Therefore, if Trump can be labelled as a populist, it is not due to the political contents he puts forward: what matters for that labelling is the articulation he does of those contents by recurring to the Populist Narrative Structure. Therefore, it is the presence – as identified by the analysts – in his discourse and performances of this narrative frame what allows calling him a populist.

6.4 Matteo Salvini

The second case study revolves around Italian politician Matteo Salvini. Like Trump, Salvini has been approached as an example of right-wing populism due to the nationalistic and nativist contents of his discourse and performances. These contents include a belief in the need to reform the European Union to grant members states more sovereignty, and a strong anti-immigration position. Since the 1990s, Salvini has been affiliated to the Lega Nord Party, one of the three Italian parties usually labelled as populist, together with Forza Italia and Movimento Cinque Stelle (Bobba & Legnante, 2017).

Since its creation, the Lega Nord was a regionalist party whose aim was to achieve independence of and/or greater autonomy for Italy's northern historical region of Padania (Albertazzi, Giovanni & Seddone, 2018; Cervi, 2020; Tarchi, 2008). The party, which in its discourse evidenced populist features, participated in government coalitions led by Silvio Berlusconi (also identified by scholars as a populist). In 2013, Salvini was elected as the new party leader after a scandal revolving around its previous leader, Umberto Bossi. Since then, the party changed its scope and, by eliminating the reference to the North from its name, became Lega and established close cooperation with Marine Le Pen and other European right-wing parties (Cervi, 2020). Therefore, if the discourse of the Lega Nord revolved around an 'other' that was Italian and *internal*, that is, belonging to the national level – the southern Italians and the centralism of 'Rome' – in *Lega*'s discourse it is *external*: non-national migrants and the dictates of the EU (Albertazzi, Giovannini & Seddone, 2018). In June 2018, Salvini was appointed Minister of Internal Affairs and, in August 2019, he was removed from the position following a government collapse.

Salvini's discourse is interesting for the purposes of this book for multiple reasons. One of them is that it displays a clear populist component, combined with nationalist contents and articulated around five main categories: the Italian 'people', mass media, clandestine migrants, the politicians and Europe (Cervi, 2020). Moreover, like Trump, Salvini has used aggressive tactics such as 'character assassination' (Berti & Loner, 2021) when dealing with his opponents. More interestingly, in more than one occasion Salvini has proudly embraced the accusations of being a populist by making of this a virtue rather than an insult or something to be worried about. In 2017, he said: '[Matteo] Renzi has attacked me and said that I am a populist. I am proud of that if being a populist means being with the people and trying to solve their problems. I prefer to listen to normal people rather than solving the problems of the banking and financial sectors'.[7] Moreover, in 2018, he declared that 'being a populist is a compliment'.

Salvini has a prototypical anti-status quo discourse and employs a confrontational attitude and tone of voice in his public performances, targeting different enemies like Europe, the traditional media and 'clandestine' immigrants that arrive in Italy. As argued, he tends to identify himself with a homogeneous common Italian collective identity, where the concept of *common sense* is placed as the main normative criterion of legitimacy for political decision-making (Addis, 2020: 138). One of the slogans used by Lega was 'The revolution of common sense' [*La rivoluzione del buonsenso*].[8]

These discursive and performative aspects can be interpreted as manifestations of the Populist Narrative Structure – namely, of the antagonistic relationship and of the collective identity 'the people', axiologized in positive terms.

While discussing the case of Trump, it was demonstrated how the Populist Narrative Structure is evidenced mainly in language use and in how he constructs specific situations and relationships within the political system. Despite the relevance of Salvini's language in his populist performance, this section focuses in how he uses social media for meaning-making. This focus aims at showing how Semiotics approaches meaning-making and signification in multimodal – or syncretic – terms, that is, through an examination of a broad array of semiotic resources of different natures.

In particular, the focus is set on Salvini's food and gastronomic contents. Paolo Demuru (2021a) analysed a set of his social media posts and discovered a number of strategies underpinning Salvini's meaning-making online. For example, in some posts, he presents dishes that feature ingredients matching the colours of the Italian flag, like tomatoes or tomato sauce (red), mozzarella or pasta (white) and basil or pesto (green) (Demuru, 2021a: 515; Terracciano, 2019: 172). It should be noted that actualizing the content of an Italian national identity – a virtual semantic unit in the form of a collective identity to be found in the level of the deep structures – through evoking its flag – a discursive manifestation of that semantic unit – is an example of *nationalism* – that is, 'the people' defined in *national* terms – and not of populism. The same occurs with Salvini's posts featuring traditional and regional Italian dishes, which is a discursive and performative strategy to demonstrate that he knows the country's diversity and its vast culinary tradition – a trait that also defines Italy internationally.

What is populistic about Salvini's food posts on social media; that is, how do these posts reflect the Populist Narrative Structure? One possible answer is that by exposing his private life – and particularly by recurring to mundane and natural basic activities like cooking and eating as the content of his posts – Salvini presents himself as a normal, ordinary, common man that eats food as everyone else does. Moreover, the dishes he uses in his posts are *popular* – in the sense that they are common dishes in the popular sectors of Italian society – and even *plebeian*, such as pasta, sandwiches, pizza and croquettes, among others, and not 'anything fancy or factitious' (Demuru, 2021a: 509).

For Demuru (2021a: 508), Salvini uses food 'to communicate individual ordinariness and authenticity, as well as the myth of a pure national-popular culture to be preserved from internal and external threats'. In this sense, Salvini's food-based contents serve a more relevant meaning-making purpose within the broader populist discourse: to build a relationship between the leader and the electorate based on virtual interactions. When a political actor posts contents online for the consumption of the general public, he is articulating a performance through the use of semiotic resources. For Demuru (2021a: 508), in Salvini's social media posts, 'food posts appear to be an ideological tool through which right-wing populism is communicated as a soft, safe, worthwhile and enjoyable political regime'.

To understand the nature of Salvini's performance of the Populist Narrative Structure online and his own placement as the political leader that is part of 'the people', also relevant is how the photographs that he posts do not demonstrate an effort of the photographer to be professional in managing and editing its visual dimension. The photographs used give the impression of a normal human being, a man like any other standard and common Italian citizen, sharing his ordinary, common and private everyday life through the communicative channels that 'the people' normally use. Hence, the divide between the political front stage and the private backstage is clearly blurred (Wodak, 2015): the intended effect of sense seems to be that the populist leader, besides being a politician, is a normal person that eats bread with Nutella and wears sports clothing at home. This is a strategy to take distance from 'politics as usual' and standard politicians and to perform as part of 'the people'.

Politicians use social media frequently and they do so in particular in the context of highly mediatized politics we live nowadays. But there is a difference between using Twitter or Facebook to produce a written utterance related to a political topic – like Trump did – and using them to showcase the politician's private life and habits – cooking and eating, what they do during the weekend or going on holiday. It is this use, also, that helps construct the collective identity of 'the people' *by modelling it,* although the effect of sense is grounded on the illusion of *mirroring* it. In this sense, while Salvini performs a 'form of life' assumed as existing and that defines who and how the Italian 'people' are, with his online performances he actually showcases how that 'form of life' *should be* through a repertoire of practices assumed to be *an expression* of it.

Demuru (2021a: 510) argues that the nature of social media platforms supports the *disintermediation* of the relationship between the leader and the audiences. Hence, these platforms contribute to creating the illusion of togetherness between the leader and 'the people' identified by Landowski. This occurs based on the use of non-standard, disruptive and challenging communication strategies within the political, like showcasing the leader's private, ordinary and everyday life. To refer to this sort of 'disintegration' of the populist leader in the collective identity 'the people', Demuru (2021a: 511) prefers the term 'anonymity', understood as the strategy of becoming 'unremarkable, average, banal, people just like everybody else'. This is precisely the performative strategy that Salvini implements when posting the contents like the ones discussed here.

In Semiotics, it is common to analyse the paradigmatic substitutions possible to do in a given text or situation and study how these substitutions could change their overall meaning. Paradigmatically – that is, by replacing one cultural content with another – what would happen if Salvini posted images of himself preparing or eating fancy dishes instead of popular ones, even if Italian? What effect would a substitution of pizza with caviar or champagne, for example, have in the meanings he produces when posting those images? What if instead of typical Italian dishes Salvini were cooking and consuming non-Italian dishes that are nevertheless consumed by the popular sections of society? In the first case, it would be hard to argue that he is enacting 'the people', because eating caviar and drinking champagne rather conveys *elitism* and other meanings that are not connotatively attached to 'the people', the popular sections of society or the plebeians. In the second case, he would be definitely be popular and plebeian but not expressing the nationalist component that his online performances actually express. Therefore, food-related cultural contents serve as *semiotic resources* that political actors can use in their performances to articulate specific meanings that are culturally codified.

Salvini's food-related posts reflect his overall performative strategy on social media. As evidenced by Cervi (2020), the contents that Salvini creates on Facebook also bring the backstage into the front stage; that is, they show his private life in everyday, normal and ordinary situations – at home, at work, in a car driving somewhere, interacting with his children – frequently wearing informal clothes and so on. This performance aims at creating an effect of sense of *transparency* and of a direct relationship with the followers through the exploitation of *deixis*, that is, a type of enunciation that brings the leader to life by affirming 'I am here, right now, doing this and talking to you'. Deictic utterances are anchored to the moment of the enunciation and serve the purpose of creating the illusion of a live *situation* between the enunciator and the addressee.

It has been argued that it seems to be an *elective affinity* between populism and social media (Gerbaudo, 2018; Sedda & Demuru, 2018b; 2019), most probably due to the meaning-making mechanisms these platforms offer to convey a sense of togetherness and of being part of the same collective identity. Facebook's *live* feature, for example, generates an online interaction in which audiences can *be part* in real time of what is going on, even if they are not physically present. This reinforces the illusion of co-presence and togetherness that is typical of the interactional regime of adjustment (Landowski, 2018). In this sense, for Hawkins (2009: 1047), 'actions are ultimately "populist" because of the meaning that is ascribed to them by their participants, not because of any objective quality that inheres in them'.

In conclusion, Salvini's use of social media platforms to expose his private life through the use of food-related contents serves to show how populist leaders dispose of a broad repertoire of semiotic resources for meaning-making. These transcend the mere use of language and production of messages revolving around political topics. As argued, although posting an image of food on a social media platform might seem innocuous, it nevertheless contributes to the populist performance of the Populist Narrative Structure, even if not evident as in the case of language use. In this sense, it could be concluded following Panizza (2005: 21) that 'as a political figure who seeks to be at the same time one of the people and their leader, the populist leader appears as an ordinary person with extraordinary attributes'. This is so even if those attributes are related to everyday, common and ordinary events, habits and practices.

6.5 Hugo Chávez

Hugo Chávez, head of state of Venezuela from 1999 until his death in March 2013, has been a key political figure in the field of populism studies (Hawkins, 2009; Casullo, 2019; Gualda, 2019). This is the case not only due to the use of the Populist Narrative Structure in his speeches but also thanks to the peculiarities of his performances as a populist leader. According to Ricardo Gualda (2019: 60), Chávez was 'probably the earliest and most successful populist leader of the twenty-first century'. He definitely was a prototypical example of the 'charismatic strongman' type of populist leader (Mudde & Rovira Kaltwasser, 2017: 63).

Kirk A. Hawkins (2009: 1040-1) opens his article 'Is Chávez a Populist? Latin America Measuring Populism' quoting a passage from Chávez's closing campaign speech held in Caracas, Venezuela, in December 2006:

> Let no one forget that we are confronting the Devil himself. Sunday, 3 December at the ballot box we will confront the imperialist government of the United States of North America [sic]—that is our real adversary, not these has-beens here, these lackeys of imperialism. [...] You the people are the giant that awoke, I your humble soldier will only do what you say. I am at your orders to continue clearing the way to the greater Fatherland [...] Because you are not going to reelect Chávez really, you are going to reelect yourselves, the people will reelect the people. Chávez is nothing but an instrument of the people.[9]

Multiple aspects of the passage evidence the Populist Narrative Structure. To begin with, there are direct references to 'the people' [*el pueblo*], depicted as 'a giant that awoke'. Second, there is the idea of a confrontation against an 'other', a 'real adversary' that is equalled with 'the Devil himself'. Here, the axiologization – in this case, in moral terms – that is typical of populism is clearly visible. Third, that 'other' is constructed as 'the imperialist government of the United States of North America', but there is also a reference to an internal 'other' in the form of 'these has-beens' [*bate quebrados*] and 'lackeys of imperialism' [*lacayos del imperialismo*]. Capitalism, imperialism and the United States come together in Chávez' use of the Populist Narrative Structure as an 'other' through a chain of equivalences (Savage, 2018). Finally, Chávez positions himself as the populist leader in terms of a 'humble soldier' [*diminuto soldado*] who 'will do what you say'.

In his discourse, Chávez proposes an equivalence between himself and 'the people' in a tautology that is illustrative of populism's mechanism of manipulation through the illusion of togetherness: it is 'the people' who will reelect Chávez, a member of 'the people'. In a different speech, Chávez performed the role of the leader in a more evident way, as the one with the power of changing social reality through his speech acts (in this case, in the form of a declaration): 'I declare the people to be the only and the true owners of their sovereignty. I declare the Venezuelan people the true owners of their own history' (quoted in Panizza, 2005: 4).

In Chávez' discourse, the semantic unit 'the people' gains value through the existence of an external enemy – the United States, Bush and capitalist imperialism – and also through an equivalence with Venezuela's poorer sections of society. This discursive construction reflects the left-wing political contents that Chávez articulates in his discourse and performances with the Populist Narrative Structure. Besides its populist component, his discourse is based on a revolutionary Marxist social premise reinterpreted in Latin American terms: according to Chávez's world view, his mission is to implement in Venezuela the bigger Latin American project of a *Bolivarian revolution* aimed at gaining autonomy from the historical influence that the United States – and other imperialistic forces – has had in the continent (Navaja de Arnoux, 2008; García-Marín & Luengo, 2019; Bermúdez & Martínez, 2000; Churmaceiro, 2004). In discursive terms, in Chávez's world view, 'only those who reject and fight against this enemy can be part of the people's crusade', as argued by Hawkins (2009:

1044). Those who do not – even if they are Venezuelans and hence part of 'the people' in national terms – are 'traitors', 'pipsqueaks' [*frijolitos*], 'incompetent', 'irresponsible', 'liars' and 'un-patriots', among other attributions that reflect a negative axiologization that divides society in two groups (Hawkins, 2009: 1044).

Hawkins conducts research on populism by examining discourse in a restricted sense, that is, through the study of the words used by populist leaders like Chávez in their public speeches. Hawkins proposes a holistic view that does not only count the frequency of a word use but also looks at the tone and style of language use, given that 'the ideas that constitute the content of the discourse are held subconsciously'. In Hawkins's study, Chávez leads the ranking of populist political actors with an average populism score of 1.9, followed by Velasco Ibarra (Ecuador), Alexander Lukashenko (Belarus) and Evo Morales (Bolivia).

One of Hawkins's conclusions is that the batch of populist political actors whose speeches he analysed shows commonalities with the discourses of previous populist actors like Perón, Vargas and others. This is an interesting epistemological step that might serve to explain why the label *populism* became so popular at the beginning of the twenty-first century to make sense of concrete political actors: by establishing similarities with previous populist political actors, the concept might have undergone a process of overstretching, losing its original meaning and covering only a portion of the semantic field covered by the original concept.

Gualda (2019) identifies how Chávez places himself in discourse as a leader through the establishment of a lineage with mythological national heroes such as Simón Bolivar and Jesus Christ. In spite of this chain of equivalences in historical terms that Chávez uses to position himself as a saviour, he also 'resembles the traditional Hispanic literary figure of the "pícaro"'; that is, he performs his role as a leader as someone funny, even laughable, that does not fully match the values normally linked to the figure of a virtuous and mythical hero.

Gualda's (2019) study of Chávez's appearances in *Aló Presidente* [*Hello President*] are relevant for a semiotic perspective. *Aló Presidente* was a weekly television show hosted by Chávez on Sundays without a fixed duration. In the show, Chávez spoke directly and freely to the audience, and eventually answered their questions and telephone calls. The fact of a president having a TV show is itself a clear result of the mediatization of politics and of how the use of media – both traditional and online – become central in exercising power in a context in which the logic of the media has colonized other social domains (Hjarvard, 2013). But the show was also a great tool for creating the illusion of togetherness discussed earlier: according to Gualda (2019: 65), 'people loved him. He was one of them; he made sense; he was going to change everything, and it was fun'.

The TV show was a unique stage for Chávez to perform his role as one more among 'the people' through the creation of *a situation of co-presence*, even if it was not in person but mediated by television. According to Gualda (2019: 76), Chávez always acted as if he were 'unconcerned about acting "presidential" and ceremonial while telling his many stories or performing (even singing, which he did frequently)'. Even if being on TV might not be something that occurs to 'the common people', the mediation of the medium is forgotten and an illusory bond between the TV audience and the featured individual on TV emerges (Verón, 1983, my translation).

This effect of sense is strengthened thanks to a series of semiotic mechanisms that define the nature of syncretic/multimodal acts of enunciation such as TV appearances. To begin with, Chávez's discourse exhibited a permanent recurrence to an 'I-you' dialogic structure. Besides, Chávez normally looked at the camera when speaking. He also established dialogues with members of the audience as if he were involved in relationships – family, for example – with them (Gualda, 2019: 76). According to Gualda (2019: 83), Chávez 'treats older women as mothers, flirts with adult women (something one would not expect from a father/husband), motivates the youth and acts lovingly with children'. As Gualda (2019: 84) concludes, 'at every step of his performances, he portrays himself in a position of leadership, power, and as a reliable provider'.

Gualda (2019: 85) distinguishes between a technocratic and a populist mode of establishing relationships with the audiences: 'in technocratic, institutional liberal democracies, the relationship between the public and their leaders is professional and anonymous. In the case of populist, common-sense personalist autocracies, the relationships are personal, affective, and based on group (family, tribe . . .) loyalties'. The cases of Salvini and Chávez seem to be paradigmatic in this sense. Trump's discourse and performances, though, do not seem to reflect this general principle because he usually took extreme care of his appearance – attire, make-up, hair and so on – in public events and did not usually expose his privacy on social media.

Arditi (2005: 73) identifies a number of 'trademark characteristics' of Latin American populism during the 1930s and 1940s. Among others, he mentions 'the cult of personality that aggrandises the stature of the leader and turns him or her into a quasi-messianic figure'. The case of Chávez is in line with the discursive and performative strategies of his Latin American predecessors. Moreover, it has also been an inspiration for other 'Bolivarian populist actors' (García-Marín & Luengo, 2019) in Latin America. Briefly, Chávez can be considered 'the icon of twenty-first-century Latin American populism', as Savage (2018: 5) argues.

The three examples studied in this chapter evidence how political actors dispose of multiple semiotic resources for meaning-making, ranging from words to practices and including the tone of voice, the clothes they wear, what they post on social media, their appearances in the media and in public events, how they refer to their opponents or even the quality of the photographs they share online. Moreover, it has been demonstrated how different scenarios and stages exist where populist political actors can perform their role as leaders by displaying a relationship of closeness and proximity with 'the people'.

Arditi (2005: 82) argues that in populist discourse the gap between the represented and the leader is vague and that it is 'bridged by a "presentation" that forgets the iterability at work in the "re-" of representation'. Populist political actors construct representations in and through their discourses and performances to potentiate their identities as being part of 'the people'. But at the same time, they construct a special narrative role for them within those representations. Therefore, populist discourse is 'a mirror game, an alleged double and simultaneous full presence, of the people and of those who act for them', giving place to a 'presumed immediacy of the relation between the people and the leader or his movement' (Arditi, 2005: 82).

As discussed, a manipulative regime of interaction underpins populist meaning-making. This is the case because populist actors operate within democratic systems and hence need to convince the electorate to support them and vote for them autonomously. For Adamidis (2021: 22), the strategic objective of populist leaders is 'the effective manipulation of "the people's" thoughts and emotions, by artfully interpellating them as a homogeneous group with putatively common identity and interests'. In this sense, due to the nature of the message they convey, populist leaders have a strong agency to construct the political 'contest over meaning' in populist terms.

Other specific sociocultural variables play a role in how populist actors perform their identities as political leaders. Mudde and Rovira Kaltwasser (2017: 77) argue that in more traditional societies where the macho culture is accepted as the norm, the 'strongman' type of leadership is more likely to succeed, while entrepreneur-populists 'will probably be attractive in more capitalist and materialist societies'. This thesis demonstrates how populist meaning-making is embedded in specific cultural webs of signification. Moreover, depending on the values that are hegemonic in a given society, outsiders to the political sphere coming from different fields will be accepted as legitimate political leaders. As Panizza (2005: 20) argues, 'the populist leader often places him/herself symbolically outside the political realm, by claiming that he/she is not a politician, or at least that he/she is "not a politician like the others"'. This strategy is aligned with populist actors' intended effect of sense presented in this chapter.

To conclude, this chapter has demonstrated how examining the discourses and performances of political actors from a semiotic perspective implies taking into account all the possible channels and resources that can be used for meaning-making, with a particular focus on *enunciation*. However, examining meaning-making with an exclusive focus on enunciation does not suffice to understand how populist discourse is meaningful to voters. Intersubjectivity and interactions must also be taken into account because they are crucial for the co-construction of meaning between social actors. In politics, meaning is above all *sense*, that is, something *felt* and *experienced* in the body. This phenomenological stance is crucial to a social Semiotics interested in grasping how lived experience becomes meaningful to people. In the political field, voters perceive through their senses a complex semiotic system that articulates words, images, videos, texts, objects, attitudes and so on, aimed at making them feel part of the political in its quality of a public sphere: how discourse is actually meaningful to people is something that still needs to be researched. It is here where interpretative Semiotics will be crucial.

7

Right-Wing Populism

So far, the book has revolved around populism as a concept to make sense of a number of social – and hence discursive – practices within the political field that can be found both on the right and the left sides of the political spectrum, in different historical moments and in various geographical areas. If these political practices are made sense of through the same analytical category that is because they share some commonalities. Scholars have, however, struggled to identify to which type of phenomenon or domain – an ideology, a strategy, a performative style and so on – those commonalities belong.

The previous chapters argued that populism is a discursive practice used in the political field that implies employing a specific narrative structure as the ground for meaning-making. Moreover, it was argued that populist leaders are crucial players in filling the empty spaces of the Populist Narrative Structure with context-dependent contents that are relevant within the cultural semiospheres in which they are politically active. In semiotic terms, it is them who, thanks to their capacity to enunciate texts, *actualize* the virtual Populist Narrative Structure through the use of a broad spectrum of semiotic resources.

This chapter and the following examine the two standard types of populism identified and studied in a consensual manner by political scientists, communication scholars and discourse analysts: right-wing and left-wing populism. The fact that these labels exist in different languages evidences how these two manifestations of populism are *codified in culture*: while there could be other types of populism, it is usually these two that structure scholarship on populism and political comments.

In approaching these two manifestations of populism, the same challenges linked to the concept of populism occur: speaking of *right-wing populism* implies postulating the existence of an underlying discursive practice that is shared by the discourses and performances of multiple political actors. Therefore, right-wing and left-wing populism are also phenomena of a discursive nature to be inductively identified as underlying specific discourses and practices and that, once they have achieved a status of cultural codification, are used deductively to make sense of the commonalities that these political manifestations show.

7.1 What is right-wing populism?

Right-wing populism is a discursive phenomenon that occurs within the political field and that is characterized by the combination of the Populist Narrative Structure with ideological contents and policy issues and items that, as a result of cultural codification, are located on the right side of the political spectrum, like conservatism, nationalism, nativism, national sovereignty and anti-immigration, among others. This combination has given place to the establishment of what could be conceived of as a *subgenre* of populist discourse. This subgenre is characterized by features that have been of interest for discourse analysts and political scientists, who have used specific expressions to refer to it (Akkerman, de Lange & Rooduijn, 2016; Mudde, 2007; Betz, 1994; Wodak, 2015). The combination of the Populist Narrative Structure with right-wing political contents is a phenomenon of a *discursive* nature in which different ideas and concepts are brought together in a process of bricolage that produces meaning within the public sphere. The textual result of that process of bricolage is closely related to the idea of a *thin-centred ideology* that scholars have used drawing on Freeden's work (1996; 2013) to explain what populism is (Mudde, 2004; 2017; Stanley, 2008). As argued in a previous chapter, these scholars claim that populism is a type of ideology that due to its 'thinness' can be easily combined with other ideological contents. As it was argued, political ideologies are *discursive artefacts*: they are meaningful articulations that relate political concepts and build narratives and world views – *Weltanschauungen* – around them. Therefore, conceiving of populism as a thin-centred ideology might be another way of expressing the intuition that it is in the nature of this political phenomenon to merge and blend with other discourses or ideas.

The expression *right-wing populism* presents some challenges that can already be evidenced by examining its grammar. In the formulation, *populism* is a noun modified by the qualifying adjective *right-wing*. Therefore, the denotative reference of the expression would be *a type of populism* that has a right-wing component. However, the expression is in fact used to refer to political actors, parties and movements that put forward right-wing political contents by framing them in populist terms, that is, through the use of the Populist Narrative Structure. For Taggart (2017: 321), this framing consists in a 'populist politization of the issues involved'. Therefore, it would be more appropriate to use the lexical unit *populism* as an adjective – *populist* – rather than as a noun, and the lexical unit *right-wing* as the noun that defines the type of parties or actors being examined based on the ideological and policy issues they put forward.

In line with this argument, Mudde (2007) prefers the denomination *populist radical right* to refer to this type of political parties and actors. This inversion might seem a simple wordplay, but it is not: what matters in researching these parties and actors is their *right-wingness* and how it is expressed through the use of – and articulated with – the Populist Narrative Structure. According to Mudde (2007), the populist radical right is composed of three core elements: nativism, authoritarianism and populism. *Nativism* is "an ideology, which holds that states should be inhabited exclusively by members of the native group ("the nation") and that nonnative elements (persons and ideas) are fundamentally threatening to the homogenous nation-state' (Mudde, 2007: 22). Nativism combines nationalism with xenophobia. *Authoritarianism* is defined as 'the belief in a strictly ordered society, in which infringements of authority are to be punished severely' (Mudde, 2007: 23). The third ingredient is *populism*, which Mudde (2007: 23) defines as a thin-centred ideology and, hence, as 'an ideological feature, and not merely as a political style'. Akkerman, de Lange, and Roodujin (2016: 5), on their part, use the label *radical right-wing populist parties* to underline the three core features of these parties: they are *radical* – that is, they do not take centre positions on ideological terms – *right-wing* – they reject individual and social equality – and populist.

Given that populism is *only one* of the components of these radical right-wing populist parties, it seems more appropriate to speak of a radical right (noun) that is *populist* (adjective) rather than speaking of a type of populism (noun) that is *right-wing* (adjective). However, given that this book studies *populism*, it seems more appropriate to maintain the denomination *right-wing populism* to refer to the discursive articulation resulting from combining the Populist Narrative Structure with right-wing political contents. As it can be seen, the sole denomination of the phenomenon evidences the challenges linked to the use of words to refer to social practices and their outputs.

This is a relevant aspect since there are radical right-wing parties and actors that are not populist (Mudde, 2007: 45–52). According to Pappas (2019a: 64), populist radical right parties and actors express nativism over populism. This means that their defining feature is related to the use of specific political contents revolving around the political Subject 'the nation', who belongs to it and who does not. Populism is only *an ingredient* of a number of radical right parties and actors that intensifies the nationalistic and nativist components by polarizing society and by filling the empty space 'the people' mainly with nationalistic contents, although not only.

Right-wing populism began to gain attention from scholars as a political phenomenon when it mushroomed in Europe, during the 1990s (Betz, 1994; Rovira Kaltwasser et al., 2017). In particular, it became a popular object of study when right-wing populist parties stopped begin marginal within the party systems they belong to and gained relevance in elections (Akkerman, de Lange & Rooduijn, 2016). One of the first case studies was Austria's party FPÖ under the leadership of Jörg Haider: it was the first European right-wing populist party that accessed government thanks to a political coalition (Mouffe, 2005b). In the United States, it was Donald Trump's speedy ascension to power that triggered a widespread interest in right-wing populism. In Latin America, the label *right-wing populism* began being used when conservative and authoritarian politicians like Jair Bolsonaro made it into the political mainstream, although some researchers also conceive of the neoliberal presidencies of the 1990s as manifestations of populism on the right.

For a semiotic perspective, the main research interest is how right-wing populist politicians produce meaning in a multimodal/syncretic manner by recurring to the Populist Narrative Structure. The work of discourse analysts like Wodak (2015) and Charaudeau (2011) is precious in mapping the discursive strategies used by the populist radical right. According to Wodak, these parties and actors have a tendency to work with a strategy that taps on and constructs *fear*. Independently of what the Object – or Subject – causing fear might be – the 'other', globalization, change, the loss of welfare, climate change – there is a specific emotion that is expected to be awakened by the discourses produced by right-wing populist politicians. As Wodak (2015: 5) argues, 'in principle, almost anything can be constructed as a threat to "Us", an imagined homogeneous people inside a well-protected territory'. To achieve that effect, they employ specific *topoi*, such as 'urgency', 'threat', 'the saviour' and 'history'.

With regards to right-wing populism as a *politics of fear*, Pappas (2019a: 51) argues that 'the contemporary surge of populism in various parts of the liberal democratic world – first imperceptibly, later on with astonishing force – is associated with the growing fear of the middle classes that the benefits they were able to win during the earlier post-war decades are being lost'. According to the author, 'when large segments in society lose their faith in liberal democracy (and reason is substituted with resentment, long-term interest with contentious passion), it is likely that opportunistic leaders – authentic demagogues in the classical Greek sense of the word – may emerge and produce a populist outcome' (Pappas, 2019a: 51).

Besides the contents evidenced in their discourses and performances, populist right-wing political actors tend to enact a particular style of relating to and placing themselves into the political. Bergmann (2020: 7) claims that this style is normally anti-establishment and fights the liberal order by challenging the rules of 'politics as usual'. According to the author, they pose 'challenges to what we deem being proper and professional politics'. That is why Mouffe (2005a: 51) argues that right-wing populism constructs 'an opposition between "the people" and the "establishment"' and not necessarily with 'the elites'. Therefore, their main strategy seems to be to reshape how voters imagine the political field and, with it, to redraw the core and the boundaries of the political semiosphere (Moreno Barreneche, 2019a).

As Mouffe (2005b: 50) claims, right-wing populist parties and actors were originally considered *marginal* from the political systems where they operated. Their existence was usually explained by specific national idiosyncrasies, like in the case of Austria. However, since the mainstreaming of these parties and actors, they have been and still are considered by many a serious threat to liberal-democratic institutions due to the challenging and anti-establishment politics they put forward. Through the combination of nativist contents with a performative style that challenges 'politics as usual', populist right-wing political actors produce a specific 'structure of feeling' in discourse that voters can identify with based on their perceptions, feelings and opinions towards the political system. By defining the empty space 'the people' in national terms and through the construction of an 'other' that is external to the national semiosphere – that is, 'non-native' – they build 'an illusory hope, founded on false premises and on unacceptable mechanisms of exclusion, where xenophobia usually plays a central role' (Mouffe, 2005b: 56).

To sum up, when populism occurs combined with contents and ideologies that are traditionally labelled as being part of the right side of the political spectrum – conservatism, nationalism, nativism, patriotism – the Populist Narrative Structure is filled with contents that tend to draw the core and boundaries of 'the people' through a mix with a national imagined community, that is, a group of individuals that is depicted as sharing some traits that bind them and that serves as a criterion for the exclusion of others that are not part of that community (Anderson, 1983; Appiah, 2018). As Mouffe (2005b: 69) argues, this usually turns into some type of xenophobia that can be evidenced in discourse: for example, 'immigrants are presented as a threat to the identity of the people, while multiculturalism is perceived as being imposed by the elites against the popular will'. Therefore, examining the link between populism and nationalism in the discourse of the populist radical right seems in order.

7.2 Populism and nationalism

Scholars working within Laclauian discourse theory have argued that nationalism and populism have usually been conflated due to the commonalities that exist between the two concepts (De Cleen, 2017; De Cleen & Stavrakakis, 2017; Katsambekis & Stavrakakis, 2017; Anastasiou, 2019; Stavrakakis et al., 2019). However, as argued in a previous chapter, populist discourse revolves around the empty category of 'the people', which is characterized by its multiple possible meanings (Canovan, 1984). One of those possible meanings implies imagining 'the people' as a semantic unit equivalent to 'the nation', that is, as a group of individuals that are bounded through a particular common history that makes of them a distinct collective identity that is limited and sovereign (Anderson, 1983) within the continuum of all possible national identities. For De Cleen and Stavrakakis (2017: 302), the distinction between the two concepts lies in that nationalism constructs discursively 'the people' as nation, while populism does it in terms of 'the people' as underdog.

It is true, though, that nationalism and populism share some basic features. This is the case because, as De Cleen and Stavrakakis (2017: 301) argue, 'the nation-state remains the primary context for democratic political representation and public debate'. Moreover, nationalist and populist political actors on the right-wing of the political spectrum tend to equate 'the people' with the *ethnos* – that is, an imagined community articulated around the belonging to a group based on tangible shared traits – rather than the *demos* (De Cleen, 2017; De Cleen & Stavrakakis, 2017; Akkerman, 2003). However, De Cleen (2017: 342) claims, 'including elements of nationalism in definitions of populism hinders the application of the concept to other (non-nationalist) forms of populism'. As argued, populism is a discursive practice revolving around 'the people', an empty signifier that can be filled with multiple meanings – among them, one that is equivalent to the national imagined community.

Anastasiou (2019: 335) claims that 'in actual practice, the nationalism/populism distinction is often blurred by political acts that (attempt to) establish an analogous connection between "the people" and "the nation" (and/or their respective family resemblances)'. When an equivalence is established between 'the people' and 'the nation', it does not come as a surprise that the occurrence of populism – that is, the presence of the Populist Narrative Structure – becomes *exclusionary* and that the 'other' is not so much or only *internal* – 'the establishment', 'the elites' and so on – but also *external* – that is, all those who are not conceived of as being part of the semantic unit 'the nation'.[1] In this sense, it does not come as a surprise that the populist radical right demonizes social actors that are external to the imagined national community, such as immigrants, supranational political organizations (like the European Union), countries that are treated as social actors with a threatening agency (like Mexico and China in Trump's discourse), or members of cultures and groups that are imagined – and represented in discourse – as being different from an Us with national colours.

To grasp this meaning-making process of inclusion and exclusion, it is useful to conceptualize collective identities through Lotman's notion of the semiosphere: the in-groups and out-groups are placed within or outside the boundaries that are set around the semiotic core that defines the identity of a cultural/national semiosphere. If the social space is divided into two groups, then there is a gap that serves to distinguish – in imaginary terms – who belongs to 'we' and who to 'they' in two processes that evidence dynamics of inclusion and exclusion, respectively.

For Bowman (2005: 119), 'the Manichean opposition of 'us' and 'them' evidenced in both the nationalist imaginary and populism is [. . .] the result of processes by which a number of people are induced to recognize that they share a common antagonist, and to participate in the projects of overcoming of the community of those that enemy antagonizes'. According to the author, the difference between populism and nationalism lies in the fact that, in the former, 'the antagonistic relationship of 'us' and 'them' is played out within the constraints of a single system – with resolution imagined in the ultimate defeat and purging of the antagonist' (Bowman, 2005: 119). De Cleen and Stavrakakis (2017), for their part, argue from a discourse-theoretical perspective that while nationalism has its nodal point in the signifier 'the nation', conceives of 'the people' in national terms and offers a subject position of 'citizen of the nation' – that is, the constitutive outside is horizontal, reflecting an in/out logic – populism has its nodal point in 'the people' as underdog, offers a subject position of being a member of 'the people' and has a vertical (down/up) orientation. In either case, collective identities are used to make sense of the social space in *spatial* terms, that is, through a positioning of groups imagined as different within or outside the boundaries of the collective identities of 'the people' and 'the nation'.

In this book, populism has been characterized as a discursive practice within the political that implies using a narrative structure that depicts the social space as divided between 'the people' and those who are not conceived of as part of that collective identity. The Populist Narrative Structure frames the relationship between these two social actors in antagonistic terms. The same could be argued of nationalism: it is also a social discourse grounded on a specific empty and antagonistic narrative structure, only that 'the people' is replaced by 'the nation', whatever this label might refer to (Anastasiou, 2019). Even if nationalist political actors can indistinctly speak of 'the people' to refer to the basic structure of 'the nation' assuming a synonymic equivalence between them, the narrative structures underlying these two types of discourses are different: the collective identity that is axiologized in positive terms is different in each case.[2] That is why it makes sense to distinguish between *popul*ism, whose political Subject is 'the people', and *national*ism, whose political subject is 'the nation'. As argued, both concepts do not only share commonalities due to their historical reasons of emergence (Hermet, 1997) but also overlap in semantic terms, with many assuming they are synonyms.

De Cleen (2017: 347) argues that 'as a consequence of the predominantly national organization of political representation, most populist politics operate within a national context'. This fosters the conflation of the meanings – both in semantic and in pragmatic terms – of 'the people' and 'the nation': within a given political field, it is hard to disentangle references to one or the other since the boundaries of the two imagined communities tend to coincide. In his '*Discurso al pueblo*', former Uruguayan president José 'Pepe' Mujica addressed the Uruguayan people in the sense of the *citizens of Uruguay* and hence, the *members of the Uruguayan nation*. How could one clearly distinguish between uses of 'the people' in the senses they gain within populist and nationalist discourse?

A good example to evidence the conflation of 'the people' and 'the nation' is transnational populism (De Cleen et al., 2019; Moffitt, 2017), that is, a type of populist politics that is supranational, like in the case of politics revolving around the European Union, a supranational power structure whose 'people' are citizens of different nations. In this case, when conceived as equivalent to 'the nation', 'the people' would not have a specific nation-state as its reference – 'the European Nation' – it would rather be equivalent to a European *demos*, that is, the citizens of the European Union or 'the European people'. Theoretically, the European *demos* could be conceived of as a nation – that is, an imagined community with a shared past that is limited and sovereign – but it would not be precise to speak of the European Union as a nation in the same sense used to refer to its member states. In pragmatic terms, the signifier 'Europe' works as a diffuse and vague semantic unit that is placed in discourse as the 'national' ground for collective identification.

Before proceeding to the semiotic analysis of cases of right-wing populism in Europe, the United States and South America, it should be noted that not only right-wing populist parties and actors use nationalist contents to fill the empty spaces of the Populist Narrative Structure. Left-wing populist actors like Podemos have also recurred to reference to the nation and the homeland [*la patria*] for meaning-making (Custodi, 2021; De Cleen & Stavrakakis, 2017). However, they do not tend to equal 'the people' with 'the nation' in ethnic or exclusionary terms as right-wing populists tend to do: as Jacopo Custodi (2021) claims, Podemos uses nationalistic contents to redefine in populist terms what the Spanish nation should be, and something similar occurs in the case of Argentina's Cristina Fernández's discourse, as will be discussed in Chapter 8.

Finally, it should also be noted that filling the empty collective identity of 'the people' with nationalistic contents is not a necessary condition for populism to be right-wing. Actually, 'the people' can be filled with any other content that presupposes an identity based on shared traits and that is used in discourse as the material anchorage to fill the semiotic core of 'the people' and to establish boundaries towards an external 'other'. Religion, the colour of the skin, gender and speaking a language, among others (Appiah, 2018), are all traits that can be used to produce an exclusionary type of populism, that is, one that excludes in discourse from a collective identity a group of individuals imagined as alien and axiologized in negative terms (Mudde & Rovira Kaltwasser, 2013).

In short, the defining feature of right-wing populism seems not to be so much its specific contents, but the practices of othering and of semiotic expulsion of groups that are imagined as not being part of the fuzzy category of 'the people'. Due to the prevalence of the nation-state as the principle that organizes the political sphere in our contemporary age, this practice of othering has a tendency to be framed in national terms, like in the claims for greater national sovereignty, avoiding external interference, building walls, recovering or protecting the values of a given cultural group and stopping migration.

7.3 Right-wing populism in Europe: Marine Le Pen and the Front National

Since the beginning of the twenty-first century, Europe has been the continent where right-wing populism has been most visible: several politicians and political parties have been approached and studied as examples of right-wing populism. This section studies the case of Marine Le Pen, candidate for France's Front National (FN), a political party founded in the 1970s and renamed in 2018 Rassemblement National that is considered a model for the radical right in Western Europe (Ivaldi, 2016). As Mudde (2007: 41) claims, it is 'the most famous populist radical right party' and 'considered the prototype by various scholars'.

In the early 2000s, Jean-Marie Le Pen's daughter, Marine, started gaining visibility within the party he had led since the 1970s and, in 2011, was elected as its leader. After her takeover, Marine Le Pen made significant efforts to mainstream the FN into the French party system by de-demonizing it (Taggart, 2017; Shields, 2013; Ivaldi, 2016). Her success in a number of elections from the 2010s evidence how this textbook right-wing populist party stopped being considered as an anomaly that needs to be excluded through a *cordon sanitaire* and was normalized (Shields, 2013; Ivaldi, 2016; Hubé & Truan, 2016).

Since its origins, the FN dealt with the topic of immigration as if it were a threat to the *nature* or *essence* of French society. According to Taggart (2017: 322), the party is characterized by 'a strong emphasis on French national identity, opposition to immigration, and a policy of national preference designed to oppose multiculturalism'. Even if Marine Le Pen abandoned the most radical right-wing positions and views embraced by his father and opted for a populist articulation, she nevertheless remained close to political contents that are typically right-wing, such as an opposition to immigration, the proposal of abandoning external forces and actors that hinder national sovereignty, like the European Union, and the exaltation of French national values and traditions – the process of Islamization of French society has been a constant subject in Le Pen's discourse.

Le Pen's populism is evidenced in various instances of her discourses and performances, like when she speaks of 'a little Parisian elite' that hinders the interest of 'the French people' (Shields, 2013: 182). It is also clearly visible in the narrative structure and the contents of one of her spots for the 2017 French presidential election.[3] The semiotic analysis of this spot – with a focus on its enunciation strategy and its underlying narrative structure – will help visualize how the Populist Narrative Structure is articulated with right-wing, nationalistic and exclusionary contents. This is the text of the spot (my translation):

> Since I can remember, I have always felt a visceral, passionate attachment to our country and its history. I love France. I love from the depths of my heart, from the depths of my soul, this millenary nation that does not submit, this impetuous people that does not give up. I am a woman, and as a woman I experience as extreme violence the restrictions on freedoms that are multiplying throughout our

country through the development of Islamic fundamentalism. I am a mother, and like millions of parents, I worry every day about the state of the country and the world that we will leave to our children as heritage. I am a lawyer, and I have kept from my years as a member of the Bar a deep attachment to the respect of public liberties and a particular sensitivity to the faith of victims confronted with the impunity of criminals. Deep down, if I had to define myself, I believe I would answer simply that I am intensely, proudly, faithfully, evidently French. I receive insults towards France as if they were addressed directly to me. Whether it is insecurity and violence or the misery that touches in excess numerous compatriots, I feel the suffering of the French people as a personal suffering.

The choice you will make in the upcoming presidential election is crucial, fundamental. It is a true choice of civilisation. Either you decide to continue with those who have lied, failed, betrayed; with those that led the people astray and lost France, or you decide to put France back in order. Yes – I want to put France back in order. I want that the French people can live free in an independent France. I want that the French people can live in security in a respected France. I want that the French people can live protected in a prosperous France. I want that the French people can live united in a proud France. I want that the French people can live well in a sustainable France. I want that the French people can live their dreams in a fair France. That is the whole sense of my commitment. That is why I am fighting for. That is the project I will put in practice at the head of the State, in your name, in the name of the people.[4]

Studying enunciation implies examining how the uttered text carries traces or marks of the act of enunciation: every text is produced by someone in a given moment and a given place; however, these deictic traces are not always present in the utterance. When confronted to the spot, audiences *know* that the message is uttered by Marine Le Pen thanks to the nature of the discursive genre as it is codified in culture: in an electoral spot that supports a political candidate's running for office, it is highly probable that the candidate will not only be featured in the texts produced for the campaign (spots, billboards, brochures, etc.) but also address the audience directly in the attempt to build a sense of trust (Pezzini, 2001).

Besides the standard presence of the political candidate in this discursive genre as it is codified in culture, the contents of Le Pen's spot are highly self-referential and autobiographical. Moreover, when the written text is read out loud in this multimodal/syncretic audiovisual product, it is Le Pen's herself speaking. These *isotopies* – that is, repetitions of items in the level of discourse that conduct to a same semantic unit on the level of the 'deep structures' – make clear that the 'I' that speaks is referentially tied to the person Marine Le Pen. However, this referentiality is for Semiotics never pure or transparent: in the spot there is *a discursive construction* of Marine Le Pen through the use of semiotic resources of diverse nature like words, tone of voice, images, music and a narrative tempo. The Marine Le Pen that is the subject of the spot is the result of placing Marine Le Pen as an object – in Laclau and Mouffe's terms – embedded in and shaped by a social discourse; therefore, the Marine Le Pen featured in the spot is a discursive *simulacrum* (Landowski, 1983) – anchored in a real person – aimed at creating a specific impression in the audience – in the sense of Goffman's (1956) impression management – and at achieving specific effects of sense, like emotional sympathy, faith in her project and a motivation to vote for her.

As is common practice in politics, the written text might have been written by an expert in political communication or by a speechwriter. Independently of who might have written it, a deliberate and evident intention to create an effect of sense of Marine Le Pen talking *directly* to the electorate is evidenced in the spot. *Pronouns* are one of the many semiotic resources of a linguistic nature used to create this effect of sense: the personal pronoun *je* [I] appears in the text around twenty-five times. Moreover, the use of possessive pronouns in the first person singular *mon/ma/mes* [my] strengthens the intended effect of the enunciator addressing directly the addressee: 'du plus profond de *mon* coeur', 'du plus profond de *mon* âme'. These pronouns evidence the presence of an 'I' that is speaking.

Reflecting Verón's (1987, my translation) theory of political enunciation, it is precisely in the use of pronouns that Le Pen's spot constructs the illusion of her being part of 'the people': the occurrences of the possessive pronouns in first person singular *mon/ma/mes* are limited and alternate with the possessive pronouns in the first person of plural *our*: '*notre* pays' [*our* country], '*nos* enfants' [*our* children] and so on. With the use of these pronouns, Le Pen constructs a *pro-addressee*, that is, a collective of identification that reflects the assumption of an inclusive relationship that groups into a unique collective identity the enunciator and those who experience the world as she does. The text of the spot is an interesting semiotic construction of the assumed continuity between the leader and 'the people' that is typical of populist discourse: it starts by evoking the personal experience of the populist leader and finalizes making explicit the purpose of her engagement in politics: to do something in the name of 'the people'.

In the text, the empty category 'the people' is actualized through various linguistic resources. In the first place, there are direct references to 'the people' [*le peuple*], for example in 'ce *peuple* impetueux' [this impetuous *people*] or 'au nom du *peuple*' [in the name of the *people*]. There is also a strategic use of the pronoun *vous*, which in French refers to the second person both in singular and in plural: Le Pen addresses *you* individually as a voter but also collectively as 'the people'. This strategy blurs the boundaries between the individual person and 'the people' in the sense of a group of individuals, which become 'the people' (in populist terms). There are also references to 'the French people' [*les français*], which are discursive manifestations of the vague category 'the people' filled with a *national* content. It is here where the *bricolage* between populist and nationalist contents occurs: Le Pen establishes an implicit equivalence between *le peuple, les français, la France* and *notre pays*. In her discourse, all these expressions are isotopies that refer to the same semantic unit in the plane of the content: the empty category of 'the people', which in her discourse are *French*.

France is (re)presented in the text of the spot as a great nation that has come to a state of decadency. It is a country that awakens passionate and visceral feelings, a country that one can love from the deepest bottom of one's heart, a millenary nation with an impetuous people that does not give up. It is a country currently threatened by insecurity, violence – one that must make 'a choice of civilization'. France and its 'people', defined in national terms, are semantic units axiologized in positive terms. In these descriptions of the positively axiologized semantic units, 'the people's other(s)' appear(s): these are Islamic fundamentalism and those who have lied, failed and betrayed the country. While the first type of content is clearly *nationalist*, the second is more diffuse and vague: are 'those who have lied, failed and betrayed' 'the elites' or 'the establishment'? As argued in Chapter 5, although these semantic units might be frequent within populist discourse, they do not seem to be a necessary condition for populism to exist. Le Pen's spot is a good example of this thesis.[5]

In the spot, these two 'people's others' share the fact of being defined as opposed to 'the people' and, hence, merge into a single 'other', even if vague and unclear. The 'other' is characterized and constructed in discourse through the use of language and images of a strong *emotional* character: the members of the collective 'other' have not tried, done their best and failed – they have simply lied and betrayed. Hence, they cannot be trusted because their actions are not mistakes guided by goodwill: they are guided by who knows which evil and morally condemnable intentions. As a result, they are not legitimate adversaries: they are the enemy, axiologized in negative terms, in a polarized society where the electorate needs to make a choice of civilization following a logic of 'either with them or with me/us'. This reflects the antagonistic component of the Populist Narrative Structure.

The text is also a good example of how relevant the populist leader is in bringing the Populist Narrative Structure to life by filling it with specific contents: Le Pen does not only thematize France, the French people and the threats they face, but tells also the story of a French woman, mother and lawyer that will change things once she is in power as a result of the strong feelings that France and being French – the semantic units of Le Pen's discourse that are axiologized in positive terms – awake in her. In this sense, it is worth noting the use of adverbs such as *intensely, proudly, faithfully* and *evidently* to describe her feeling French: all evoke strong emotional connotations.

In narrative terms, Le Pen's declared goal (the Object of Value) is to restore France's reputation as a respected, prosperous, proud, sustainable and fair nation: she would like to 'make France great again'. The story being told is that of a normal French woman who loves her country and that wants to stand for its national 'people' against the threats posed by a diffuse 'other' that is constructed in discourse in an exclusionary manner, both in internal and external terms.[6] It is not a coincidence that a book authored by Le Pen and published in 2012 is entitled *Pour que vive la France*, another discursive articulation that works as an isotopy in Le Pen's discourse: all these references to France are markers of a textual and ideological coherence that allows the identification of a clear narrative programme in Le Pen's discourse.

So far, the analysis of the spot has examined only linguistic resources. As argued in Chapter 3, Semiotics is also interested in how non-linguistic resources intervene in meaning-making. In the spot, the visual and musical resources are also central in producing the desired effect of sense. The images alternate between (1) Marine Le Pen as a contemplative individual – in multiple fragments of the spot she is alone, on her own, withdrawn; (2) Marine Le Pen as a human being with a private life – she shares her personal story and looks at photographs from her past; (3) Marine Le Pen as a social and public figure – in a bar drinking coffee, talking to the press, reading a document in a setting that looks like a presidential office; and (4) Marine Le Pen as a mythical figure – navigating in a boat, looking into the horizon. The locations chosen to shoot the spot are also meaningful due to their connotations: the beaches of Normandy, the *Arc du Triomphe* and the *Tour Eiffel* are all symbols of France's greatness as a nation.

The music is also crucial in this multimodal product. The upbeat melody is played by strings, drums and, at the end, trumpets. All these belong to the semiotic universe of orchestral music and, as such, have a connotation of greatness and classicism. The beat of the melody and the fact that the majority of its chords are minor create a feeling of tension that strengthens Le Pen's message. In semiotic terms, the melody of the spot resembles those frequently used in promotional trailers of movies, series or videogames to create an effect of a sense of *tension*, particularly when war and struggles for power are involved. That tension could be approached as a manifestation of the antagonistic relationship that is constitutive of the Populist Narrative Structure.

As discussed in Chapter 3, one of Semiotics' research traditions is the *interpretative*. While Greimas and Greimassian circles focused mainly in how *semiosis* occurs in texts as the passage from the plane of the content to that of the expression, interpretative semioticians have been interested in understanding how individuals make sense of signs and texts, that is, how the plane of the expression leads to the plane of the content. Eco (1968; 1976), for example, identified the relevance of the encyclopaedic competences of the reader in grasping the sense of a text (Paolucci, 2017: 104–37; Lorusso, 2008). What are the possible interpretations granted by Le Pen's spot? How can audiences make sense of what they see and hear when confronted with it?

In a 2012 poll – that is, five years before the release of the analysed spot – respondents were divided between seeing Marine Le Pen as a representative of 'a patriotic right attached to traditional values' or of 'a nationalistic and xenophobic extreme right'. The percentages attributed to each statement were 41 per cent and 45 per cent, respectively (Shields, 2013: 192). The same exercise could be done after exposing an audience to the 2017 spot: depending on various factors, participants might interpret the video in one or the other sense. The generative/structural study of how a text signifies and creates a proposal of meaning that can be segmented in smaller units and described using semiotic meta-language does not shed much light on how people will read it or relate with it in cognitive and emotional terms.

Hubé and Truan (2016: 187) argue that 'even though many researchers might designate the right wing FN party [. . .] with the qualifying adjective of *populist*, they tend to make a very clear distinction between the party's excluding *ideology* (clearly xenophobic and anti-Semitic in the FN's case) and the party's populist *rhetoric strategy* that they develop in this ideological frame'. This might be the case if one considers the whole history of the FN within the French party system. However, the spot analysed here shows *a proud nationalism* – that is, a positively axiologized discourse about France and being French – rather than focusing on concrete facts about the 'other' that might be read as open xenophobia.

The complexity of the social domain does not always fit neatly into the conceptual categories that researchers develop. Although nationalism is a clear and salient content of Marine Le Pen's discourse, it does not only fill the empty category of 'the people' with nationalistic contents in the sense of 'the people' as nation (as is the case of the spot analysed here): she has also frequently addressed *les oubliés*, that is, those who have been forgotten by the system, in an attempt to find new enunciative positions (Fernández Vázquez, 2017). Ivaldi (2016: 231) quotes a passage of a speech that Le Pen gave in Metz, France, on 10 December 2011, where she said:

> Farmers, workers, job seekers, young people, craftsmen, shopkeepers, employees, civil servants, pensioners, people in rural areas, you are the forgotten ones, you are the invisible majority [. . .] crushed by the madness of the financial system which has become the sole horizon for the ruling political caste. For them and their God, the triple A, you are triple nothings.

This passage evidences how Le Pen established a chain of equivalences between collective identities to construct 'the people' in positive terms. Her spot from the 2017 campaign, *'J'ai bessoin de Marine'* ['I need Marine']⁷ does exactly the same: by articulating together in an audiovisual spot twelve stories of common and ordinary individuals – a fisherman, a student, a pensioner, a farmer, a healthcare worker, a policewoman, a rugby player – that claim that they need her, Le Pen fills the empty space 'the people' with figurative content that models who 'the people' are. In this spot, the nationalist contents that were so salient in the spot analysed before are not prominent compared to its populist component.

The articulation – or not – of nationalism and populism shows the challenging nature of populism as a discursive phenomenon: collective identities are not built once and forever; they are rather constructed *dynamically*, in open processes of meaning-making that occur in different situations over time and that might change even from one passage of a specific speech or text to another. When the nature of the collective identity that is at the base of a given social discourse is ambiguous and vague – as is the case of 'the people' – the possibilities of merging multiple cultural and political contents to fill it with meaning are many. This is the reason why distinguishing analytically between nationalist and populist contents might not be so straightforward in some cases.

The analysis of the 2017 spot – which is only *one* text among others that construct Marine Le Pen as a public figure and a political leader – evidences how a political leader can use different semiotic resources – pronouns, nouns, narrative strategies, music, images, connotations – to create a discursive position for herself within the public sphere by embracing specific contents that fill the empty spaces of the Populist Narrative Structure. In 2022, Le Pen ran again for president. Unsurprisingly, the first spot of the campaign used the same discursive strategies to place herself within the French political semiosphere as the candidate who can 'make France great again', not only in terms of what Le Pen says but also of the visual and musical resources used.[8] Already the selection of the Museé du Louvre as the place where enunciation occurs is relevant in terms of meaning-making since it evidences the mythification of the French past and greatness underlying Le Pen's discourse.

7.4 Right-wing populism in the United States: Donald Trump revisited

The United States were the scene of one of the first historical occurrences of populism as a political phenomenon: the People's Party from the 1890s was an agrarian movement that opposed the urban elites (Canovan, 1981; Hofstader, 1969; Tarragoni, 2021; Rovira Kaltwasser et al., 2017; Priester, 2007). In the fight of their representatives for more inclusion and benefits for the rural sections of society, this manifestation of populism was – in principle – exempt from ideological contents that could allow an interpretation as being a type of right-wing populism. It was rather a left-wing phenomenon aiming at a more robust social inclusion.

In the twentieth century, a number of political actors were considered populist, such as Huey Long, George C. Wallace and Ross Perot (Priester, 2007: 78–141). In 2015, when Donald Trump announced his intention to run for the presidential office as a Republican candidate, the terms 'populism' and 'populist' were used to make sense of his discourse and performances. In particular, these words were used to *accuse* Trump rather than in descriptive terms, that is, to make sense of his policy proposals. How could one of the wealthiest men in the United States be a representative of the underprivileged groups of society like the rural workers represented by the People's Party were? Evidently, a new meaning was ascribed to the concept of populism in a process of conceptual stretching that allowed seeing in Trump a populist.

As it has been argued here, the overstretching of the concept of populism might be grounded in the identification of a specific narrative structure as underlying the discourses and performances of political actors across time and space. As discussed in Chapter 6, Trump's discourse and performances evidence the use of the Populist Narrative Structure and fill its empty spaces with nationalist and political contents that are typically right-wing. The slogan 'Make America great again' conveys a message similar to the one underlying Le Pen's discourse. While the previous chapter examined the presence of the Populist Narrative Structure in some of Trump's speeches, this chapter focuses on studying some of his audiovisual spots with the purpose of showcasing the uses of the structure in multimodal/syncretic texts.

The 2020 clips 'Break in',[9] 'Abolished',[10] and 'You won't be safe in Joe Biden's America'[11] revolve around insecurity in the United States under a hypothetical presidency of Joe Biden and under the allegations that he planned to cut funding for the police. The overarching narrative of these spots proposes that those cuts would lead to situations of emergency where there would not be operators available to answer to 911 emergency calls. Therefore, the spots reflect the discursive strategy of *a politics of fear* identified by Wodak (2015). Trump is not present as a candidate in any of these clips, apart from the closing reference and his endorsement of the advertisements. These spots were clearly created with the aim of constructing fear in the electorate through a sense effect of *crisis*.

Moffitt (2014), Moffitt and Tormey (2014) and Rooduijn (2014) identify the attempts to discursively construct the sense of crisis as one of the defining features of populism. Even in those contexts where social crises might actually be evidenced through specific indicators, crises are *social* phenomena that have a constitutive discursive dimension. There might be an economic crisis taking place, defined in economic terms as a slowing down or recession of the economy of a country, but *how* that economic fact is thematized, narrated and discursively employed is a relevant part of how that crisis is actually perceived in a country's public sphere.[12]

The three spots of the campaign do not show, however, elements that can be identified as populist or nationalist (at least as conceived in this book). A further clip, entitled 'America First',[13] also displays a tone of crisis, but it adds other elements that evidence the presence of the Populist Narrative Structure. In the spot, Trump reads the following text:

> For too long, Washington flourished, politicians prospered. The establishment protected itself, but not the citizens of our country. Their victories have not been your victories. Their triumphs have not been your triumphs.
>
> That all changes starting right here and right now. From this day forward, a new vision will govern our land. It's going to be only 'America first'. Buy American and hire American. No challenge can match the heart and fight and spirit of America. We will not fail. Our country will thrive and prosper again.
>
> We will reinforce old alliances and form new ones, and unite the civilized world against radical Islamic terrorism, which we will eradicate completely from the face of the Earth. We will be protected by the great men and women from our military and law enforcement. We will bring back our jobs. We will bring back our borders. We will bring back our wealth. And we will bring back our dreams. We will face challenges. We will confront hardships. But we will get the job done. Together we will determine the course of America and the world for many, many years to come. This moment is your moment. It belongs to you.

The text of the spot – but also the images, the music, the narrative tempo and other semiotic resources used strategically for meaning-making – reflect a similar underlying strategy as Marine Le Pen's spot analysed in this chapter. In narrative terms, the plot revolves around a crisis that poses a threat to the nation – France in the case of Le Pen; America in the case of Trump – and a hero – the populist leader – that will solve it in the name of 'the people'. In Trump's spot, the utterance 'that all changes starting right here and right now' is accompanied with his entry into the spot and, with it, in the narrative: it is he who can stop and revert the critical situation caused by a number of 'others'; it is he who can 'bring back' everything that has been lost.

The orchestral music that begins when that phrase is uttered and the footage of Trump – used for the first time in the spot – reveals much about the intended emotional effect: he is a hero that comes into the narrative with magnificence and grandeur. The similarities between the music used in this clip and the one used in Le Pen's do not come as a surprise. Moreover, the fast and swift editing used for Trump's irruption into the clip contrasts with the slow tempo of the first part of the spot.

In Trump's spot, 'the people' is filled through various semiotic resources. In the first place, there is a reference to 'the citizens of our country'. The noun *citizens* does not reflect the Populist Narrative Structure *per se* but is one of the possible resources available to actualize the empty semantic unit. Second, the use of pronouns in '*our* country', '*your* victories', '*your* triumphs', and '*our* land' merges the leader with the audiences in a same collective identity (the *pro-addressee*). Moreover, the pronoun *we* is used as the subject of verbs such as *reinforce, unite, eradicate, be protected, bring back jobs and borders, confront hardships* and *get the job done*. While the use of the plural pronoun *we* can be out of politeness to avoid the use of the *I*, it can also be read as a strategy to construct 'the people' in discourse. Finally, there are plenty of references to America and that what is American, not only in the text but also in the images: several American flags are featured in the spot. This meaning-making strategy evidences how Trump fills the empty category of 'the people' with nationalistic contents: in his discourse, 'the people' is above all *American*. The phrases 'Made in America', 'Made in the Unites States' and 'Made in U.S.A.' featured in the footage are part of this discursive strategy.

While Marine Le Pen's spot was intimate and personal, Trump's style and tone of voice are more assertive. While Le Pen established a clear distinction between 'Marine as a woman' and 'Marine as part of the people', Trump's enunciation strategy in the spot analysed blurs the borders between the 'I', the 'we' and the 'you'. However, the final sentences clearly address a 'you' as a call to action, in a message that can be read as 'while all the electoral promises will be ours, the vote is yours'.

Regarding othering, the spot begins with a clear strategy of dichotomization: the words 'Washington', 'politicians' and 'establishment' are used to construct an internal 'other' that is distinguished from the addressee through the use of the pronoun *their*. Through this very simple mechanism of enunciation, the category of 'not-the-people' – a *counter-addressee* – is created. Visually, images from Trump's adversaries (Hillary Clinton, Nancy Pelosi, Bill Clinton, Barack Obama, Joe Biden) are used to guide interpretations regarding who the words that express the category of 'the people's other' allude to. In this sense, the spot reflects the dichotomization between 'the people' and 'the elites'/'the establishment' that many identify as the essence of populist discourse. However, as in Le Pen's spot, other 'others' are present in the delimitation of 'the people', like *Islamic terrorism* (Le Pen's formulation was *Islamic fundamentalism*).

In the spot, the relationship of antagonism that characterizes the Populist Narrative Structure is expressed through multiple resources. The text itself presents a competition between 'the people' and multiple 'other'. Moreover, Trump's tone of voice adds tension to the message. The music and the tempo of the edition also add to the creation of tension. Finally, the images chosen also contribute to this intended effect of sense: the military, border control officers, airplanes and other state-owned resources revolving around defence are prominent in the spot.

A third product worth discussing is another spot from Trump's 2016 presidential campaign[14] since it helps visualize the Populist Narrative Structure at work without the nationalist content of the previous spot. In fact, if the spot were not based on a speech Trump gave, it could be an example of left-wing populism. This is the text:

> Our movement is about replacing a failed and corrupt political establishment with a new government controlled by you, the American people. The establishment has trillions of dollars at stake in this election. For those who control the levers of power in Washington and for the global special interest, they partner with these

people that don't have your good in mind. The political establishment that is trying to stop us is the same group responsible for our disastrous trade deals, massive illegal immigration and economic and foreign policies that have bled our country dry. The political establishment has brought about the destruction of our factories and their jobs as they flee to Mexico, China and other countries all around the world. It is a global power structure that is responsible for the economic decisions that have robbed our working class, stripped our country of its wealth and put that money into the pocket of a handful of large corporations and political entities.

The only thing that can stop this corrupt machine is you. The only force strong enough to save our country is us. The only people brave enough to vote out this corrupt establishment is you, the American people. I'm doing this for the people and for the movement, and we will take back this country for you, and we will make America great again.

This text does not include references to nationalist or traditionally right-wing contents. As discussed in the following chapter, the references against the global elites present multiple similarities with the discourse of left-wing populism. In the text, Trump's alternation of pronouns between *we/us/our* and *you/your* creates the illusion of him being part of 'the people', although neither in the sense of the working classes – he is certainly the opposite to that social imaginary – nor in a national sense; in this spot, 'the people' are similar to Le Pen's *oubliés*, that is, those who have been forgotten by the system/establishment. In the clip, several images of random individuals are used to fill the semantic unit 'the people' with figurative content.[15]

This spot is strongly focused on the 'other' as a strategy of constructing 'the people' in oppositional and relational terms. The 'other' is referred to with the expressions 'political establishment' – labelled as 'failed' and 'corrupt', what evidences a negative axiologization – 'those who control the levers of power in Washington', 'the global special interest' and 'these people that don't have your good in mind'. To represent the actions of that 'other', Trump uses verbs and expressions that connote illegality and breaking the law: *robbed, stripped*, 'put the money into the pocket'. This situation of disadvantage for 'the people' is what justifies in narrative terms Trump's irruption into politics as an outsider saviour that will fulfil a heroic task in a scenario of danger, tension and threat to save 'us', 'you' and 'the people'.

When analysing multiple political actors' texts and products, the challenges of labelling political movements become evident. The spots discussed in this section share commonalities but also present differences among them. What is it that justifies labelling a politician a *populist*? Is the adjective *populist* appropriate to label political actors, movements and parties, or would it be more precise to use it to refer to the *texts* and *products* that use the Populist Narrative Structure? These challenges might evidence how populism is a discursive practice of a *continuous* nature that political actors can stretch and use for meaning-making within the political: while some of Trump's messages are clearly right-wing in that they create fear and fill the empty space of 'the people' with nationalistic and nativist contents, his discourse also reflects other type of contents that also fill the empty spaces of the Populist Narrative Structure.

7.5 Right-wing populism in South America? Jair Bolsonaro

As argued earlier, Europe has been the hotspot for occurrences of populism linked to the right side of the political spectrum. In the United States, Donald Trump triggered a resignification of the concept of populism due to the nature of his discourse and performative style, which due to their resemblances with those of a number of politicians from European countries began being labelled as 'populist'.

South America has been traditionally studied as the hotspot of left-wing populism. During the twentieth century and the first fifteen years of the twenty-first, scholars have approached political actors such as Juan Domingo Perón, Getúlio Vargas, Hugo Chávez, Carlos Menem, Alberto Fujimori, Rafael Correa, Evo Morales and others as cases of populism in the continent. Among them, only Menem and Fujimori cast doubts about the nature of their populism due to the neoliberal programmes they implemented in Argentina and in Peru. In the case of Menem, this is particularly interesting because of his affiliation to Peronism, a left-wing political movement that originates in the politics of Perón (Grimson, 2019).

In this context of left-wing and inclusionary South American populisms, the rise to power of Jair Bolsonaro in 2018 after being elected by the Brazilian citizenry has caused discussions on right-wing populism in the continent. However, the discussions do not always manage to distinguish properly between Bolsonaro's *populism* and *authoritarianism*.[16] Is Bolsonaro a populist political actor? Do his discourse and performances evidence meaning-making being based on the Populist Narrative Structure? Or is Bolsonaro rather a traditional authoritarian, conservative and right-wing politician?

In the same article where he studies Matteo Salvini's social media posts, Demuru (2021a) studied the case of Bolsonaro's use of social media to present himself as *an ordinary man*, that is, as any other Brazilian that is part of 'the people'. According to Demuru, Bolsonaro's posts allow to identify a type of *gastropopulist*, nationalistic and patriotic performance. According to the author, Bolsonaro's strategy 'appears to be more oriented to ordinary everyday food, beverages and culinary habits, which are, nonetheless, culturally and socially identified as expressions of national popular culture' (Demuru, 2021a: 515). These include drinking coconut water at beach kiosks and eating corn, *queijo mineiro* – a cheese variety from one of Brazil's regions – barbeque and other industrial food products consumed by the Brazilian popular – in the sense of *plebeian* – sections of society. This conclusion, however, means that Bolsonaro performs a *popular* identity, what does not necessarily equals *being a populist*. Social actors can perform specific identities without making of them the main political Subject. In Uruguay, former president José 'Pepe' Mujica also performed a popular identity that was close to 'the people' in the sense of the plebeians, but on the left-wing side of the political continuum and without a conception of the 'other' as an enemy. The malleability of social identities is what explains that a politician performing a popular identity might be placed in the left and in the right sides of the political spectrum, as in the cases of Mujica and Bolsonaro, respectively.

Barbosa Gouvêa and Villas Bôas Castelo Branco (2021: 141) also consider Bolsonaro to be a populist politician and claim that his 'populist movement is characterized by the use of political and religious moralism, the unbridled drive for misinformation and fake news, polarization, and militarization of politics'. How are these traits *populist* in the sense used in this book? For Demuru (2021b), Bolsonaro's discursive performances share some traits with those of other right-wing politicians like Trump, Salvini and Orban. Bolsonaro performs the sense of a crisis in his discourses and speaks of the need of *saving* Brazil.[17] Moreover, the fact that Bolsonaro is an open admirer of Trump fuels his identification with Trump's politics and, in doing so, as a populist (Fechine, 2020; 2021). For example, in more than one occasion, Bolsonaro has accused 'the Left' – and not 'the elites', 'the establishment', 'terrorism' or 'the immigrants' – of trying to impede his ascension to power. Moreover, Bolsonaro performs a type of strong and confrontational leadership that shares traits with how populist political actors like Le Pen and Trump perform their roles as populist leaders. However, the Populist Narrative Structure is not identifiable straightforwardly in Bolsonaro's electoral spots or speeches, as it is in the cases of Le Pen and Trump.[18]

The nature of Bolsonaro's performances as a political leader has given place to the analytical category of *messianic populism* (Demuru, 2021b). While traditional right-wing and left-wing varieties of populism tend to focus on the political subject of 'the people', the messianic type focuses on the role of the leader as a saviour. As demonstrated in the analyses conducted in this chapter, both Le Pen and Trump could also be described as messianic populists. The question remains, though, if this discursive practice that revolves around the political leader as a saviour is actually populism or if it is rather another variation of the phenomenon of personalization of politics. According to how populism is conceived of in this book, Bolsonaro would not constitute a case of populism: although he polarizes society, demonizes his opponents, criticizes the establishment and performs his role as a leader in a fashion that coincides with that of other political leaders that are populist, his references to the empty category of 'the people' – *o povo, os brasileiros* – are not central and hence do not seem to justify the use of the label *populism* – that is, the *-ism* of 'the people' – to describe his discourse.[19]

Researchers and analysts that label Bolsonaro as a populist might do so by identifying commonalities between the discourse and performances of the Brazilian politician and those of other populist political actors, such as the idea of a societal crisis in their countries or the use of conspiracy theories to explain social reality (Demuru, 2021b: 276). Nevertheless, it might be more appropriate to speak of a *messianic personalization* to refer to the particular way in which a leader performs his political role. If it is defined as a type of performance in which the leader poses as a saviour that comes to save society from specific internal and/or external threats, this style would definitely serve to make sense of Bolsonaro's style as a politician. Moreover, it could shed light on the discursive practices used by certain populist leaders that might not be necessarily populist *per se*, but rather the result of an *elective affinity* between populist discourse and a specific mode of positioning oneself as a leader in the public sphere. In the case of Bolsonaro, the high religious content of his messianic discourse overshadows the popular – in the sense of populism's 'the people' – component.

Since it is a trait he shares with other populist leaders, a comment on Bolsonaro's strategy of personalization seems in order. In a campaign event that took place in Juiz de Fora, Brazil, Bolsonaro was stabbed in the abdomen and survived. Since then, he has used the episode as a symbolic resurrection in the sense that he is the chosen one to put Brazil back on track and keep 'the Reds' – left-wing and popular politicians like those of the Worker's Party [*PT*], including former presidents Lula da Silva and Dilma Rousseff – out of power. His performance as a conservative, anti-Left, anti-establishment and religious politician is evidenced not only in his communication products – such as the slogan of one of his campaigns 'Brazil above everything. God above everyone' [*Brasil acima de tudo. Deus acima de todos*] – but also in his use of the body as a semiotic resource for meaning-making (Demuru, Rodríguez de Oliveira, & Cuevas Calderón, 2021): looking normal, ordinary, popular and even buffoonish might serve the purpose of expressing anti-establishment contents but not necessarily populist contents.

This chapter studied one of the standard forms – in the sense that they are codified within the political semiosphere – that populism might take when combined with right-wing political contents such as nationalism, nativism and anti-immigration. In classificatory terms, sub-types of right-wing populism could be identified depending on the combination of the Populist Narrative Structure with other contents. Nevertheless, due to the still valid utility of the dichotomy between right and left to make sense of the political domain – at least in analytical terms – it seems logical that the populist waters are split in two.

This chapter has demonstrated how right-wing populist political actors bring the Populist Narrative Structure to life by filling it with right-wing political contents that are relevant in the contexts within which they are active. This is nothing else than a discursive practice of *bricolage* that implies articulating pre-existent cultural contents to produce new sense and meanings. Specifically, the chapter demonstrated how populist performances and discourses from different geographical areas share some commonalities that might justify the use of the label *populism* to make sense of them. Moreover, through the discussion of the case of Jair Bolsonaro, it was demonstrated how some traits normally ascribed to populist actors – like personalism, messianism, authoritarianism – might in fact not be *per se* populist. Since the concept of populism is easily stretchable, political actors might be easily labelled as populist based on these commonalities with populist political actors, even if their discourses are not people-centric. In this sense, the fact that tigers, cats and lions are animals that have four legs and a tail does not imply that dogs, who also have four legs and a tail, are felines.

The semiotic examination of the discourses and performances of political actors normally said to be populist proves to be useful to solve this conceptual challenge. While the commonalities between Le Pen's and Trump's discourses and performances are based on the use of the Populist Narrative Structure, they match Bolsonaro's in a different aspect. Contemporary politics is full of actors, parties and movements that question and challenge the establishment, technocracy and 'politics as usual'. This might explain why so many outsider political actors are successful in elections: although they do not have previous political experience, their discourses and performances are appealing to disaffected and disillusioned voters – Le Pen's *oubliés*. Political actors must develop strategies to mobilize these people and gain their electoral support. Therefore, diverse discursive strategies are used to propose a 'structure of feeling' that can be appealing to them, not only in cognitive but also in emotional terms. Creating a sense of crisis and fostering fear; posing as a messianic leader that does not fear challenging the system; accusing politicians, the establishment and elites; and focusing on the greatness of a nation are all discursive strategies aimed at achieving specific goals. They are used to produce meaning and, with it, motivate action.

However, calling all these meaning-making strategies 'populist' just because they aim at touching the hearts and guts of the electorate is conceptually wrong. Questioning the establishment and 'politics as usual' is not something that can be encompassed with the term 'populism', as many analysts and scholars do. For a politician, party or movement to be properly labelled as populist, the semantic unit of 'the people' must be the main Subject of its discourse, and an antagonistic relationship must be established with an 'other' that is defined in logical terms as 'not-the-people'. In other words, for a discourse to be populist, it must be grounded on the Populist Narrative Structure. Otherwise, political actors, parties and movements might be conservative, reactionary, anti-establishment, anti-elite, anti-globalization, anti-EU, Eurosceptic, anti-system, messianic, authoritarian, conspirative, even fascist or any other label but not populist.

8

Left-Wing Populism

The previous chapter examined right-wing populism, which was defined in semiotic terms as the articulation of the Populist Narrative Structure with political contents that traditionally belong to the right side of the political continuum. This chapter focuses on left-wing populism, a discursive practice used within the political field that is defined symmetrically to its right-wing counterpart, that is, as the use of the Populist Narrative Structure to frame political contents that belong to the left-wing side of that continuum.

Studying populism on the Left has a number of challenges that are not present when studying populism on the Right. On the one hand, given the common lexical ground of the words 'populist' and 'popular' in the Latin word *populus*, it is not straightforward to draw a clear line between which type of politics would be populist and which popular, let alone between populist and popular political actors, parties and movements. The case of Jair Bolsonaro discussed in the previous chapter already points out towards this challenge. As is argued in the following, the Populist Narrative Structure serves to distinguish one type of politics from the other. The case of the South American Left serves to illustrate this first challenge.

On the other hand, left-wing populism has been normally dealt with in normative terms, that is, as a political movement that can *strengthen* democracy. This thesis opposes standard scholarship on populism that sees in it a threat to democracy. The semiotic definition of left-wing populism put forward in this book must take into account the hegemonic conception of left-wing populism as a political *strategy* that could revitalize the Left and achieve a more inclusive democracy. This normative posture draws on the theory put forward by Laclau and Mouffe (2001; Laclau, 2005a; Mouffe, 2018).

After discussing the nature of left-wing populism as a discursive practice that can be approached from a semiotic perspective, the chapter focuses on examining the constitutive relationship of left-wing populism with neoliberalism and globalization, as these economic models are usually used as the reason why social exclusion has been fostered within the national contexts where left-wing populism emerges. To illustrate the theoretical argument presented in Sections 8.1 and 8.2, the last three sections of the chapter study the complex relationship between the popular and populism in South American politics (8.3), the case of the Spanish political party Podemos (8.4) and Bernie Sanders's presidential campaigns in the United States. In examining these cases, it is argued that the degree of populism in the discourses and performances of political actors, parties and movements on the Left will depend on the centrality that the Populist Narrative Structure has in their discursive articulations, as evidenced in specific textual products. As is argued, due to the nature of left-wing populism, distinguishing between populist and popular political actors is not always an easy task.

8.1 What is left-wing populism?

Left-wing populism is a discursive phenomenon that occurs within the political field and that is characterized by the combination of the Populist Narrative Structure with ideological contents and policy issues and items that, as a result of cultural codification, are located on the left side of the political spectrum, like *egalitarianism, equality, social inclusion, recognition* and *fairness*, among others. This combination has given place to the establishment of what could be conceived of as a subgenre of populist discourse. This subgenre is characterized by features that have been of interest for discourse analysts and political scientists, who have used specific expressions to refer to it, like *left-wing populism, left populism* or *populist radical left* (García Agustín, 2020; Damiani, 2020; Mouffe, 2018; Katsambekis & Kioupkiolis, 2019; Prentoulis, 2021; Charalambous & Ioannou, 2020).

The previous paragraph is almost the same as the one used in the previous chapter to define right-wing populism, only that the words in italics replace those linked to that specific subtype of populism. This deliberate repetition aims at arguing that, from the semiotic perspective put forward in this book, *there are no structural or formal differences between the two types of populism*: the two subgenres of populism imply that political actors – individual or collective – use the Populist Narrative Structure to frame political contents – from the Right and the Left, depending on how these contents are culturally codified – and fill its empty spaces with contents that are relevant in their public spheres. These contents are not only context-dependent but also draw on other social discourses revolving around the political sphere and, particularly, the vague and ambiguous category of 'the people' as opposed to an 'other'. In semiotic terms, it is due to this narrative, structural and formal component that populism can be found on both sides of the political spectrum.

In contrast to what occurs with right-wing populism, left-wing populism has been a topic of interest for analysts engaged not only in descriptive research but also in normative debates regarding the nature and status of the political in our present age. In *For a Left Populism*, Chantal Mouffe (2018) embraces this type of populism in normative terms since she sees it as an opportunity for the expansion of democracy (rather than a threat). In this sense, although right-wing populism and its counterpart on the Left are phenomena that share discursive commonalities, their normative implications are different. This is the result of the presence of other contents – besides populism – on the discursive articulations that these movements, parties and actors use for meaning-making within the political field.[1]

Although Mouffe embraces left-wing populism normatively as a political strategy to strengthen democracy – a political position that is not relevant for Semiotics – she defines populism in discursive terms: for Mouffe (2018: 5), populism is 'a discursive strategy of construction of the political frontier between "the people" and "the oligarchy"'. This short definition presents commonalities with the conception of populism presented in this book. First and foremost, populism is a *discursive phenomenon*, that is, a mode of doing things through the use of semiotic resources. Second, it is a *strategy*, that is, an instrumental action aimed at producing specific effects on the social realm. Although this book prefers to use the broader label of *discursive practice* to define the genus of populism, it makes sense that Mouffe defines it as a *discursive strategy*, that is, something to be implemented with the purpose of achieving specific political goals. In the third place, the strategy aims at *constructing a political frontier*, which is one of the features that define the Populist Narrative Structure. Finally, the main actors of that discursive strategy are for Mouffe 'the people' and 'the oligarchy'.

In Mouffe's definition, what characterizes left-wing populism is that the empty position of 'the people's other' is invested with positive content – as explained in Chapter 5 – through an equivalence with another empty category: 'the oligarchy'. This semantic unit brings together and homogenizes social actors, simplifies reality and axiologizes an 'other' that is defined in logical terms as 'not-the-people'. This negative semantic unit is filled with positive content through the establishment of an equivalence or synonymy with another semantic unit: 'the oligarchy'. This semantic unit is normally internal to a society and a constitutive part of the public sphere where left-wing populism occurs. Moreover, it implies a division of the social space in a vertical, that is, bottom-up axis: within a society there are those who have privileges and power and there are those who do not.[2]

Left-wing populism is a form of populism that stems from the Left and, when embracing populism, does not leave aside the political contents that are traditionally associated with the Left in the political imaginary (García Agustín, 2020: 3). In left-wing populism, the left-wing component is *always* visible, as opposed to what occurs in right-wing populism, where right-wing political contents might not always be there. Theoretically, it would be hard to place a populist movement, actor or party on the left side of the political spectrum if their discourse and performances did not revolve around greater social inclusion and more privileges for the dispossessed. This claim is challenging from a conceptual perspective since it might be hard to decide whether a candidate, party or movement from the Left is populist or not, as it occurs in the cases of South American politicians and Bernie Sanders discussed next.

The case of Chávez comes in handy to illustrate this point. Besides being a populist – due to the salience of the Populist Narrative Structure in his meaning-making – Chávez was a clear representative of the Latin American Left as evidenced in the specific contents he used to fill the Populist Narrative Structure. Given that the populist component is so salient in Chávez's discourse and performances, it would be incorrect to label him only as a leftist without acknowledging the central populist component of his discourse and performances. This is also the case for European populist political actors and parties like Pablo Iglesias, Podemos and SYRIZA: they are certainly populist, but they are also clearly left-wing. Due to the nature of the Left, in some cases it might be challenging to distinguish between *populism on the Left* and *left-wing political contents*. In this sense, García Agustín (2020: 3) points out the importance of 'taking diverse socio-political contexts into account in order to understand how populism is embedded within different left-wing traditions'.

In Latin America, political actors like Evo Morales and Cristina Fernández de Kirchner have been usually labelled as populists since their discourses and performances tend to revolve around the semantic unit 'the people' [*el pueblo*]. However, the salience of or amount of references to 'the people' in the discourse of a political actor is not a sufficient condition for it to be populist: an enumeration of the references to 'the people' in party discourse (Stavrakakis & Katsambekis, 2014: 127) does not say much about its populist component. As is argued later in the chapter, Morales and Fernández might make of 'the people' the main Subject of their political performances due to the centrality that this semantic unit has in South American politics, in particular to refer to the popular and plebeian sectors of societies that are highly unequal. Therefore, distinguishing between populism and left-wing political contents in their discourses and performances based on the presence of a popular component is not an easy task. According to Damiani (2020: 35), 'the distinction can be identified in the distance that separates the "class left" from the "people left"'. However, such a distinction is not always transparent when analysing discourses and other texts.[3]

As any other form of populism, left-wing populism revolves around the semantic unit 'the people' and makes of it the main political Subject. However, since left-wing populism's 'other' tends to be *internal* to the society where populism occurs, the extension of 'the people' is segmented differently than in right-wing populism: left-wing populist actors tend to fill the empty space 'the people' not in nationalist, nativist or exclusionary terms but rather aim at extending the scope of who is/are part of 'the people' in their efforts to strengthen democracy. In opposition to the *cultural* type of othering that is characteristic of right-wing, left-wing populism seems to prefer an *economic* type of othering, even if the empty space of the 'other' is sometimes filled with contents linked to this collective identity's habits and 'forms of life'. In particular, left-wing populists aim at fighting social inequalities within their societies. These are usually presented in discourse as the result of external forces, such as neoliberalism, capitalism and globalization. Hence, egalitarianism, transversality, inclusiveness and participation are central to left-wing populism (García Agustín, 2020: 10).

According to García Agustín (2020: 10), left-wing populism is 'the combination of the populist impetus of expanding representation (through the appeal to "the people" against the elites) and higher participation and of the left tradition to promote equality and social justice'. This definition could be reformulated in semiotic terms as follows: left-wing populism is the discursive practice within the political field that uses the Populist Narrative Structure combined with the traditional Left to expand representation, achieve a higher participation and promote equality and social justice.

Left-wing populism does not conceive of 'the people' as a homogeneous collective identity. As if following Laclau and Mouffe's theory, populist political actors on the Left usually aim at *creating a people* through the establishment of a *chain of equivalence* in their discourses and performances between different and heterogeneous collective identities that are seen as subjects of exclusion, dominance, inequality and subalternity.[4] While right-wing populism and the traditional Left tend to speak of '*the people*' as a given and pre-existent collective identity – the definite article *the* is used to denote referentially a specific entity of the world – left-wing populism seems to revolve around the need to construct '*a* people'. While right-wing populism and the traditional Left see in 'the people' a homogeneous collective identity that pre-exists the discursive exchange within the political and is considered an historical, natural fact, left-wing populism has a different approach and sees 'the people' as the product of bringing together heterogeneous social identities. For Damiani (2020: 35), left-wing populism's categories 'are non-homogenous groups united by a shared sense of existential insecurity who express new social needs and the demand for a renewed model of *laissez-faire* with the aim of interrupting the decline of the middle class and the further impoverishment of working people to the benefit of a small privileged elite'.

In our present time, discourses of the Left normally present Damiani's 'sense of existential insecurity' as a result of the hegemony of neoliberalism, capitalism and globalization. If before the 1980s, the Marxist Left tended to conceive of oppression mostly as the result of a country's social structure – that is, as something *internal* – over the last four decades and due to the expansion and intensification of globalization, there was a tendency of explaining inequality, subalternity and dominance mostly by recurring to causes that are *external* to a country's social structure, like globalization, capitalism, neoliberalism, global elites and transnational corporations. This dynamic of using external forces, causes and actors as scapegoats can be found both in left-wing and in right-wing types of populism. Nevertheless, it would be wrong to consider it a defining feature of populism, especially when examining the historical and pre-globalization occurrences of this political phenomenon.

8.2 Left-wing populism, neoliberalism and globalization

In several countries, the combination of left-wing political contents with the Populist Narrative Structure occurred following concrete economic crises, such as the one that hit Europe in 2008 (García Agustín, 2020). This crisis fuelled social discontent in countries like Spain and Greece. It was in those countries that the parties Podemos and SYRIZA capitalized on that social discontent following the austerity measures that the governments implemented following indications from the European Union. Something similar happened in the United States, where Bernie Sanders's campaigns capitalized on the social discontent that fuelled the Occupy movement.

In *For a Left Populism*, Mouffe (2018) argues that following these crises, a 'populist moment' built up. Mouffe conceives of this moment as a weakening of the combination of liberalism and democracy that characterizes the contemporary Western political systems. For Mouffe, neoliberalism became hegemonic since the 1980s and, in the mid-2010s, the neoliberal global order experienced a moment of fracture due to the inequalities it has created. These are Mouffe's first sentences in that book:

> At the origin of this book is my conviction that it is urgent for the left to grasp the nature of the current conjuncture and the challenge represented by the 'populist moment'. We are witnessing a crisis of the neoliberal hegemonic formation and

this crisis opens the possibility for the construction of a more democratic order. (Mouffe, 2018: 1)

According to Mouffe (2018: 18), the 'populist moment' is characterized by 'the emergence of manifold resistances against a politico-economic system that is increasingly perceived as being controlled by privileged elites who are deaf to the demands of the other groups in society'. This moment is the right one for left-wing political actors to construct 'a people' through a strategy of social mobilization that establishes chains of equivalences between different unmet social and political demands. This is what (left-wing) populism is about according to Laclau's (2005a) latest work: a political logic that renders visible the essence of democratic politics. Subsequently, Mouffe embraced it as a political strategy based on discourse.

While right-wing populism became originally appealing to the electorate – at least in Europe – in the context of globalization 'by drawing a frontier between the "people" and the "political establishment"' through a translation 'into a nationalistic vocabulary [of] the demands of the popular sectors who felt excluded from the dominant consensus' (Mouffe, 2018: 19), left-wing populism does not necessarily embrace a nationalist component in exclusionary terms – at least not as one of its central contents. This is the case even if some left-wing – and even left-wing populist – movements tend to conflate the popular with the national due to the history of these concepts in their public spheres (like in some South American countries).

Left-wing populists also use the Populist Narrative Structure to draw a frontier between 'the people' and an 'other'. As Mouffe (2018: 23) argues, 'both types of populism aim to federate unsatisfied demands, but they do it in very different ways. The difference lies in the composition of the "we" and in how the adversary, the "they," is defined'. The difference between the two types of populism lies *in the contents, not in the structural or formal aspects*. This is also something that Laclau could see clearly.

It does not come as a surprise that the most paradigmatic cases of left-wing populism – Podemos, SYRIZA, Latin America's 'third wave' – occurred in countries that are located in the periphery or the semi-periphery of the world, and whose economies depend on variables – like foreign investments – that are external to their economic actions, policies and programmes. In Europe, Spain and Greece are the two most discussed countries when studying left-wing populism: both were severely hit by the 2008 economic crisis and citizenry mobilized to complain about the austerity measures taken in its aftermath. Something similar occurred in France, where Jean-Luc Mélenchon capitalized on the effects of the economic crisis, and in the United States, where Bernie Sanders did the same. In South America, several political actors usually labelled as populists became relevant within their national political spheres following the social and economic results of the market-oriented reforms from the 1990s governments (MacDonald & Ruckert, 2009; Grugel & Riggirozzi, 2009).

There seems to be a correlation between the economic domain – crises, measures, policies and so on – and the emergence of left-wing populist movements. It has also been argued that being a colonized or colonizer country also plays a role in explaining the emergence of inclusive or exclusionary forms of populism (Filc, 2015). A correlation is established between these economic and structural aspects and the existence and growth of inequalities within a society. Faced to these inequalities that are usually suffered by the so-called losers of globalization – another empty category that equals the collective of 'the less privileged members of society' – left-wing populists confront in their discourses the neoliberal global system and try to awake in the disaffected citizens of their countries the feeling that they need to take over the guidance of the political destiny. Against the interest of global elites and corporations, the plebeian sections of society need to awake: this is the core message of left-wing populism, as is demonstrated in the following. In this sense, it seems logical that populism triggered such interest over the last three to four decades, which are the decades of globalization.

Neoliberalism is one of the keywords used by political actors from the Left since this logic became hegemonic in the 1980s (Dardot & Laval, 2009; Boas & Gans-Morse, 2009; Harvey, 2005). Left-wing and other critical scholars have a tendency to see in the neoliberal economic logic – or *governmentality* – the fuel of globalization and the liberal economic order that is hegemonic in our globalized world. According to Mouffe (2018: 11–12), neoliberalism is 'a set of political-economic practices aimed at imposing the rule of the market – deregulation, privatization, fiscal austerity – and limiting the role of the state to the protection of private property rights, free markets and free trade'. As such, these practices oppose the essence of Marxism, Keynesianism and other ideas from the domain of political economy that see the state as a key player in achieving a more equal and just society. This has always been the main normative goal of the Left.

According to these critics, the neoliberal order has left thousands and millions of individuals in situations of dispossession, oppression and subalternity. These individuals are the losers of globalization. If the Left has historically fought for the less privileged – and, in particular, for the working classes – then an assimilation between the Left and an anti-globalization attitude seems evident. This assimilation consists in broadening the causes of the situation of dominance or lack of privileges to forces that are not only internal to a country – the hegemonic sectors of a given society, who want to maintain their economic, political and social privileges and power – but also external, such as the interest of global elites, multinational corporations and major world powers and organizations. Confronted to these external forces, populists on the left – but also on the right – fight to give 'the people' a central role within the political system. Nevertheless, left-wing and right-wing populism do it by filling this empty category with different political contents.

In left-wing populism, references to 'the economic and political establishment', 'the oligarchy', 'the rich' and 'the billionaires' are frequent, as is discussed in the following. Due to the nature of the semantic unit 'the people' within the discourse of the Left, it seems normal for left-wing populism to have an inherently *anti-elite* component. In left-wing populism, 'the people' equals the plebs, the underdog and 'the common and ordinary people'. For Tarragoni (2021), populism is essentially left-wing because it seeks a 'plebeian revitalization of democracy against neoliberalism'. To construct in discourse the idea of 'the plebeian', the empty category of 'the people' is filled with social imaginaries of *normality* and *commonality* that are dominant in a given culture and society. In turn, the empty space of 'the people's other' is normally defined based on the lack of that common, normal and ordinary component.

In left-wing populism, lifestyles and the socio-economic milieu play a key role in the distinction between 'the people' and 'the oligarchy'. As an example, while 'the people' goes to work by bus, the 'other' drives expensive cars; while 'the people' go on holiday in their own countries, the 'other' travels to fancy places that do not match the common and ordinary component of 'the people's' lifestyle as it is imagined in the dominant social imaginary; while 'the people' work hard and pay their taxes, the 'other' commits fraud and does not work hard. A thorough semiotic and comparative study of how the 'standard', 'average' or 'ordinary' citizen is imagined in different cultures could shed light on how populist political actors – both on the left and the right – capitalize on these social imaginaries for meaning-making. In this task, the Semiotics of the 'forms of life' could be of help.

8.3 Left-wing populism in South America: The challenge of distinguishing between populist and popular politics

In South America, the label *populism* has a particular history that is strongly intertwined with a type of inclusionary politics that shows multiple commonalities with the type of politics put forward by the European Left. Juan Domingo Perón, Getúlio Vargas and Lázaro Cárdenas are consensually considered populists not only due to their strong, personalistic and charismatic leadership but particularly because of their discourses – and measures – aimed at including the interest and well-being of the unprivileged masses into the political system. Since they mainly addressed the popular sections of society, politicians like Perón and his wife Evita were *popular* leaders, not only because the focus of their discourses and policy-making was set on 'the people' as the popular and plebeian sections of society, but also because they were adored by the electorate and, hence, were *popular* in the sense of something that is successful in terms of its social acceptance.

In South America's political history, two further rounds of populism have been identified after Perón, Vargas, Cárdenas and others. Scholars see a neoliberal type of populism in the governments of Carlos Menem in Argentina and Alberto Fujimori in Peru, among others, who embraced neoliberal economic policies but nevertheless appealed to the masses. More recently, scholars have identified a third wave of left-wing populism in the continent, which began with Hugo Chávez and expanded to also include, among others, Evo Morales in Bolivia, Cristina Fernández de Kirchner in Argentina and Rafael Correa in Ecuador (Casullo, 2019).

If the concept of populism is defined in line with its history in South America, then the political leaders from the third wave are populists, not only because their discourses and performances are personalistic and charismatic – in line with those of Perón, Vargas and others – but also because they address, appeal to and are capable of mobilizing the masses. However, when the concept of populism is approached as a discursive practice that implies using the Populist Narrative Structure for meaning-making within the political, besides the evident case of Hugo Chávez studied in Chapter 6, it is hard to find political actors in South America that are 'full fledged' populists. This subchapter addresses the challenges of distinguishing between the Left and left-wing populism in South American politics. Through the study of the cases of José 'Pepe' Mujica (Uruguay), Cristina Fernández de Kirchner (Argentina) and Evo Morales (Bolivia), the subchapter will shed light on the challenges of establishing a clear distinction between *popular* and *populist* politics in South America.

In Chapter 6, it was argued that Chávez's discourse and performances evidenced in a clear manner the use of the Populist Narrative Structure combined with salient left-wing and Latin Americanist political contents. Within the context of South American politics, even if the populist component of his discourse is salient, Chávez was above all a representative of 'the Latin American Left' not only due to the contents he used for meaning-making but also due to his rhetoric. Here, the label *Latin American Left* serves to make sense of a number of contemporary political actors, parties and movements that share some traits and that, due to the salience of 'the people' [*el pueblo*] in their discourses and performances, are usually labelled as populists. However, they might actually be doing a type of *popular* politics, that is, a type of politics oriented towards the inclusion and well-being of the popular masses that defines the nature of the Left in South America. In this sense, even if Chávez had not recurred to the Populist Narrative Structure – that is, 'the people' versus an 'other' – for meaning-making, he could have still been a representative of the Left and of a type of *popular* politics, that is, politics for the masses and revolving around the semantic unit 'the people'.

Revisiting the case of former Uruguayan president José 'Pepe' Mujica is a good starting point for the discussion of the challenges of distinguishing between popular and populist politics in South America. Mujica's discourse included constant references to *el pueblo* ['the people']. His 'Speech to the People' reflects the dominant conception of 'the people' in the Uruguayan cultural encyclopaedia: in the speech, *el pueblo* is the result of a discursive articulation of the popular and plebeian sections of society and 'the people' as the Uruguayan *demos*, that is, the electoral base of democracy in Uruguay.

In Uruguay and in other South American political semiospheres, the noun *pueblo* has specific connotations linked to the Left, independently of what it might denote or refer to. In semiotic terms, this noun underwent a process of *mythification*: specific connotations that were not part of the original denotation of a word became part of its sedimented meaning (Barthes, 1957). In the post-colonial configuration of South American societies, economic and political elites held positions of privilege, and the plebeian and popular sections of society were the losers in that process. As a result, in South America the word *pueblo* has sedimented connotations linked with the Left and activates a semantic field that overlaps with left-wing populism's 'people'. Unsurprisingly, in the continent the words 'populism' and 'populist' have been frequently used to discredit movements that are actually *popular*, in the sense that they seek a broader inclusion of the popular, plebeian and massive sections of society, together with a reduction of social inequalities. The noun *plebeianism* could be used to distinguish from populism a type of popular politics that does not recur to the Populist Narrative Structure for meaning-making.

In this sense, much theoretical confusion could have been spared to populism scholars if Mouffe and Laclau had chosen the noun *plebeianism* rather than *populism* to refer to their normative conception of 'politics for the people' as a way to expand democracy. This book tries to show why the concept of populism is used to refer to discursive strategies that work both for the Left and the Right. If the word 'populism' is reserved for one of those occurrences only – for example, on the Right and with an exclusionary character – and *plebeianism* is used to refer to this type of inclusionary politics on the Left, it would be easier to characterize these two types of people-centric politics, and even to assess them in normative terms: while populism would pose a threat to democracy, plebeianism would aim at strengthening it. Another option for naming these phenomena would be using the lexical unit *populism* as an adjective to qualify nationalism and plebeianism: right-wing populism would be a *populist exclusionary nationalism* and left-wing populism would be a *populist inclusive plebeianism*. In both cases, the use of the adjective *populist* is conditioned by the use political actors do of the Populist Narrative Structure. Nevertheless, since the noun *populism* is currently used to refer to right-wing and left-wing political manifestations, it is fundamental to understand what it is that right-wing and left-wing populism share. As argued here, that would be the use of the Populist Narrative Structure.

In semiotic terms, the meaning of the noun *pueblo* in South American politics seems to be the result of an operation of semiotic construction that reflects the logics of construction of 'the people's other' in populist discourse: while populist political actors normally construct their country's 'people' by establishing a frontier with an 'other' that is defined in negative terms as 'not-the-people', *popular* politics normally does the opposite – based on an identification of an 'other' in terms of accumulation of wealth, resources and power, it constructs a popular collective identity as one that is homogeneous, unitary and, above all, a majority in society (Remedi, 2019). In popular politics, the noun *pueblo* is used to refer to that collective identity. In Evita's discourse, for example, the plural nouns *negritos* [blackies], *descamisados* [shirtless] and *grasitas* [greasy] were used to create a 'people' as the popular and plebeian sectors of Argentinean society through the employment of semiotic resources that are stereotypically linked in Argentinean culture to the physical appearance – skin colour, clothing, *habitus* and taste – of the working classes, and in particular of the groups that migrated from the inland to the cities to work in factories in severely unprivileged conditions.

The adjectives *populist* and *popular* share the same lexical root: the Latin noun *populus*. How to distinguish what is *populist* from what is *popular*? The case of Mujica demonstrated that a political actor can be popular – or *plebeianist*, in the sense of doing inclusive politics for the popular and plebeian sections of society and appealing to them electorally – without being a populist. A spot from Mujica's 2019 presidential campaign includes images of random people that look like common and ordinary Uruguayan citizens. The voice-over says: 'We are different. Do you mind? Neither do I. The President of all of us: Pepe Mujica.'[5] Even if in that spot the semantic unit of 'the people' is constructed in terms of a plurality of individuals – the Uruguayans – that share a common political interest, Mujica's campaigns, discourse and performances are characterized by the use of semiotic resources stemming from the cultural repertoire of Uruguay's popular and plebeian sectors, such as folkloric music, carnival choirs and a performative style that is humble and popular (in the plebeian sense). Mujica's discourse and performances do not evidence an antagonistic and polarizing relationship of 'a people' with an enemy. Hence, the adjectives *popular* or *plebeian* might be more appropriate to describe his discourse and performances than *populist*.

In the previous chapter, it was argued that political actors can be populist without anchoring their discourses and performances in their country's popular repertoire. While Bolsonaro's performances connote commonness and an ordinary lifestyle similar to that of an imagined standard Brazilian (Demuru, 2021a), Trump constructs the American 'people' without employing semiotic resources taken from a popular repertoire, like country music, barbecues, cowboys or any other folkish cultural tradition or social imaginary. Trump's lifestyle clearly does not reflect in any way that of the popular/plebeian sectors of the American society. However, he establishes a clear antagonistic relationship between the American 'people' and an 'other'. Hence, it is possible for populism to exist without the popular or plebeian component, and popular or plebeian politics can exist without being populist.

In South American politics, the boundaries between the popular/plebeian and the populist are not easy to draw. Hence, political actors whose discourse and performances have a strong and salient popular/plebeian component have been frequently labelled as populist, even if their discourses and performances do not evidence meaning-making being grounded first and foremost on the Populist Narrative Structure. The cases of Cristina Fernández in Argentina and of Evo Morales in Bolivia serve to illustrate this argument.

The argument begins with the examination of an electoral spot by Cristina Fernández, president of Argentina between 2007 and 2015. In her discourse and performances, Fernández capitalized on the cultural myth of Eva Perón (Sebreli, 2008) to position herself within the Argentinean political semiosphere, in particular since she became a political leader when her husband Néstor Kirchner passed away.

Fernández was *a Peronist*. This is a complex and polysemic label used in the Argentinean public sphere, which is the result of an articulation of popular and nationalistic political contents anchored in Juan Domingo Perón's political activity (Grimson, 2019; Sigal & Verón, 2003). Therefore, depending on the viewpoint and the interpretations of Perón's actions in the Argentinean political domain, Peronism could be regarded as either a left or a right-wing phenomenon. As Fernández and her husband capitalized on it, this pre-existing social discourse served to refer to an inclusive, mass, popular and leftist political project, which is referred to as *Kirchnerismo* (Cingolani & Fernández, 2019: 19–20).

This is the text of a spot from Fernández's 2011 presidential campaign:[6]

> When a people [*pueblo*] is not joyful and has no self-esteem, it can be easily dominated. To change History, the will of one crazy man [*reference to Néstor Kirchner*] or of one crazy woman [*reference to herself*] are not enough. More crazy people are needed: 40 millions of crazy people, 40 millions of Argentineans ready to continue changing History.[7]

The text includes a reference to *el pueblo* in the sense of the Argentinean *demos*. The noun *argentinos* used at the end works as an isotopy that fills the semantic unit 'the people' with a national content. Actually, it was frequent for Fernández to use the word *Argentines* [*argentinos/argentinas*] rather than 'the people', although when holding speeches in public and open spaces she addressed the crowd as *el pueblo*. Her repertoire also includes the noun *compatriotas* [compatriots], like in her last speech as a president in December 2015,[8] where she mentioned that her government was *popular* and that it had the hegemonic media and local and international corporations against it. In that speech, Fernández claimed that 'we love the homeland [*patria*]'; 'we believe in the people [*pueblo*]', and concluded saying: 'that is the biggest I have given to the Argentinean People: popular empowerment, citizen empowerment'. These words evidence an enunciation that oscillates between a collective *pro-addresse* (we) and the individuality of the leader (I).

References to *el pueblo* and other nouns that refer to the semantic unit 'the people' are certainly present in Fernández's discourse and performances, and so is the use of an antagonistic relationship with an 'other'. This 'other' normally takes the form of the hegemonic media, large financial corporations and the political opposition. Moreover, she frequently used the binary opposition 'we' versus 'they' (La Nación, 2015) to create an antagonism that fostered political polarization in the Argentinean public sphere (Villegas, 2020). Besides being popular/plebeianist, Fernández's discourse and performances evidence a resource to populism as a mode of framing the popular/plebeianist political contents.

The images used in the spot focus exclusively on constructing an Argentinean 'people' through three semiotic resources: showing large groups of individuals, normally in public spaces – 'the people' as a group – common and ordinary individuals – 'the people' as the common Argentinean citizen, that is, the popular/plebeian sections of society – and national contents like flags, rural traditions and carnival – 'the people' in national terms. Here, nationalistic contents are used not in exclusionary terms, but because they serve the purpose of figurativizing who 'the people' are. The spot does not include any visual footage aimed at constructing an 'other' as 'not-the-people'. Therefore, while its content is certainly popular/plebeianist, it is not populist.

In South American politics – and in particular, in Argentina – the public space plays a crucial role in the construction of the 'people' in spatial-semiotic terms. In Argentinean history, Plaza de Mayo – Buenos Aires' main square – has been mythified with connotations that make of it *the* space of 'the people' (Dagatti & Gómez Triben, 2020; Sigal, 2006). In her last public speech as the president – and in many of her speeches – Fernández addressed the massive group of individuals present in the square as *el pueblo*. That crowd of individuals is inherently popular and left-wing, as evidenced in the symbols they carry with them – flags of Che Guevara, the Andean community, trade unions and pro-abortion – and how they behave – like when jumping, waving the Argentinean flag and chanting as if they were in a football stadium. At the beginning of the speech, the crowd on the square sings '*Oh le le, oh la la, si este no es el pueblo, ¿el pueblo dónde está?*' ['Oh le le, oh la la, if this is not the people, where is the people?'].[9]

Also interesting in this regard is the speech that Fernández gave at Plaza de Mayo in 2019, after being appointed the vice-president.[10] In that speech, she advised the newly elected president Alberto Fernández as follows: 'Always trust your people. They do not betray. They are the most loyal. They only ask to be defended and represented.' Then, she encouraged him to 'have faith in the people' because 'History is always written, sooner or later, by the people'. Finally, she advised: 'recur to this wonderful people that never abandons those that take risks on their name, any time you feel alone or in need', because the people will 'always be there to fight for just causes'.[11] Immediately after Fernández uttered those words, the crowd started chanting '*Alberto querido: el pueblo está contigo*' ['Dear Alberto, the people is with you'].

As in Mujica's 'Speech to the People', the references to 'the people' as the result of an articulation of 'the people' as *demos* and 'the people' as the popular and plebeian sections of society evidence a type of *popular* politics, but not necessarily *populist* politics. In this sense, in Cristina Fernández's discourse and performances, the popular/plebeian and the populist components coexist. In fact, Fernández used to refer to her government as *gobierno popular* [popular government], not populist. How can the popular and populist contents of a discourse be disentangled? Can they be disentangled at all? The identification (or not) of the Populist Narrative Structure in the text that a political actors enunciates could be a first step in this direction.

In Bolivia, former president Evo Morales – in office between 2006 and 2019 – is also frequently included in the list of South American left-wing populists. However, due to Bolivia's ethnical composition, the category of 'the people' gains in Morales's discourse interesting shades that are not present in societies that are more homogeneous in ethnic terms. Raúl Madrid saw in this phenomenon the rise of *ethnopopulism* in Latin America. However, in a book from 2012 on the same topic, he preferred to replace that category with *ethnic politics* and listed Morales as one of its examples. Although according to Madrid's definition of populism, Morales constitutes a clear case of a populist political actor, this does not occur when conceiving of populism in semiotic terms, that is, as the discursive practice grounded in the use of the Populist Narrative Structure.

Morales's discourse and performances revolved strongly around the popular sectors of Bolivian society, with a particular focus on collective identities historically excluded, like the ethnic groups that were oppressed in Bolivia since the time of the Spanish colonization. As Mujica and Fernández did, Morales also used to refer to *el pueblo*, as evidenced in an electoral spot from 2014:[12]

> Sisters and brothers: our great nation has awakened. Bolivia grew as never before, as we always dreamt. Today, our Nation is full with dignity and respect. We improved the quality of life of the Bolivians. We are going to give the biggest step in our history. We will be the energetic hearth of South America and we will illuminate our future even more.
>
> [*Evo Morales:*] Sisters and brothers: Long live the Bolivian people! Long live! Long live democracy with the people![13]

The spot includes footage of anonymous and unknown individuals looking directly into the lens of the camera. Due to their physical appearance, many of them can be easily identified as individuals with an indigenous background and, hence, as members of the Bolivian popular and plebeian sectors, that is, those opposed to 'the oligarchy' and that have been historically marginalized from power positions. The vast majority of the anonymous people featured in the first scenes of the spot can be easily identified based on their bodily traits as part of indigenous ethnic groups, which constitute a significant part of the Bolivian population (Madrid, 2008: 484).

Hence the label of *ethnopopulism* or *ethnic politics* to refer to Morales's discourse and performances: in his discourse, Morales definitely constructs a 'people' in inclusionary terms that is labelled by many as typically leftist.[14] This discursive construction gave place to the discursive construction of Bolivia as a *plurinational* state, that is, one that is not ethnically homogeneous. This social diversity reflects in how Morales constructs Bolivia's 'people' in his discourse. As García-Marín and Luengo (2019: 88) argue, his discourse is characterized by a definition of Us through the use of pronouns – *us, our* – references to the nation as a brotherhood – 'sisters and brothers', in the spot – and nouns such as *Bolivia, the workers, the Motherland [patria]* and *the people [pueblo]*.[15]

That is why it makes more sense to regard Morales and other ethnic political actors and candidates from South America as *indigenist* rather than populist, even if they might occasionally recur to the use of the Populist Narrative Structure for meaning-making and, hence, be populists. However, if 'the people' these actors construct in their discourses and performances is strongly linked to a specific collective identity that is segmented taking into account the ethnic element, the label populism might not be the most accurate to make sense of them. Nevertheless, as it can be seen, in South American politics it is not always easy to disentangle the popular and the ethnic collective identities since, historically, the ethnic groups have been the plebeian groups (in the sense of 'not-the-elite').

In the discourses and performances of ethnic/indigenist/plebeianist politicians, some elements might actualize the virtual ethnic collective identity, while others might do so with the popular identity. Moreover, political actors can also activate a populist 'people' whenever antagonisms are used to construct 'the people' in discourse. One of Morales's slogans was *Evo y pueblo* ['Evo and People'][16] and his Twitter account is @evoespueblo ['Evo is People']. What sense of 'the people' do these strategic formulas intend to construct? What semantic functions do the conjunction *and* and the verb *to be* intend to fulfil? Independently of what conception of 'the people' Morales embraces, the formula establishes an equivalence between the leader and 'the people': in the first case, the leader is *with* 'the people'; in the second, he *is* 'the people'.

Besides its indigenist/ethnic component, Morales's discourse was also clearly leftist and aligned with the South American Left. The name of the party Morales represented included a direct reference to the left-wing character of his political platform: *Movimiento al Socialismo* (MAS) means 'Movement for Socialism'. The party was created in the 1990s and strategically targeted voters from the low and middle classes, disaffected by the market-oriented policies that the governing parties had implemented in that decade (Madrid, 2012: 36). According to Madrid (2012: 36), the electoral rise of MAS at the beginning of the 2000s was based on a combination of ethnic and populist appeals and the centrality it gave to the figure of the leader, who aimed at mobilizing the popular masses. For García-Marín and Luengo (2019: 82), the MAS 'borrows the discourse of the leftist tradition and the movement endorsing ethnic identification'.

An electoral spot from 2019[17] evidences a clear leftist and egalitarian content: in the spot, random Bolivian citizens are placed in a sort of 'race of privileges' where a hostess makes questions about their lifestyles; those who had access to solutions for their problems can give a step forward. At the end, only one is in the frontline and the hostess asks who had the opportunity of finding other solutions thanks to Morales's measures. At the end of the race, the hostess says: 'This is the result of distributing wealth, of valuing the people and of building a more just country. Thanks to the work of Evo and People,[18] now everyone has the opportunity to achieve their dreams.'

To sum up, when scrutinizing the discourses and performances of South American political actors that scholars, the media and other political actors consensually identify as populist, analysts should be careful with regard to two aspects. On the one hand, it is imperative to disentangle and distinguish clearly the popular/plebeian and the populist components in a political actor's discourse and performances. As it has been argued here, referring to 'the people' is not a sufficient condition for a discourse to be populist. On the other hand, it should be clearly stated what the labels *populism* and *populist* refer to when discussing a South American political actor's discourse and performances. Mujica's discourse is highly popular/plebeian but hardy populist. Cristina Fernández's discourse oscillates between – and merges – the popular/plebeian and the populist. Morales's discourse is highly popular/plebeian but adds an indigenist component that is marginal, for example, in the Uruguayan public sphere. In opposition to these three political actors, the discourses and performances of Chávez are popular/plebeian and also strongly populist.

As it was suggested previously, the labels *populism* and *populist* have different conceptual histories and hence meanings in Europe, the United States and South America (Rooduijn, 2014). Therefore, while Mujica, Fernández and Morales might be populists in the sense that is prevalent in South America – that is, charismatic leaders aiming at mobilizing the popular masses and achieving greater social inclusion for them – they might not be populists when approached using other definitions, like the semiotic one proposed here. In this sense, the semiotic approach could provide a clear criterion to identify populist political actors and distinguish them from other types of politics revolving around 'the people'.

8.4 Left-wing populism in Europe: Podemos

In Europe, scholarship on populism was usually focused on its right-wing manifestations. However, in the aftermath of the 2008 economic crisis and the austerity measures it triggered, some parties, actors and movements embracing left-wing political contents started being labelled as populists. The two most visible European populist parties were SYRIZA, in Greece, and Podemos, in Spain. Following these examples, observers began identifying other political actors as populist, and even some actors identified themselves as such, like Jean-Luc Mélenchon, leader of the La France Insoumise Party, in France.[19]

The party Podemos was founded in Spain in 2014, in the aftermath of the Indignados movement that took place in 2011 as a consequence of the 2008 crisis. Quickly, the party achieved a central role within Spanish politics following its electoral success in the 2014 European Parliament elections. Since then, it challenged the traditional Spanish two-party system (Orriols & Cordero, 2016).[20] As Mazzolini and

Borriello (2021: 3) argue, Podemos is 'the most iconic example of a trend that has seen the emergence in Europe of a new type of strategy previously circumscribed to Latin America: left populism'.[21] For García Agustín (2020: 16–17), the European cycle of left-wing populism began when the Left was declining in Latin America.

From a semiotic perspective, the analysis of the party's name is already relevant: *podemos* is a verb conjugated in the first person plural that can be translated as 'we can'. This naming strategy creates from the beginning *pro-addressee* (Verón, 1987), that is, the illusion of a 'we' that includes both the enunciator and the addressees. The option for the modal verb 'to can' [*poder*] is also relevant in semiotic terms, as this is one of the semiotic modalities in Greimas's theory, together with to want [*vouloir*], to must [*devoir*] and to know [*savoir*] (Greimas, 1983; Badir, 2020). The name of the party is in itself a semiotic artefact that constructs an Us and affirms its agency through the combination of grammatical – morphology – and lexical – a modal verb – resources.

According to Sanders, Berganza and De Miguel (2016: 253), Podemos's communications were originally centred in four themes: (1) 'the corruption of mainstream Spanish politics'; (2) a 'constant use of the term *casta* (caste, ruling class)' as a means to position itself as being on the side of 'the people'; (3) the idea of a new type of participatory politics; and (4) its positioning beyond the Left-Right dichotomy that is hegemonic in Spanish politics. These four themes evidence the use of the Populist Narrative Structure: the party emerges in a moment of a perceived economic and political crisis; criticizes established politicians, parties and 'politics as usual'; and uses a discourse in which 'the people' are encouraged to recover popular sovereignty – in narrative terms, a Subject must achieve a state of conjunction with an Object of Value. This narrative programme implies a struggle against an 'other' – the anti-Subject – that is constructed around the semantic unit of 'the caste' [*la casta*], a generic noun that in Podemos's discourse is equivalent to 'the political establishment'. In this narrative scheme, Podemos positions itself as the helper that will achieve a state of real democracy thanks to its challenging way of doing a transversal type of politics (Arroyas Langa & Pérez Díaz, 2016: 53).

In Podemos populist discourse, the role of Pablo Iglesias as the populist leader is salient. Since the origins of the party in 2014, Iglesias performed his role as a politician in a relatively informal manner. For this meaning-making purpose, he made a strategic use of the bodily dimension with the aim of producing the effect of sense of being an ordinary citizen like any other 'standard' or 'common' Spaniard. Not wearing a tie, avoiding suits and his ponytail challenged the standard looks and attires of standard politics.[22] Moreover, reflecting the spatial-semiotic strategy described in the analysis of Fernández's case, the party's rallies and events during the electoral campaigns used to take place in ordinary and public places from the everyday circuit, like schools and streets (Sanders, Berganza & De Miguel, 2016: 254).

On social media, Iglesias's use of Twitter evidences commonalities with the communicative strategies of other populist politicians (Arroyas Langa & Pérez Díaz, 2016). Some examples are a narrative articulation grounded in an antagonism between 'us' and 'them', a vague and abstract construction of the adversary and the exaltation of the party's honesty against the corruption of the political caste. The axiologization of the 'other' in negative moral terms reflects the strategy of othering that is characteristic of populism. Podemos's 'other' is a discursive construction that capitalizes on the 15-M demonstrations, where the slogan '*No nos representan*' ['They do not represent us'] was used. Those who were imagined as the (omitted) subject of the verb *to represent* were later transformed in discourse into 'the caste'. Before that positivity, the semantic unit of 'not-the-people' existed as a vague reference to a 'they' that is not Us.

Two electoral spots evidence Podemos's use of the Populist Narrative Structure, albeit in a different fashion. The first spot dates from 2014 and introduces the party and some of its main representatives – including Pablo Iglesias – to the electorate in the wake of the European Parliament election.[23] The text of the spot is read by six members of the party, who are featured in the footage and are introduced with their names and a definite description. This is the text:

> They say it is not possible to stand up to Merkel. They say we should tighten our belts even more. They say it is normal to live in constant fear. They say it is time to pack our bags. They say it is not possible to choose anything beyond Them and That. They say that corruption is an isolated problem. They say that we need to give up to having the country and the future sold in pieces.
>
> They are taking us to misery. They have broken every single compromise. Is it not possible to wish for a better country for your children? I say we are many more and that we can win. We can [*podemos*] put the people's [*la gente*] needs first: that is democracy. We can sit the caste and their friends in the dock. Of course we can.
>
> [*Pablo Iglesias*:] When was the last time you voted with hope?
> [*Voices in the background shout collectively* 'Yes, it is possible!']
> [*Pablo Iglesias*:] Of course we can.[24]

The images included in the spot revolve around the six party members that read the script out loud, plus Iglesias, who is featured at the end of the clip and introduced as the party's leader. Like in the case of Morales's spot, these individuals look at the lens of the camera, as if attempting to establish an intimate relationship with the addressee. Also like in Morales's spot, the music has a high emotional component: contrary to the cases of Le Pen and Trump, it does not evoke connotations of a heroic plot in the sense of preparing for combat but rather evoking hope – it has an inspirational component. The musical selection along these lines matches Iglesias's question at the end of the spot, 'When was the last time you voted with hope?', which aims at activating an emotional dimension in the electorate that can trigger their vote in positive terms, as opposed to when fear is used by right-wing populists to awaken the passions of the electorate.

With regards to the structure of the text, the Populist Narrative Structure is evidenced thanks to a number of semiotic resources. To begin with, there is a discursive construction of 'the people' through direct reference: *la gente*.[25] Moreover, the use of verbs conjugated in the first person plural – in particular, the repetition of the formula 'we can' – also constructs this collective actor in discourse. In the third place, pronouns such as *we* and *our* contribute to the construction of an inclusive Us that embraces the enunciators and the addressees. Finally, a group of people chanting, 'Yes, it is possible!' [*¡Sí, se puede!*] at the end of the spot is another semiotic resource used to create the effect of sense of a social actor that is collective.

The text also constructs an 'other' not only through the use of verbs conjugated in the third person of plural – 'they say', 'they are taking', 'they have broken' – but also through specific references such as 'the caste and their friends'. In this discursive construction of 'the people's other', the reference to Angela Merkel functions to create the effect of a sense of an external issue that divides opinions in two: 'they' say it is not possible to stand up to Merkel, but 'we' believe it is possible. This evidences the antagonistic relationship that the spot establishes between the 'we' and the 'they'.

The axiologization in moral terms of the two actors is also evident in the spot: the enemy needs to be sat in the dock and judged, is taking 'Us' to misery and has broken every single compromise. According to Arroyas Langa and Pérez Díaz (2016: 58), in Iglesias's discourse – and also of Podemos – values serve 'the purpose of sustaining the populist narrative of antithesis'. In this sense, while the 'Us' is characterized as transparent, honest, noble, authentic, pure and a carrier of hope, the 'other' is depicted as morally decadent since their representatives have lost the civic sense of politics. Hence, they *are* corrupt, defend political privileges and, in doing so, create inequality and suffering (Arroyas Langa & Pérez Díaz, 2016: 59). In this sense, Podemos's discourse also revolves around a sense of crisis, not only in economic terms – following the 2008 financial crisis and the austerity measures it gave place to – but also in political and moral terms.

In 2014, when Podemos was being introduced to the Spanish electorate, the party needed to buy a van for campaigning purposes. For that occasion, the party produced a spot[26] with the following text and the song 'People have the power', by Patti Smith, in the background:

> Some are used to travelling always in first class. Comfortable seats, gin tonics or martinis on the plane. Full luxury and comfort paid by who knows who. Others are satisfied [*otros nos conformamos*, reflexive verb conjugated in the first person plural] with more humble means. But even the humble means are expensive when they are used to do something big. In Podemos we have always said that we do not want to owe anything to banks. And that is why we will not ask them for money. We believe that the people [*la gente*] must finance our electoral campaign. Thanks to your contributions we are independent. This is a campaign van – you have paid for it: Thank you![27]

Here, it is interesting to analyse how the 'we'-'they' dichotomy is constructed in discourse and how each of these groups is characterized through the semantic opposition *comfort-humility*. But more interesting is to analyse how Iglesias appeals directly to 'the people' [*la gente*] for them to finance their campaign and includes the addressee in that group through the use of a plural *you*.

The second spot to be analysed in search of the Populist Narrative Structure dates from 2019,[28] a year in which the party was already using the name 'Unidas Podemos' following a coalition with other Spanish left-wing parties. The formation of the coalition involved embracing contents linked to the radical Left – in particular following the South American example – such as using gender-inclusive language,[29] criticizing capitalism and its effects on local economies and trying to appeal to social groups whose demands could potentially be set in a chain of equivalence. The spot begins with a clip of former French president Nicolas Sarkozy arguing in French for the need to moralize capitalism and the market economy instead of getting rid of them:

> The most insatiable capitalism devoured itself and, in doing so, sunk countries, evicted families from their homes and destroyed jobs. Those who provoked the disaster were also in charge of the recovery, congregated around a sole creed: austerity.
> [. . .] Many lost, but a few won. These were also the years of big benefits for companies, of millionaire salaries, of corruption, of traps, of putrefaction. Yesterday, elites wanted to reform capitalism; today, they declare that the crisis is over.
> [. . .] But they did not take into account that we had awaken. Our breath originates in the dignity of the working people [*la gente trabajadora*] that fights with determination for a habitable present, in the courage of millions of teenagers that want to save the planet, [. . .] in women, who mark the path towards a free and enjoyable life. They have always told us it was impossible, that History was written by them. And that is not true.
> We could. [. . .] A country can be made by putting the people [*la gente*] in the centre. We are not scared. We feel like keep going on and are certain that History will not be dictated from above: neither twenty families nor 35 boards of directors nor the spokespersons of the powerful. Next to their cold lies, there are warm truths, such as that democracy bleeds out when it is kidnapped, [. . .] that government is for the people [*la gente*], [. . .] that the future is ours, that it is possible, [. . .] that, whatever they say, it is you who writes History.[30]

In semiotic terms, this spot is more complex than the one from 2014. For example, the editing links the possible interpretations of the overall meaning of the spot to the multimodality/syncretism resulting from the coexistence of the text and the images chosen to accompany it. The text evidences similarities with that of the first spot analysed, such as the assumption that there is 'a people' that was disregarded, awoke and now has political agency. Moreover, the 'we'–'they' dichotomy is present in two spots.

Regarding the images, the meaning-making repertoire of the 2019 spot is broad: some evoke economic crisis, others serve as metaphors to guide interpretations about capitalism – for example, animals fighting fiercely, footage shows common and ordinary people suffering, crying, being hit by the police, leaving their countries, while images of rich people that actualize the semantic unit 'the caste' are smiling, laughing and arriving to airports. Footage of specific politicians like Nicolas Sarkozy, Emmanuel Macron, Angela Merkel, Mariano Rajoy and José Luis Rodríguez Zapatero figurativize the semantic unit of 'the establishment'. In general terms, the first part of the 2019 spot shows a situation of disadvantage for 'the people', and of privilege for its 'other'.

When the text reads 'we awoke', a change in the plot occurs. The images feature groups of people on the streets. Through the use of these images, there is a semiotic construction of 'the people' as a crowd that gets together and occupies the public space, like the Argentinean people in Plaza de Mayo. When the text reads 'we awoke', the music changes to a more heroic tone: the second half of the narrative revolves around the hero: 'the people'. This capitalizes on the social imaginary that emerged based on the 2011 popular demonstrations in Spain. Here, footage of Iglesias and other Podemos parliamentarians is used in an editing that merges the leader(s) and 'the people'. Finally, Iglesias appears for a couple of seconds walking in a relaxed manner, looking directly at the camera without saying anything: the leader is here and knows what to do to save Us.

As it can be seen, spots from different moments in Podemos history evidence in a clear manner the centrality of the Populist Narrative Structure as the mould for meaning-making. However, as Mazzolini and Borriello (2021: 7) argue, in the process the party stopped being a 'transversal populist party hostile to the whole party system and aiming at winning an overall majority' and 'progressively "normalized" and transformed into a renewed version of the Spanish radical left'. In spite of the differences between the two moments (2014 and 2019), the populist component is present, as evidenced in the corpus analysed in this section.[31]

8.5 Left-wing populism in the United States? Bernie Sanders

In the wake of the 2016 presidential election in the United States, Bernie Sanders ran to be the Democrats' nominee. His discourse and performances resembled in several of their traits those of European left-wing populist parties and candidates like Podemos. As a result, Sanders began being identified as a populist, in a political context where, due to historical events (as argued in a previous chapter), left-wing populism seemed to be the only logical possibility for populism to exist. Therefore, while Trump's identification as a populist might have been surprising for the reasons presented in the previous chapter, Sanders's did not.

When populism is defined as the ideology or the political movement that was embraced by the members of the agrarian People's Party in the nineteenth century – that is, as an ideology that stands for the less privileged and rural sections of society against the interests of an urban elite – then Sanders is definitely a populist: his political project goes in line with more political inclusion and a reduction of social inequalities through cutting privileges to the minority powerful sections of society. Therefore, when considering the political history of the United States, it does not come as a surprise that scholars, observers and political commentators saw in Sanders a populist. However, if populism is defined as the discursive practice of employing the Populist Narrative Structure for meaning-making within the political, it is more challenging to argue straightforwardly that Sanders's discourse and performances are of a populist nature.

This is the case because the left-wing contents and policy proposals were more salient in Sanders's campaign than the populist framing. While Podemos is above all a populist party that fills the empty spaces of the Populist Narrative Structure with left-wing political contents like equality, transversality and inclusion, in Sanders's discourse the populist component seems to be rather secondary compared to its left-wing contents. This was also the case in the discourses of Cristina Fernández and Evo

Morales. In fact, Sanders's political platform during the 2016 US election did not differ much from the type of platforms embraced by politicians and parties from the Left in South America: ideas like the need for a political revolution – Sanders wrote a book entitled *Our Revolution* – the fight against inequality through conquering more and better rights for the less privileged sections of society – universal healthcare, better wages and working hours, free university education and so on – and a self-definition as 'progressive' and as a 'democratic socialist' were the main contents of his proposals (Staufer, 2021; Macaulay, 2019).

The electoral spot 'Fight for Someone You Don't Know', from 2019, evidences the logic of solidarity that characterizes the discourse of South American parties on the Left:[32]

> Take a look around you and find someone you don't know. Maybe somebody doesn't look kind of like you. Are you willing to fight for that person as much as you're willing to fight for yourself? If you and millions of others are prepared to do that, not only will we win this election, but together we will transform this country.

The text does not evidence references to the collective actor 'the people'. In exchange, the idea of individuals that should look around and find others like them is central. Instead of constructing in discourse a homogeneous 'people', the text is grounded on the notion of *heterogeneity*. In the spot, what that homogeneity means is filled with visual content through a focus on individuals that represent minorities within the US society, like individuals of an Arab, Hispanic and African origin. In the spot, the footage that does not focus on the crowd standing around Sanders – as the Argentinean 'people' did in Cristina Fernández's speeches on Playa de Mayo – focuses on individuals that reflect these minorities.

Sanders's discourse assumes that US society is diverse and heterogeneous. Therefore, his discourse and performances had a focus on the semantic unit 'America', a label that was used to refer at the same time to the country and to its 'people', as in the case of Trump. In some of his electoral spots from 2016, the song *America* by Simon and Garfunkel was used to structure the audiovisual products. The spot 'America'[33] includes images of Bernie Sanders in direct contact with the American 'people' – in the sense of the common, normal and ordinary people of the United States – and that collective identity is filled with some national tones, albeit in a strictly different mode than the nationalist component was featured in Trump's discourse.

When examining Sanders's discourse and performances, they seem to be democratic socialist, progressive and leftist rather than populist. However, his discourse and performances also evidence the use of the Populist Narrative Structure, even if the left-wing political contents prevail over the populist component. The Populist Narrative Structure is clearly visible in the spot 'Vote Together',[34] from Sanders's 2016 campaign, where images and photographs of random individuals that are identifiable as part of different collective – gender, ethnic and so on – identities are used to construct the idea of an heterogeneous 'people':

> Our job is not to divide. Our job is to bring people together. If we do not allow them to divide us up by race, by sexual orientation, by gender, by not allowing

them to divide us up by whether or not we were born in America or whether we are immigrants. We stand together. White, black, Hispanic, gay, straight, woman and men. When we stand together and demand that this country works for all of us rather than the few, we will transform America. And that is what this campaign is about: it's bringing people together.

The text reflects clearly the logic of left-wing populism as a normative project. Differently to what occurs with the previous examples studied in this book, Sanders does not seem to assume the existence of *a* or *the* people – think of Podemos and the use it makes of footage of groups of individuals on the streets. Sanders clearly *constructs* a 'people' by bringing people – different individuals – together through the concept of *togetherness*. This move reflects Laclau and Mouffe's concept of a chain of equivalence between existing unmet demands within a society. Sanders's discourse does not include a reference to '*the* people', as Trump's discourse did; it rather revolves around a homogeneous collective identity that *needs to be constructed*. Sanders's discourse is about *people*, that is, a collection of heterogeneous individuals that need to group to conduct the political revolution he put forward.

The spot has formal similarities with Morales's construction of the Bolivian people in one of the spots analysed before. The two spots use images of random and anonymous individuals to create the sense of a collective group. In both cases, a majority of the individuals featured in the spots are stereotypically recognizable as members of minority or excluded social groups. However, the effects of sense that guide the two spots are different when examined from a semiotic perspective: while Morales seems to assume that there is a Bolivian 'people' that is characterized by an ethnic and indigenous component, Sanders seems to be more interested in grouping individuals without committing in any form to how 'the people' are; while Morales puts on the table the marginalized sectors of Bolivian society and hence models who are meant to be part of it, Sanders has a more open strategy that does not model who can be part of the political Subject that will follow him in conducting his revolution.

In the process of constructing a 'people', Sanders performs the role of the populist leader in a different manner than Trump. As Macaulay (2019) argues, while Trump posed at the same time as a helper and as a Subject of a political change that will make America great again, Sanders posed only as a helper: he will help 'the people' group up, discover their unified collective identity and 'find America' to change the system. Contrary to Trump, he does not present himself as a necessary link in achieving this change: Sanders's discourse does not evidence a self-positioning as part of 'the people's' unmet demands. For Macaulay (2019: 188), 'Sanders' populism does not construct leadership through one individual as central to the effectuation of demands; rather he constructs leadership as constructed through metaphorically-related individuals, "our brothers and our sisters and our co-workers and our neighbours," to effect structural societal change that will in turn bring about a realization of popular demands.' Macaulay (2019: 193) adds that 'Sanders' populist narrative provides agentive roles for his audience that are not realised in Trump's narrative'. In Sanders's discourse, there are also references to an 'other' which, contrary to the case of Trump, is *internal* to the American society. These references occur through the expressions *people on top*, *the billionaire class, Wall Street, corporate America, a handful of billionaires, oligarchs* and *the establishment* (economic, political and in the media). According to Staufer (2021: 234), Sanders's main antagonist is 'the billionaire class', 'whose schemes are aided and abetted by "establishment" politicians from both major American parties'. As in any other left-wing political programme, Sanders's aim is to include the excluded, that is, to create a political system that benefits the 99 per cent and not the 1 per cent only. The spot 'For All', from the 2019 campaign, revolves on inequality between 'the people' and 'the rich':

> Huge tax breaks for the rich while the middle class continues to struggle. That's what happens when billionaires are able to control the political system. Our campaign is funded by the working people of this country, those little people that I will represent. No more tax breaks for billionaires. We're gonna fight for equal pay, for equal work, healthcare for all of our people and a liveable wage. I am Bernie Sanders and I approve of this message because we need an economy that works for all of us, not just wealthy campaign contributors.[35]

To sum up, it seems hard to label Sanders's discourse and performances as neatly populist. They are rather a textbook example of a progressive, socialist and left-wing type of politics aiming at broader social inclusion and more equality within the scope of a national society. However, some of his utterances reveal the use of the Populist Narrative Structure. Labelling Sanders a populist evidences the challenges linked to the concept of populism: if it is used to refer to a specific historical ideology within the United States stemming from the People's Party, then Sanders reflects that ideology. However, in contemporary terms, 'populism' does not seem to be the right word to refer to a plebeian and popular type of politics located on the left side of the political continuum only. If *populism* is used to refer to a normative project of constructing 'a people' through the establishment of a chain of equivalences between demands that are *popular* – that is, revolving around 'the people' in any of the senses this word might have – then Sanders is a left-wing populist in the normative sense embraced by Mouffe (2018) and others.

However, if populism is approached as the discursive practice of using the Populist Narrative Structure as the basis for meaning-making, it seems harder to label Sanders a populist: although in his discourse there are elements that reflect the structure, its place within his broader meaning-making is limited compared to the salience of Sanders's progressive and social-democratic beliefs. These beliefs are present in the speech 'Democratic Socialism' that Sanders pronounced at Georgetown University on 19 November 2015 (Macaulay, 2019).

This chapter has demonstrated the challenges of identifying left-wing populism empirically. Although it might be clear what left-wing populism is in normative and in historical-ideological terms, it is not easy to disentangle the popular from the populist in specific discourses and texts uttered and produced by political actors on the Left. In spite of the challenges in distinguishing between the Left, popular/plebeian politics and left-wing populism, some commonalities arise between them, such as the criticism of capitalism, neoliberalism and globalization, together with the discursive construction of an 'other' that corresponds with a small and privileged sector of society that seems to be protected against the dynamics of neoliberal globalization. Moreover, as evidenced in the analyses of this chapter, depending on the salience of the populist component in a candidate's or party's discourse, it might seem more or less appropriate to refer to them as populist. By studying enunciation and examining the narrative emplotment, evidence was gathered regarding how populist political actors present themselves as populist leaders and, at the same time, as part of 'the people' (or not).

In spite of the challenges of distinguishing between discourses and performances revolving around 'the people' as leftist, popular/plebeian or populist, the discursive articulation of the Populist Narrative Structure with specific political contents culturally codified as being on the left side of the political spectrum allows a rapid identification of left-wing populists. In Spain, the discourse of Podemos does not differ much from the discourses of socialist or other left-wing parties in South America content-wise: social inclusion and recognition, more social equality, extension of rights for minorities and other egalitarian contents are also embraced by the Spanish political party. However, its use of the Populist Narrative Structure is salient compared to the South American cases studied in this chapter. Bernie Sanders also made claims in favour of those standard left-wing contents and policy issues. As argued, these contents are not populist *per se* but first and foremost leftist. What makes them populist is their framing by articulating them with the Populist Narrative Structure. In a nutshell, apart from popular/plebeian politics that are populist (Chávez, Podemos) or that can exhibit some degree of populism (Cristina Fernández, Sanders), there can be popular/plebeian politics that are not populist at all (Mujica) and populist politics that are not popular/plebeian (Trump, Le Pen).

In this sense, the study of left-wing populism in South America evidences the challenges linked to the concept of 'the people'. In a previous chapter, it was argued that translating the noun 'the people' into Spanish is challenging since a number of words could be used, like *pueblo* and *gente*. If they had been active in a Spanish-speaking context, would have Trump and Sanders used the same word to refer to 'the people'? South American politicians on the Left refer constantly to *el pueblo* but certainly not in the same sense Trump and Le Pen use the nouns *people* and *peuple*.

The Left's historical use of the political Subject 'the people' makes the distinction between the Left and populism not easy to establish. While the case of Sanders serves as an example of a left-wing project that uses a certain degree of populism for meaning-making, those of South American candidates and of Podemos demonstrate how the distinction between the Left's 'people' and populism's 'people' is not straightforward. This seems to be the reason why the Left embraced left-wing populism with a great degree of continuity, and why it was electorally successful: in building 'a people' following the logic of equivalence of unmet social demands identified by Laclau and Mouffe, democracy can be reinvigorated thanks to the reestablishment of 'a people' as democracy's ground. How the polysemic nature, openness and vagueness of the concept 'the people' facilitates this needs further examination.

To sum up, a semiotic approach to left-wing populism can shed light on the commonalities that this subtype of populism shares with right-wing populism, and also on how the empty signifier 'the people' might be filled with popular contents that can be hard to disentangle from the populist narrative framing. Although the specific political contents and 'others' that different left-wing populists construct in their discourses might differ, for a leftist movement to be populist there needs to be an evidence of the Populist Narrative Structure as underlying meaning-making. Otherwise, it might be a case of popular politics, radical Left or plebeianism, but not necessarily of populism.

Conclusion

The title *The Social Semiotics of Populism* refers to the two main objects of interest of the research presented in this book. In the first chapter, it was stated that the book aimed at putting Semiotics's conceptual and theoretical apparatus to the test with the purpose of finding out if it can be of use in clarifying the nature of populism. This is a goal that focuses on strengthening Semiotics's potential as a social science and, in particular, to position it as a discipline that can shed clear light on the dynamics of the political field (which has a constitutive discursive dimension).

Second, in that same chapter it was mentioned that the book's main objective was to shed new light on the challenging phenomenon of populism by examining how meaning-making occurs in the discourses and performances of populist political actors. As it was argued throughout the book, Semiotics's focus and methodology would be in a position to contribute to this perspective by throwing light on aspects of populist meaning-making that are usually not taken into account when approaching populism as a type of discourse or performative style. This is a goal that revolves around the phenomenon of populism.

Finally, throughout the book it was argued that political science and theory could profit from embracing Semiotics when dealing with discourse and meaning-making. It is the time to assess the semiotic approach to populism with a focus on how it contributes to (1) semiotic theory, (2) populism studies and (3) political science and theory.

It is a fact that over the last decades Semiotics has lost its popularity. It is currently hard to find departments or institutes of Semiotics within a university. Normally, semioticians work in departments and institutes of communication, linguistics, philosophy and other related social sciences and humanities. Nevertheless, in spite of its marginal position within the academic circles, Semiotics exists in the form of a discipline articulated around a vast and heterogeneous semiotic theory produced during the twentieth century. Moreover, *semiosis* and meaning-making – Semiotics's objects of study – are crucial for a number of disciplines and research traditions within the social sciences and humanities, as argued in Chapter 3.

One of the reasons why Semiotics is said to have lost its popularity is due to the complexity and obscurity of its theoretical apparatus. It is true that becoming proficient in semiotic theory implies dealing with concepts, arguments and a meta-language that require significant efforts and that are not always reader-friendly. Moreover, the lack of translations does not help in the attempts to grasp Semiotics in its broad heterogeneity and complexity. One first contribution of this book goes in that direction: it provides a general mapping of semiotic theory explained in a simple and accessible manner.

Moreover, it presents some of the key texts produced by semioticians working in English, French, Italian, Portuguese and Spanish.

To avoid the effect of an echo chamber in which jargon does not contribute to clarity, one of the possible ways to reposition Semiotics as a key social science consists in *applying* its theoretical and conceptual apparatus for the study of concrete objects. This is precisely what the vast majority of social semioticians discussed in Chapter 3 tend to do: they normally choose objects of study that can be approached by focusing on *semiosis* and meaning-making. Depending on their academic backgrounds, these researchers will use one or the other concept, tool or theory to make sense of what they are studying.

This book has been another attempt to do that: populism is an object of study that belongs to the political domain and that due to its social nature has an inherent discursive component. Therefore, the book aimed at exploring how Semiotics could shed light on the challenging phenomenon of populism. The difference of this book with the work of other semioticians is that it does not commit to a single semiotic tradition or theory but uses different concepts, methods and models to make sense of populist sense-making. This is a deliberate option that has advantages and disadvantages.

The aim of the book was not only to contribute to Semiotics and semio-political theory through the study of populism. Rather, it tried to demonstrate to students of populism how Semiotics can be of help in trying to articulate the different existing accounts on what populism is and, with that move, in making sense of populism as a political activity based on sense- and meaning-making. The semiotic approach to populism implies conceiving of sense- and meaning-making as a whole. Therefore, the ideological, performative, discursive and strategic are only *different dimensions* of a multifaceted social phenomenon. This purpose implied sacrificing semiotic rigour and depth: the authors, concepts and theories are presented in this book in a simplified and general manner. Some semioticians might even find the book too general due to its dealing with different semiotic traditions, concepts and tools and not committing to only one of them, as is the common practice.

This is a risk the author is willing to take. Semioticians know semiotic theory and, in case they are interested in studying populism, they will be in a position to make sense of this political phenomenon using the theories, methods and concepts of their preference. However, the situation is not the same for students of populism. Within populism studies, the discursive accounts are strongly anchored in the work of Laclau and the Essex school, which is a peculiar type of theory hard to categorize following the standard classification of the social sciences. In this sense, it is enlightening that Laclau's work is usually referred simply as 'discourse theory'.

The purpose of introducing semiotic theory to scholars, researchers and students of populism that might not be familiar with it was one of the main motivations in writing this book. The results are only the tip of an iceberg: Semiotics can do significantly more than what has been done in the previous eight chapters to shed light on populism. In fact, the semiotic analyses presented here are basic and generic: using the semiotic square to map the semantic organization of a given discourse, examining enunciation and narrative structures as evidenced in specific texts and using the concept of the semiosphere to approach how collective identities are constructed are basic operations that only *illustrate* what Semiotics could do to make sense of any social phenomenon. More could have been written on the aesthesic and emotional component of populist discourse, on the performativity of the populist leader, on the role of high- and low-cultural contents in populist performances, on the interactional dimension of populism, on the meanings conveyed by music when combined with the Populist Narrative Structure or on how populist discourse aims at producing alternative ways of conceiving democracy. As Greimas argued, individuals are embedded in meaning. This makes of Semiotics the discipline that can in principle study anything that is meaningful.

In particular, the study of populism from a semiotic perspective is expected to encourage political scientists, discourse analysts and other students of populism to think of populism in socio-semiotic terms, even if this does not occur in the form of an embracing of semiotic theory. Thinking of populism in socio-semiotic terms implies conceiving it above all as a *discursive practice* based on meaning-making, interactions between social actors and the circulation of social discourses that are meaningful thanks to their being part of a local cultural encyclopaedia or semiosphere. While this premise does not imply that populism is *only* discourse, it underlines the fact that it has a constitutive discursive dimension that can be studied through the lenses of semiotic theory. The discursive dimension of populism is not only expressed through words and language but also through the use of other semiotic resources such as music, audiovisual content, editing strategies, gestures, attire, use of objects and the creation of specific situations between the leader and the electorate. All these are objects of study that Semiotics is ready to deal with, with the purpose of understanding populist meaning-making.

In the previous chapter, it was argued that many of the theoretical challenges linked to populism stem from the meanings of the words *populism* and 'populist'. While some pragmatic uses of these words are not semantically accurate and reflect an intention to intervene in the political field – for example, when accusing someone of being a populist – other uses reveal the challenges linked to the semantics of the concept of 'the people'. An *-ism* of 'the people' makes sense for any competent user of language. However, what that concept actually means is a different story: as argued in these pages, 'the people' is an ambiguous and vague lexical unit based on an ancient word no longer in use and that is the root of other words that have specific meanings in different languages and contexts. As a discipline that merges semantics and pragmatics in its conception of meaning, Semiotics can also intervene in the debates regarding the concepts used to make sense of the social realm.

Besides how it can contribute to Semiotics as a discipline, this book aimed at producing new insights into the field of populism studies. In Chapter 1, it was argued that populism is better understood when conceived of as the discursive practice of producing meaning in the public sphere through the use of the Populist Narrative Structure. The structure of the book reflects the central role of the Populist Narrative Structure in studying populism. Moreover, the empirical analyses included in Chapters 6, 7 and 8 focus on identifying how the structure is evidenced in specific texts and cultural products. The working principle of those analyses has been the following: if the structure is somehow present, then the text/product is populist; if it is not, then it is not, although it might be popular, plebeian or any other type of people-centred politics.

Even if it provides a clear criterion to identify populism and to distinguish it from other discursive phenomena, this is a problematic – and arbitrary – claim. Actually, populism could be a political ideology, as Tarragoni (2021) and others argue. To understand the internal logics of the populist ideology, Tarragoni's genetic approach should be used to discover what is it that all populisms – past and present – have in common. This is an enormous task that implies dealing with texts – speeches, manifestos, advertisements and so on – from different times and latitudes. According to the theses presented in this book, only those texts that evidence the use of the Populist Narrative Structure as the ground for meaning-making would be legitimately populist. 'Other' might be popular, plebeianist or people-centric but not populist.

This statement is problematic because it might be wrong. It might be the case that it is not the Populist Narrative Structure what renders a discourse or text populist. It might be that populism actually is about mobilizing the masses and charismatic leadership, independently of how that is achieved in the discursive dimension. If populism is approached from a sociological perspective, then the Populist Narrative Structure might in fact not be a necessary condition for populism to exist. What is the point of insisting so much in the centrality of the structure to define populism?

In spite of its origins in the nineteenth century as an ideology, populism is a concept used nowadays to make sense of a broad spectrum of political phenomena. In this sense, the question 'What is populism?' should be put on hold until a previous question is answered: 'What does *populism* mean?' As it was argued in the previous pages, in 2023 the term 'populism' has a broad semantic field that encompasses diverse meanings. Populism can be found on the right and on the left sides of the political spectrum. Moreover, it can be regarded as a threat to democracy or as something positive for it. It can also be a synonym of popular/plebeian politics, demagoguery or even authoritarianism.

Therefore, the thesis that equals populism with the presence of the Populist Narrative Structure is not universal but contingent: it only points out to the fact that nowadays, the labels *populism* and *populist* seem to be used in a sense that reflects that equivalence. If Trump, Le Pen, Chávez and Podemos are all labelled as populists, this is because their discourses and performances evidence the use of the Populist Narrative Structure. Even if scholars of populism might have reached this conclusion intuitively, up to now nobody has formulated this thesis by recurring to the analytical category of 'narrative structure'.

Even if it is the case that populism does not depend on the use of the Populist Narrative Structure and is simply a type of politics revolving around 'the people' that aims at mobilizing the masses, even if a dichotomization of society and polarization are not necessary conditions for populism to occur, even if 'the people's other' is 'the elite' and 'the elite' only, this book has shed light on some structural properties of discourses and performances said to be populist. Due to its broad focus on meaning- and sense-making, it has demonstrated how words, gesture, attire, music, a narrative tempo, editing strategies and other semiotic resources can be used to convey meanings. Moreover, the book has tried to demonstrate how the adjective *populist* might be mistakenly used to refer to phenomena that are people-centric, popular, plebeianist, ethno-popular and that polarize society, when there are differences in how political actors construct the social reality in their discourses and performances between these political discourses and populism.

In this sense, this book has evidenced the challenges of populism as a polysemic concept anchored in the Roman lexical unit *populus*. As argued in a previous chapter, something popular can be many things. Hence, popular politics can also take many forms. In any case, there is no doubt that populism is a political phenomenon anchored in meaning-making and interactions. As any social activity, doing populist – but also popular, plebeianist and other types of – politics implies mobilizing semiotic resources in the public sphere to produce effects of sense that have a cognitive and emotional impact on individuals. Semiotics – and particular social Semiotics – can help shedding light in how meaning-making occurs and how populist discourse is meaningful to the point of mobilizing the electorate.

Specifically, by examining diverse texts enunciated by political actors said to be populist, the 'absent structure' called 'Populist Narrative Structure' was identified as the common mould shared by populist actors from different regions for meaning-making. In line with the argument presented in these pages, populism could be defined from a semiotic perspective as *the discursive practice by means of which a social actor – individual or collective – produces meaning within the political field by using the Populist Narrative Structure as the articulating narrative principle for meaning- and sense-making. The structure opposes in an antagonistic relationship the collective identity 'the people' against another collective identity, which is defined in semantic terms as 'not-the-people' and that might take different forms depending on the context.*

Three conclusions follow from this definition. In the first place – and in line with Laclau's thesis – populism is a formal phenomenon that is filled with contents depending on the political semiosphere where it is performed. Therefore, studying populism requires immersing oneself in that semiosphere to unveil how a political actor uses pre-existing contents and semiotic resources to produce effects of sense. For example, it would be challenging to assess Cristina Fernández's populism without being familiar with Peronism and Kirchnerism, two social discourses with a wide circulation in the Argentinean political sphere. Researchers of populism must, therefore, conduct 'thick descriptions' (Geertz, 1973); that is, they must make sense of a political actor's meaning-making through an immersion in their semiospheres and understanding how political meanings are relevant within it. In this sense, populism could be certainly conceived as a thin-centred ideology, whose meaning depends on the contents used to fill it. It is precisely this formal – or *thin* – aspect what allows populism to exist both on the Right and on the Left: although right-wing and left-wing populism differ in their nature and scope, they are forms of populism (as defined here).

The second conclusion is that almost every aspect of the definition of populism presented in these pages has already been identified by scholars who have studied it. The semiotic definition of populism is based on the works of Mudde, Laclau, Mouffe, Panizza, Aslanidis, De Cleen, Stavrakakis, Casullo and many others, in the sense that their works include theses, intuitions and insights that are defining of what populism is from a semiotic perspective. However, while the conceptions of populism these authors put forward stem from their personal and academic backgrounds, the one presented here is grounded on the semiotic research tradition: by departing from Greimas's notion of structure, it was argued how all these authors have identified aspects of the Populist Narrative Structure but only a few – namely, Aslanidis and Casullo – moved into the direction of seeing that structure as a *frame* or *myth*. If there is a gain in rewriting a definition that was already consensual within populism studies, that is its acknowledgement of *the centrality of the narrative dimension of populism* based on a structuralist premise. Moreover, this definition also poses that the essence of populism is not in the presence of the 'the people' as *a signifier* in political discourse but as a *semantic unit:* a discourse can be populist even if it does not speak directly of 'the people' but as long as its meaning-making is grounded in the assumption of the existence of 'the people'.

Last but not least, a third relevant conclusion seems to be that it might not be appropriate to label political actors, parties and movements as *populist*. Rather, texts and cultural products can be populist depending on if they were created anchored in the Populist Narrative Structure or not. Labelling a political actor 'populist' is a common trend to categorize and simplify reality that might not be theoretically accurate. Political actors can produce some texts that are populist in some occasions, and others that are of a different nature in other occasions. Depending on the presence or not of the Populist Narrative Structure, a text can be classified as populist or not.

Populism would, therefore, be a matter of *degree*, as some scholars argue (Diehl, 2017; De Cleen, 2019). Specifically, it would be a matter of degree *as evidenced in specific texts*. Therefore, it would be more accurate to speak of the 'populist component' of a political text or product rather than labelling it with the totalizing adjective *populist*. In this sense, if a politician is said to be populist, then this would mean that his/her discourse and performances show a tendency to base meaning-making in the Populist Narrative Structure.

The semiotic definition of populism leaves the normative dimension aside. Therefore, Semiotics can provide an objective and descriptive criterion to identify the populist component of specific discourses and performances. Every researcher might have his/her own opinion regarding the effect of the Populist Narrative Structure in shaping the political field and, with it, social reality. However, studying populism does not imply that researchers must take a normative posture. A quote of Panizza (2005: 30) seems enlightening in this sense: 'by raising awkward questions about modern forms of democracy, and often representing the ugly face of the people, populism is neither the highest form of democracy nor its enemy, but a mirror in which democracy can contemplate itself, warts and all, and find out what it is about and what it is lacking'. Understanding the dynamics of sense- and meaning-making that define populist discourse is a first task to accomplish before engaging in the normative debate. The social Semiotics of populism is, therefore, a useful tool to justify a normative stance on this political phenomenon.

Besides its contributions to semiotic theory and populism studies, this book tried with some insistence to demonstrate how Laclau's discourse theory and his theory of populism – as well as those put forward by scholars who work within his theoretical framework – have an inherent semiotic nature. The hegemonic position of Laclau's work in populism studies – and, more broadly, in political science and theory when a discursive perspective is chosen to study political phenomena – is a contingent fact that can be corrected. Political phenomena – including populism – can be approached from a discursive perspective without having to accept Laclau's complex, obscure and even metaphysical premises and theoretical positions. In this sense, Chapters 4 and 5 attempted at 'de-Laclauizing' Laclau's discursive approach to the political and to populism by focusing on meaning-making and *semiosis*. Semiotics is a discipline with a history of theory building rather than the world view of a single author. Therefore, its concepts and tools can be handy in making sense of the political when approached from a discursive perspective.

That said, a Semiotics of the political is a discipline that still needs to be constructed. As demonstrated in Chapter 4, there have been some relevant inputs in making sense of the political from a semiotic perspective. Nevertheless, there is work to be done not only in theoretical but also in methodological terms. This book has been a contribution in that direction.

Notes

Chapter 1

1 As any other continuum that is made sense of through the intervention of culture, time can be segmented in meaningful units to explain historic progression in narrative terms. The idea of a 'political present' is hence an abstraction that serves to affirm a 'now' that is continuous, *in vivo* and coincides with the moment of analysis, in opposition to a past – which is closed and previous to the moment of analysis – and a future – which is mere potentiality and posterior to the moment of analysis. In these lines, the *political* present is an analytical category used to denote the idea that in the present, the political domain evidences certain traits that were not present in previous historical eras and that somehow define the unity of our historical moment. Cf. Benveniste (1974) and Moreno Barreneche (2022).

2 Advancing the argument presented in these pages, this book conceives of populism as the discursive practice characterized by the use of a specific narrative structure: the Populist Narrative Structure. This structure is used by political actors within the political field as a frame for meaning- and sense-making and can be filled with specific contents depending on the context of use. This approach to populism would certainly allow conceiving of populism as a phenomenon present in Antiquity and historical eras other than the contemporary.

3 To add more evidence to the argument regarding the salience of populism in our present time, some editorial facts seem to confirm the theoretical interest in the issue: it was only in 2017 that Oxford University Press published the volumes *Populism. A Very Short Introduction* (Mudde & Rovira Kaltwasser, 2017) and *The Oxford Handbook of Populism*, edited by C. Rovira Kaltwasser, P. Taggart, P. Ochoa Espejo & P. Ostiguy (2017). On that same year, Nomos published the volume *Political Populism. A Handbook*, edited by R. Heinisch, C. Holtz-Bacha & O. Mazzoleni (2017). Finally, in 2022 Palgrave published *The Palgrave Handbook of Populism*, edited by Michael Oswald (2022).

4 Federico Tarragoni (2021: 10–11) claims that it is a-historical to qualify these experiences as populist because these presidents did not extend the democratization projects of their predecessors, but rather did the opposite by embracing free-market policies. According to the sociologist, the fact that scholars refer to those presidents as a 'second tide' of Latin American populism is based on the salience of the personality of the political actors and the 'omnipotence of their executives'. Carlos Vilas (2004) presents a similar argument.

5 Source: https://www.cam.ac.uk/news/populism-revealed-as-2017-word-of-the-year-by-cambridge-university-press#:~:text=The%20word%20'populism'%20has%20been,2017%20Word%20of%20the%20Year.

6 Source: https://www.politico.com/video/2016/06/obama-im-the-real-populist-not-trump-059801
7 Source: https://www.lexpress.fr/actualite/politique/melenchon-populiste-moi-j-assume_919603.html
8 It should be noticed that Carola Schoor (2021) has recently explored the possibility of using Greimas's theoretical framework to make sense of populism as a political style. However, her study focuses on making sense of the *concept* of populism through opposing it to elitism and pluralism, and not in using Semiotics to make sense of populist discourse as a discursive practice, which is the purpose of this book.
9 To mention only one example of how this book became the starting point for any research on populism, the first chapter of Ernesto Laclau's *On Populist Reason* (2005a) criticizes the articles by MacRae, Wiles and Minogue compiled in the volume.
10 The Russian noun *narod* [народ] can be translated in English as 'a people' in the sense of a group that is somehow bounded as a constituent nation. In other Slavic languages, the noun can be used as the basis for an adjective to refer to something that conflates the popular, the national and the folk, such as *narodni* in Croatian.

Chapter 2

1 According to Mary Beard (2015: 36), 'the "people" was a much larger and amorphous body than the senate, made up, in political terms, of all male Roman citizens [. . .] In 63 BCE that was around a million men spread across the capital and throughout Italy, as well as a few beyond. In practice, it usually comprised the few thousands of the few hundred who, on any particular occasion, chose to turn up to elections, votes or meetings in the city of Rome. Exactly how influential the people were has always [. . .] been one of the big controversies of Roman history'.
2 In this sense, one of the overarching motivations of writing this book is to provide political scientists and theorists with an alternative when approaching the political field with a focus on discourse and meaning-making.
3 The adjective 'post-Laclauian' evidences the centrality of Laclau's theory within populism studies. One of the general objectives of this book is to demonstrate how Semiotics is a more solid, robust and appropriate discipline than the work of an author – and his disciples – to approach political phenomena with a focus on discourse and meaning-making.
4 Regarding simplicity, it is not exclusive of populism: as Arditi (2005: 79) argues, 'a populist persuasion built on the strength of a simple and direct language, which entails a reduction of the complexity of the issues presented to the electorate, also seems to be characteristic of the contemporary politics generally'. On simplicity, cf. Cosenza (2018).
5 The idea of a 'structure of feelings' is relevant for Semiotics because it deals with affect. As is argued in the following chapter, Semiotics is not only interested in how texts are meaningful but also in how individuals grasp meaning from them in cognitive and affective terms. On populism and emotions, cf. Cossarini & Vallespín (2019).
6 In these accounts, the concept of *strategy* is not clear enough from a perspective interested in meaning-making. As Aslanidis (2016: 97) argues, 'if we simply lump together every type of political behavior under "strategy", we sacrifice conceptual refinement and equate populism with demagoguery, the tendency to overpromise

and "say what the people want to hear."' Moreover, as argued by semiotician Jacques Fontanille (2008) *strategies* are another type of semiotic production, together with signs, texts, objects, practices and 'forms of life'. In semiotic terms, strategies can only be accessed through the analysis of discourses and performances by political actors, parties and movements and are also 'absent structures' postulated by the analyst as a coherent principle that guides action instrumentally. The same occurs with ideologies, which are normative articulations of meaning that can be accessed only through the analysis of discourse.

7   Even if the term 'ideology' is not used in Freeden's sense, semioticians and discourse analysts and theorists have challenged the distinction between discourse and ideology and argued that every discourse is ideological and that ideology is a discursive device. Cf. Eco (1976).
8   Recent scholarship argues that populism can also exist without a populist leader. The Belgian party Vlaams Belang and the German Alternative für Deutschland are frequently used as examples of populism without clear and visible leaders. If populism is conceived as the discursive practice of using the Populist Narrative Structure as the master frame for meaning-making within the political, then this thesis is acceptable. Nevertheless, it is true that due to the media attention they attract, populist leaders are key players in performing populism within the political field.

Chapter 3

1   Some semioticians see the first step in the consolidation of Semiotics as an autonomous discipline in a book by Algirdas Greimas (1986) entitled *Sémantique structurale*, from 1966. In English, the word 'meaning' covers a broad semantic field, making the distinction between how Semantics and Semiotics approach it. In Spanish, Semantics could be defined as the study of *significado* [meaning] and Semiotics as the study of *sentido* [sense] or *significación* [meaning-making/signification]. The correspondent terms in French would be *signifié* [meaning] for Semantics and *sens* and *signification* for Semiotics.
2   Source: https://www.oxfordlearnersdictionaries.com/definition/english/semiotics?q =semiotics
3   This disciplinary construction occurred by drawing on the advances and developments within other neighbouring social disciplines. As argued by Eco (1976: 6), a semiotic approach 'may try to incorporate the results of these disciplines and to redefine them within its own theoretical framework'.
4   Although there are multiple associations, conferences and journals that include the word 'semiotics' in their names, departments and institutes of Semiotics are scarce and studying the semiotics of things is usually an enterprise of interest for scholars from various disciplines other than Semiotics, like linguistics, philosophy, social psychology, sociology, anthropology, literary studies, media studies, marketing, and communication science among others (Chandler, 2017: 3–4).
5   The thesis that poses that the relationship between signifier and signified is arbitrary has been questioned by linguists (Benveniste, 1966: 49–55) and discourse theorists (Laclau & Mouffe, 2001).
6   In Saussure's theory, Linguistics is the general pattern to study *any* sign-system, linguistic or not (Chandler, 2017; Deely, 2015; Eco, 1976).

7   According to Hjelmslev, each of those planes has a *substance*, a *matter* and a *form*.
8   As is argued in Chapter 5, the semiotic square helps visualize an interesting aspect of populist discourse: those who are normally presented in populist discourse as not being part of 'the people' do not coincide in logical terms with the position of the 'other' (e.g. 'the elite'). In logical terms, those depicted in discourse as not part of the category of 'the people' should fall under the category of 'not-the-people', that is, in a relationship of *contradiction* and not of *contrariety*. As is argued in Chapter 5, due to the dynamics of social discursivity, meaning-making is more effective when working with positive rather than with negative categories. Hence, the empty semantic unit 'not-the-people' is filled with content through an equivalence with 'the people's' *contrary* instead of its *contradictory* term.
9   The adjectives *social* and *cultural* are normally used to emphasize some risks that a general Semiotics might be faced to if it focuses only in texts as closed and stable entities and leaves aside the sociocultural dimension of *semiosis*. This is something that characterized linguistic scholarship for decades following Saussure's exclusive focus on *langue* (the signs system) over *parole* (language in use by real individuals). As a result of the dominant focus on an immanentist study of texts, the pragmatic dimension of meaning and sense was largely ignored until recent times. This dimension is constitutive of meaning-making (Paolucci, 2021a).
10 As an example of how social practices and objects connote specific meanings coded in culture, one could think of drinks and cocktails and how they connote meanings revolving around the axes of masculinity-femininity, extroversion-introversion and elegance-ordinariness, among others. Cf. Manning (2012).
11 Floch, Landowski and Fontanille are only three of many semioticians that work following Greimas's legacy. Some other relevant names are Juan Alonso Aldama, Pierluigi Basso Fossali, Denis Bertrand, Anne Beyaert-Geslin, Marion Colas-Blaise, Joseph Courtés, Ivan Darrault-Harris, Maria Giulia Dondero, Verónica Estay Stange, Manar Hammad, Anne Hénault and Claude Zilberberg, among many others. Cf. Hénault (2002; 2012).
12 In fact, many of the few existing studies of populism from a semiotic perspective have been conducted by Italian semioticians (Sedda & Demuru, 2018a, 2018b, 2019; Demuru, 2021a; 2021b; Cervelli, 2018; Addis, 2020).
13 Italian Semiotics has produced some crucial journals where semiotic research is regularly published. These are Versus, Lexia, E/C and Carte Semiotiche.
14 If it is challenging to summarize the French research tradition, even more is to do it with the Italian tradition since researchers in Italy follow diverse influences (Greimas, Eco, Lotman, etc.) and have focused on diverse and heterogeneous objects of study. Other Italian semioticians besides Eco, Fabbri and Paolucci that have studied sociocultural phenomena are Maria Cristina Addis, Omar Calabrese, Giovanna Cosenza, Cristina Demaria, Paolo Demuru, Alice Giannitrapani, Tarcisio Lancioni, Massimo Leone, Anna Maria Lorusso, Dario Mangano, Francesco Mangiapane, Gianfranco Marrone, Francesco Marsciani, Francesco Mazzucchelli, Tiziana Migliore, Paolo Peverini, Isabella Pezzini, Maria Pia Pozzato, Fransiscu Sedda, Lucio Spaziante, Simona Stano, Ilaria Ventura Bordenca, Ugo Volli and Patrizia Violi, among many other researchers mainly affiliated to the universities of Bologna, Palermo, Siena and Turin, among others.
15 The lack of translations constitutes a crucial problem within semiotic scholarship. Although this has changed over the past years, French scholars usually write in French, Italians in Italian, and so on. As an example, none of Landowski's books are available in English.

16 Concomitantly to the growth of Semiotics as a social science during the second half of the twentieth century, developments in the fields of linguistics, political theory and other social and human sciences also became interested in *semiosis* and meaning-making. Therefore, they came closer to the object of study that gives Semiotics its disciplinary identity. As a result, accounts such as Critical Discourse Analysis (Wodak & Meyer, 2001) and other approaches to discursive practices (Zienkowski, 2017) are often closely related to that of Semiotics. Although they are interested in similar phenomena and share some epistemological tenets – for example, constructivism – they differ in *how* they approach *semiosis* and meaning-making.

17 While Laclau and Mouffe elaborated their discourse theory together (Laclau & Mouffe, 2001), their theories of populism should not be considered unitary. Here they are dealt with in a unified manner to simply the exposition.

18 Laclau and Mouffe share this constructivist premise. The authors identify *class essentialism* as one of Marxism's main problems after 1968, that is, the belief that 'political identities were the expression of the position of the social agents in the relations of production and their interest were defined by this position' (Mouffe, 2018: 2).

Chapter 4

1 This distinction is purely analytical and does not necessarily imply that politics is about consensus *or* conflict exclusively. As every analytical distinction, it helps visualize the existing conceptions of what politics and the political are about.

2 A good example of the problems of not finding agreement is that of Belgium, a country that between 2018 and 2020 remained without a government for 592 days because the parties did not achieve an agreement to form one.

3 This option can certainly be a source of disagreement, as Mouffe's theoretical work is part of a normative project that aims at revitalizing the political Left. In what follows, her account is taken into consideration because it serves as a good starting point to present a theory of the political that has multiple commonalities with what semioticians have written and said about this social field.

4 Within Semiotics, some recent journal issues revolve around political discourse and communication, such as Carte Semiotiche Annali 6, Punctum 6(2) and DeSignis 33.

5 Here is an illustrative example of how this logic functions within the political field: when a new political party becomes relevant within a political system, the system needs to accommodate to the presence of that new actor. Therefore, existing political parties will most probably have to redefine the meanings linked to their identities, normally through a distancing from the new party. This is where relations, oppositions and differences are in play.

6 This mechanism explains why in Uruguayan culture attending a wedding requires that men wear a suit and a tie, whereas in Austrian culture it is acceptable for men to attend a wedding wearing traditional *Trachten*.

7 Selg and Ventsel (2020) argue that Laclau and Mouffe ignored Semiotics as a strategic move given that, at the time the book was published, poststructuralism was catchier and, therefore, they preferred to engage with it rather than with Semiotics, grounded on a structural premise.

8 As an example: it is only through the analysis of concrete poems identified as 'modernist' that the social discourse of modernism, which gives place to specific stylistic strategies and texts, can be accessed.

9. Hubé and Truan (2016: 187) quote a study by Mayaffre that revolves around Nicolas Sarkozy's use of language, where he discovered that 'the use of the pronouns *on* [one] and *ça* [it] are representative of the populist distinction between an indefinite, vague threat and a vigorous "I", which creates the ethos of a powerful politician'. This reflects Benveniste's deictic account of enunciation, which has been used by researchers in the analysis of political enunciation. Cf. Benveniste (1966: 1974), Scavino (2020).
10. For Charaudeau (2014), these are legitimacy, credibility and adherence.
11. The Brazilian folkloric dance of *capoeira* is a good example of this interactional regime. Cf. Demuru (2015).
12. The ideas developed in this section are presented with greater detail in Moreno Barreneche (2020c).
13. For a more detailed argument on the concept of collective identities from a semiotic perspective, cf. Montoro and Moreno Barreneche (2021a; 2021b).
14. The idea of establishing frontiers and setting boundaries between collective identities is discussed with greater detail in the next chapter, notably by drawing on Laclau's theory of populism and on Lotman's concept of *semiosphere*.
15. Appiah (2018) calls these statements *generics*.

Chapter 5

1. *The social* can be defined following Jan Zienkowski (2017: 51) as the ensemble of 'all identities, relationships and practices that provide a more or less stable ground for our ideological presuppositions and daily practices'.
2. This logic can be clearly seen in action when, after the 9/11 terrorist attacks in the United States, George W. Busch said: 'Either you are with us, or with the terrorists' (Panizza, 2005: 6). Political spheres from countries that are strongly divided in two sides through a discursive and ideological gap (such as Argentina or Brazil) are also examples of the hegemony of this interpretative scheme.
3. This conception of the Populist Narrative Structure reflects Greimas's (1986: 19) first definition of *structure* as presented in his book *Sémantique structurale*: 'the presence of two terms and a relationship between them' [*présence de deux termes et de la relation entre eux*]. According to Greimas, these terms are not meaningful in themselves but need the relationship as a necessary condition for them to be meaningful.
4. Laclau (2005a: 117) writes that 'by "populism" we do not understand a *type* of movement – identifiable with either a special social base or a particular ideological orientation – but a *political logic*. All the attempts at finding what is idiosyncratic in populism in elements such as a peasant or small-ownership constituency, or resistance to economic modernization, or manipulation by marginalized elites are [. . .] essentially flawed: they will always be overwhelmed by an avalanche of exceptions'.
5. As Panizza (2005: 6–9) argues, George W. Bush's discourse after the 9/11 terrorist attacks constructed an intangible enemy to strengthen the US identity as a single people that is being threatened by an external danger. For a semiotic analysis of Bush's discourse as opposed to Obama's, cf. Cosenza (2018, chapter 5). For Hawkins (2009: 1058), 'it is probably not helpful to consider Bush's discourse as populist, although it can certainly be considered as antagonistic'.
6. Source: https://www.youtube.com/watch?v=j2nULN8sCDc

7 Pappas (2019a: 83), for his part, identifies three notions of the uses of 'the people' in populist discourse: (1) the little people (in Southern Europe, Eastern Europe and Latin America), (2) the common people (in the United States) and (3) the equitable native people (in Northern and Western Europe). On a footnote, he writes that he prefers to leave aside the fourth notion of the people-as-nation, 'as it is more appropriate for the study of nationalism'.
8 Labelling cultural products as 'popular' proves particularly challenging: a song, musical genre or movie might be 'popular' in the sense of being pop, mainstream or commercially successful but not in the sense of being rooted in the folkloric traditions of a group. Context also plays a role here: the signifier *popular music* does not mean the same in Mexico than in the United States.
9 Gottlob Frege (2008) referred to this issue in his seminal essay *Über Sinn und Bedeutung*. According to Frege, the expression *the will of the people* [*der Wille des Volkes*] is not referential, although it is a formula frequently used in political discourse. One of the main challenges of contemporary populism was already addressed at the end of the nineteenth century by the founder of modern philosophy of language.
10 This logic of equivalence could be graphically represented by identifying *subgroups* within the inner circle of Figure 8.
11 Oscar Reyes (2005: 104) argues that with this move, 'the specificity of populism is altogether lost and it simply collapses into a species of nationalism'.
12 On this, Pappas (2019a: 82) believes that 'the people seldom forms a natural majority of individuals sharing objective and inalienable characteristics like class, religion, race, language, or geography, on the basis of which one can tell apart poor from rich, Catholics from Protestants, whites from colored people, southerners from northerners, etc. It follows, then, that it falls upon populist leaders and other political entrepreneurs to artificially construct, and subsequently forge, the category of "the people" within specific historical circumstances'.
13 Original text in Spanish: 'Querido pueblo: ¡gracias! Gracias por tus abrazos, gracias por tus críticas, gracias por tu cariño y, sobre todo, gracias por tu hondo compañerismo cada una de las veces que me sentí solo en el medio de la Presidencia.' Source: https://www.youtube.com/watch?v=TM7G95k2sj0
14 Chapter 8 discusses with more depth the distinction between *populist* and *popular* politics.
15 Specific occurrences of populist discourse might also combine these two aspects. The case of Venezuela's Hugo Chávez and Nicolás Maduro is interesting in this sense, as they refer both to the Venezuelan elites and the United States as the 'other', opposed to which 'the Venezuelan people' gains identity.

Chapter 6

1 In spite of the salience of populist leaders and their relevance for making sense of populism, it has also been argued (Panizza, 2005: 18) that a strong personalistic and highly charismatic leader is not a necessary defining feature of populism. Within the scope of the thesis discussed in this book, any enunciator – an individual, a group of individuals, an organization – that recurs to the Populist Narrative Structure to produce meaning could be identified as a populist. In fact, there are parties labelled as populist that do not have a unique and highly visible human face to be said to be its

leader, such as Vlaams Belang (Belgium) and Alternative für Deutschland (Germany) are frequently studied as populist political parties.

2. The extension of linguistic analysis to contemplate also texts of a visual nature is one of the defining features of English social Semiotics as practiced by van Leeuwen, Kress, Hodge, Machin and others. That is why the concept of *multimodality* is so relevant within this research account.

3. Here, the meaning that can be grasped is not so much in the sense that could be translated into Spanish as *significado* and in German as *Bedeutung* but rather in the sense of what in Spanish would be *sentido* and in German *Sinn*. In events where co-presence is a constitutive factor, meaning-making has an aesthesic and emotional component that trumps the pure cognitive decoding of meaning as *significado*. The study of emotions and passions is crucial in making sense of these situations.

4. Demuru (2021a: 524) explains that the concept of *aesthesis* was introduced in Semiotics to refer to 'the role of the senses, as well as polisensoriality and synaesthesia, in the construction of meaning'.

5. Jagers and Walgrave (2007: 323) define populism as a communication style used by political actors, but they indistinctly refer to it as 'a strategy to mobilize support' and as 'a master frame'. There are relevant differences in conceiving something as a frame and as a style: while the frame operates at the cognitive level, the style does at the performative level.

6. Source: https://edition.cnn.com/videos/politics/2018/03/10/trump-pennsylvania-speech-mocking-presidential-sot.cnn

7. Original text in Italian: 'Renzi mi ha attaccato e ha detto che sono un populista. Sì, ne sono orgoglioso, se essere populista significa essere in mezzo alla gente e cercare di risolvere i suoi problemi. Preferisco ascoltare la gente normale che risolvere i problemi di bancheri e finanzieri.' In line with the argument presented in Chapter 5, note how Salvini uses the Italian word *gente* rather than *popolo*.

8. For an interesting comment on Salvini's use of *common sense*, cf. https://www.huffingtonpost.it/gianluca-passarelli/il-non-senso-del-buonsenso-salvini-l-italia-e-il-sogno-autocratico_a_23634057/

9. Original text in Spanish: 'No olvide nadie que nosotros estamos enfrentando al mismísimo diablo, el domingo 3 de diciembre enfrentaremos en las urnas electorales al gobierno imperialista de Estados Unidos de Norteamérica, ese es nuestro verdadero adversario, no son estos bate quebrados de aquí, los lacayos del imperialismo [. . .] Ustedes, pueblo, son el gigante que despertó, yo diminuto soldado de ustedes sólo haré lo que ustedes digan. ¡Estoy a la orden de ustedes para seguir abriendo el camino a la Patria grande, buena y bonita! [. . .] Porque ustedes no van a reelegir a Chávez en verdad, ustedes se van a reelegir a ustedes mismos, el pueblo va a reelegir al pueblo. Chávez no es sino un instrumento del pueblo.' Source to the full text in Spanish: https://rebelion.org/esta-victoria-se-la-vamos-a-dedicar-a-los-50-anos-de-la-llegada-del-barco-revolucionario-gramma-a-cuba/

Chapter 7

1. It is actually hard to find manifestations of populism that do not refer to 'the elite' or 'the establishment' at all. However, thanks to the logic of equivalence discussed in Chapter 5, how 'the people's other' is constructed in discourse might vary depending

on the presence and salience of positive contents to fill the semantic unit 'not-the-people', which is defined in logical terms as a negation of 'the people'.
2 Therefore, a similar study to the one presented here can be envisaged revolving around how the Nationalist Narrative Structure is brought to life by political actors across time and space. Moreover, it would be interesting to study how the Populist and the Nationalist Narrative Structures are actually combined in the discourses and performances of right-wing populist political actors. Sections 7.3 and 7.4 partially do that.
3 'Clip de campagne officiel – Marine 2017'. Source: https://www.youtube.com/watch?v=FYWnuQc5mYA
4 Original text in French: 'D'aussi loin que je me souvienne, j'ai toujours senti un rattachement viscéral, passionnel à notre pays, à son histoire. J'aime la France. J'aime du plus profond de mon cœur, du plus profond du mon âme, cette nation millénaire qui ne se soumet pas, ce peuple impétueux qui ne renonce pas. Je suis une femme, et comme femme je ressens comme une violence extrême les restrictions des libertés qui se multiplient dans tout notre pays à travers le développent du fondamentalisme islamiste. Je suis une mère, et comme des millions de parents je m'inquiète chaque jour de l'état du pays et du monde que nous laisserons en héritage à nos enfants. Je suis une avocat, et j'ai gardé de mes années de barreau un attachement profond au respect des libertés publiques, et un sensibilité particulière au sort des victimes confrontées à l'impunité des criminels. Au fond, si je devais me définir je crois que je répondrais tout simplement que je suis intensément, fièrement, fidèlement, évidemment française. Je reçois les insultes à la France comme si elles m'étaient adressées directement. Qu'il s'agisse de l'insécurité et des violences ou de la misère qui touche de trop nombreux compatriotes je ressens les souffrances des Français comme autant des souffrances personnelles.

Le choix que vous ferais lors de l'élection présidentielle à venir est crucial, fondamental. C'est un véritable choix de civilisation. Soit vous continuez avec ceux qui ont menti, failli, trahi, qui ont égaré le peuple et perdu la France, soit vous décidez de remettre la France en ordre. Oui, je veux remettre la France en ordre. Je veux que les français puissent vivre libres dans une France indépendante. Je veux que les français puissent vivre en sécurité dans une France respectée. Je veux que les français puissent vivre protégés dans une France prospère. Je veux que les français puissent vivre unis dans une France fière. Je veux que les français puissent bien vivre dans une France durable. Je veux que les français puissent vivre leurs rêves dans une France juste! C'est tout le sens de mon engagement. C'est ce pour quoi je me bats, c'est le projet que je mettrais en ouvre à la tête de l'Etat, en votre nom, au nom du peuple.'
5 In the spot for the second round of the 2017 presidential election, Le Pen declares that 'choosing France means recovering our independence, protecting our way of life and rejecting mass immigration, communitarianism and Islamist fundamentalism'. The strategy of othering underlying this chain of equivalence draws a clear boundary between a French 'we' and the threats posed by an external 'they', which is defined at the level of the deep structures as those that are not aligned with the 'French way of life'. Source: https://www.youtube.com/watch?v=N6t5qjd01qA
6 The *internal* 'other' is clearly the group of those who lied, failed and betrayed. Islamic fundamentalism, albeit originally an *external* force 'imported' intro the historically Christian and currently secular French nation, is depicted in Le Pen's discourse as also *internal* to French society – albeit not to the French nation. That is why it constitutes a problem according to Le Pen's worldview as expressed in her discourse.

7 '"J'ai besoin de Marine" | Marine 2017'. Source: https://www.youtube.com/watch?v=KfDD8fnm6bE
8 'Déclaration du Louvre | Faites l'élection présidentielle | M La France'. Source: https://www.youtube.com/watch?v=l7Tp8gtUSEs
9 'Break in'. Source: https://www.youtube.com/watch?v=moZOrq0qL3Q
10 'Abolished'. Source: https://www.youtube.com/watch?v=AOOlOMLaFho
11 'You won't be safe in Joe Biden's America'. Source: https://www.youtube.com/watch?v=JK6K-sWTAtM
12 Interestingly, in a TV spot entitled 'Carefully' that informs about Trump's recovery of Covid-19, the message is: 'We live carefully, but we are not afraid.' The idea seems to be that, when the populist leader is in charge, fear is not part of the equation. Source: https://www.youtube.com/watch?v=emnCFyi5cuQ
13 'America First'. Source: https://www.youtube.com/watch?v=glWS3vAVhJU
14 'Donald Trump's Argument for America'. Source: https://www.c-span.org/video/?418167-101/trump-presidential-campaign-ad
15 As discussed in the following chapter, the same strategy is used by other politicians of 'the people' – *populist* or *popular*, as argued in that chapter – like Bernie Sanders, Evo Morales and José Mujica.
16 Something similar occurs with other right-wing, illiberal politicians like Viktor Orbán and Recep Tayyip Erdoğan.
17 Like in this spot: https://www.youtube.com/watch?v=LnoBReTX5IU. The text says: 'In 2018 we did not vote to choose a new president only. We voted to choose a new Brazil, without corruption, impunity. [...] We voted to rescue Brazil.' At the end of the spot, a child sings 'Beloved homeland: Brazil' [*Pátria amada, Brasil*].
18 In this example, the popular element is more salient than the populist one, for example in the selection of the music. Source: https://www.youtube.com/watch?v=Jp6QeKtHisI
19 This is the case even if in some of Bolsonaro's messages there might be a form of constructing a *pro-addressee* in discourse that mimics the logic of equivalence that populist leaders use, as in this spot where it is argued that Brazil 'cannot stop' because of the threat posed by the Covid-19. Cf. https://www.youtube.com/watch?v=OosQexo9_lk

Chapter 8

1 Even if the normative dimension is not relevant for Semiotics – a discipline with a scientific vocation and, hence, interested above all in mapping and describing meaning, sense and signification – it seems appropriate to present Mouffe's conception of left-wing populism as a strategy to overcome the shortages of the Left over the last fifty years (Laclau and Mouffe, 2001). The next section examines the relationship between left-wing populism, neoliberalism and globalization.
2 As is discussed in the cases from Sections 8.3, 8.4 and 8.5, left-wing populist actors usually construct an internal 'other' in the form of a small group on the top of society, independently of what figurative form that semantic unit might take.
3 The popular chant '*El pueblo, unido, jamás sera vencido*' ['The people, united, will never be defeated'] that is frequently heard in Latin American politics evidences the essence of the challenge: while *pueblo* can mean the popular, working and plebeian sections of society – that is, the Left's traditional political Subject – it can also be read

as 'the people' in populist terms. In this sense, it does not come as a surprise that in Latin America, the word 'populism' is usually used to refer to what actually is a type of *popular* politics.

4 Laclau and Mouffe (2001; Laclau, 2005a) assume that specific social demands pre-exist the discursive dimension of the political and argue that these demands are the basis for the establishment of that chain of equivalences that can construct a people. This is a problematic claim: from a constructivist perspective, social demands are also constructed in and through discourse.

5 Original text in Spanish: 'Somos distintos. ¿A vos te importa? A mí tampoco. El presidente de todos: Pepe Mujica.' Source: https://www.youtube.com/watch?v=TFkim-sVR_U

6 'La Fuerza de la Alegría. Cristina Fernández de Kirchner Presidenta 2011.' Source: https://www.youtube.com/watch?v=NbPT7qqOrno

7 Original text in Spanish: 'Cuando un pueblo no tiene alegría y no tiene autoestima es muy fácil dominarlo. Pero para que se pueda cambiar la historia no basta con la voluntad de un loco o de una loca. Hacen falta muchos locos más: 40 millones de locos, 40 millones de argentinos dispuestos a seguir cambiando la Historia.'

8 'Cristina: "Lo más grande que le he dado al pueblo es el empoderamiento popular."' Source: https://www.youtube.com/watch?v=gpTgqep_8DA

9 Something similar occurs in other Latin American countries, where groups of individuals that demonstrate or gather on public spaces – squares, avenues, in front of the parliament and other symbolic buildings – are usually referred to and conceived of by left-wing politicians as *el pueblo*.

10 'Discurso de Cristina Kirchner, vicepresidenta, en Plaza de Mayo. Source: https://www.youtube.com/watch?v=J7pVJce8Vrc

11 Original text in Spanish: 'Confíe siempre en su pueblo. Ellos no traicionan. Son los más leales. Solo piden que los defiendan y los representen [. . .] Tenga fe en el pueblo: la historia la terminan escribiendo más temprano o más tarde los pueblos. [. . .] Y sepa que este pueblo maravilloso, que nunca abandona a los que se juegan por él, convóquelo cada vez que se sienta solo o sienta que los necesitan. Ellos siempre van a estar acá cuando los llamen por causas justas.'

12 'El spot más emotivo de Evo Morales.' Source: https://www.youtube.com/watch?v=5BqdFNQn-4k

13 Original text in Spanish: 'Hermanas y hermanos: nuestra gran nación ha despertado. Bolivia creció como nunca antes, como siempre soñamos. Hoy, nuestra nación se ha llenado de dignidad y respeto. Mejoramos la calidad de vida de las y los bolivianos. Vamos a dar el salto más grande de nuestra historia. Seremos el corazón energético de nuestra Sudamérica y, así, iluminaremos aún más nuestro futuro. [*Evo Morales:*] Hermanas y hermanos: ¡qué viva el pueblo boliviano! ¡Qué viva! ¡Qué viva la democracia con el pueblo!'

14 Madrid's definition of populism goes in line with how this phenomenon has been historically conceived of in South American politics: a personalistic and charismatic leadership, an appeal to the masses and an anti-establishment component, among others. It is not related to the use or not of the semantic unit 'the people' or the Populist Narrative Structure.

15 In semiotic terms, it is interesting to compare the music used in Morales's spot with the one used in Le Pen's and Trump's spots analysed in the previous chapter. While right-wing populists used music aimed at creating tension and awakening emotions like fear, the sense of a crisis and of a threat, the music of Morales's spot is soft, emotional and connotes hope. Moreover, the editing of Morales's spot in slow motion

also contrasts with the swift editing of one of Trump's spots analysed in the previous chapter.

16. Cf. 'Spot – Evo Morales 1.' Source: https://www.youtube.com/watch?v=OyrFy1HGb44. Besides the slogan, this spot does neither reflect the Populist Narrative Structure nor the semantic unit 'the people.'
17. 'Spot de Evo Morales.' Source: https://www.youtube.com/watch?v=6fx59rhjhNU
18. The syntagm '*Evo y pueblo*', translated in English as 'Evo and People', misses the definite article *el* [the] and sounds anomalous in grammatical terms. However, it is so that it was used as the slogan of Morales's campaign.
19. A proper study of European left-wing populism should include SYRIZA and Podemos at least. However, due to the language limitations of the author, this chapter will focus on Podemos only.
20. An official spot from May 2014 illustrates in a creative manner Spain's two-party system through a comparison with the commercial concurrence between Coca-Cola and Pepsi. Cf. https://www.youtube.com/watch?v=kCzawZUV6Gc
21. As discussed in the previous section, Latin American Left populism might actually not be populism as defined in this book. Podemos, in turn, is an example of a populist party due to the salience of the Populist Narrative Structure in its discourse.
22. A number of changes occurred in Iglesias's look after Podemos became part of the Spanish government following a coalition with the PSOE, in December 2019. For a general discussion of how the party changed over the years, cf. Mazzolini and Borriello (2021).
23. '¡Claro que podemos!' Source: https://www.youtube.com/watch?v=unFxEn2gcTs
24. Original text in Spanish: 'Dicen que no se puede plantar cara a Merkel. Dicen que nos apretemos más el cinturón. Dicen que es normal vivir siempre con miedo. Dicen que nos toca hacer las maletas. Dicen que no se puede hacer otra cosa más que elegir entre ellos y ello. Dicen que la corrupción es un problema de casos aislados. Dicen que hay que resignarse a que nos vendan el país y el futuro a trozos. Nos llevan a la miseria. Han roto todos los compromisos. ¿Es que acaso no se puede desear un país mejor para tus hijos? Yo digo que somos muchos más y que podemos ganar. Podemos poner primero las necesidades de la gente: eso es la democracia. Podemos sentar a la casta y sus amigos en el banquillo. Claro que podemos. [*Pablo Iglesias:*] ¿Cuándo fue la última vez que votaste con ilusión? [*Voices in the background shout collectively* "¡Sí, se puede!"] [*Pablo Iglesias:*] Claro que podemos.'
25. Podemos's use of *la gente* differs from South American politician's use of *el pueblo* to refer to 'the people'. This issue was discussed in Chapter 5.
26. 'La furgo de Podemos.' Source: https://www.youtube.com/watch?v=Ir2G06BBSkY
27. Original text in Spanish: 'Algunos están acostumbrados a viajar siempre en primera clase. Asientos cómodos y confortables, gin-tonics o martinis en el avión. Todo lujo y comodidad pagado por vete tú a saber quién. Otros nos conformamos con medios más humildes. Pero incluso los medios humildes, cuando se trata de hacer cosas grandes, son caros. En Podemos hemos dicho siempre que no queremos debernos a los bancos. Y por eso no vamos a pedirles dinero prestado. Creemos que debe ser la gente la que financie nuestra campaña electoral. Gracias a vuestras aportaciones somos independientes. Esta es una furgoneta de campaña y la habéis pagado vosotros. ¡Gracias!'
28. 'UNIDAS PODEMOS (Spot 2019).' Source: https://www.youtube.com/watch?v=3G6yuQkh2o4
29. In Spanish, the plural adjective *unidas* refers to a collective of women, while *unidos* refers both to a collective of men and one comprised both of men and women. In

recent years, advocates of the gender-inclusive language have insisted in using the feminine plural to refer to the mixed collectives, as is the case with Podemos, who instead of naming the coalition 'Unidos Podemos' named it 'Unidas Podemos'. For an analysis confronting populism and feminism in Podemos's discourse cf. Caravantes (2020).

30 Full text in Spanish: 'Hay cosas que cuesta creer, aunque en francés todo suene mejor. La crisis estallaba dos años antes del discurso de Sarkozy. El capitalismo más insaciable se devoraba a sí mismo y por el camino hundía países, expulsaba familias de sus casas y destruía puestos de trabajo. Los mismos que habían provocado el desastre quedaban a los mandos de la recuperación, congregados en torno a un único credo: el de la austeridad. Y la austeridad sacudió Europa con fuerza. En España incluso se hizo hueco en la constitución. Fueron los años crueles del derrumbe económico, del exilio de millares de jóvenes, de la vuelta a unos niveles de pobreza dolorosos. Muchos perdieron, pero unos pocos ganaron. Fueron también años de grandes beneficios empresariales, de sueldos millonarios, de corrupción, de trampas, de podredumbre. Ayer, las élites querían refundar el capitalismo, pero hoy nos aseguran que la crisis está superada. Pasan página a sus miserias y afirman que la suya es la única verdad, que cualquier alternativa es imposible.

Pero no contaban con que habíamos despertado. Nuestro aliento nace de la dignidad de la gente trabajadora que pelea con firmeza por un presente habitable. Del coraje de millones de adolescentes que se han propuesto salvar el planeta. De la tenacidad de un puñado de valientes convocadas a defender de nuevo el paso de las Termópilas. Del compromiso generoso de los pensionistas con el futuro. De las mujeres, que señalan el camino hacia una vida libre y plena. Siempre nos han dicho que era imposible, que la historia estaba escrita de su puño y de su letra. Y no es verdad.

Pudimos. A un ritmo más lento del que nos hubiera gustado, pero estamos pudiendo. Se puede hacer país colocando a la gente en el centro. No tenemos ningún miedo. Lo que tenemos son ganas de seguir, y la certeza de que la historia no nos la van a dictar desde arriba. Ni veinte familias, ni 35 consejos de administración, ni todos los voceros de los poderosos. Ante sus gélidas mentiras, hay verdades que abrigan. Como que la democracia se desangra cuando está secuestrada. Que ya no hay que elegir entre lo mismo y lo mismo. Que la patria es hacer comunidad. Que la palabra es el único camino. Que se gobierna para la gente. Que la suerte no está echada ni el camino marcado, ni los números cerrados. Que el futuro es nuestro. Que se puede. Que sí se puede. Que, pese a lo que te dicen, la Historia la escribes tú.'

31 In that evolution, also nationalism became more prominent in Podemos's discourse, mainly through the concept of *patria* [homeland], which gained centrality in 2016 and then slowly was put on the back page (Custodi, 2021). As argued in the previous subchapter, the strategic use of patriotism to intensify a type of plebeian politics is interesting and poses some challenges for the conceptualization of the existing varieties of populism.

32 'Fight for Someone You Don't Know.' Source: https://www.youtube.com/watch?v=3mu-K6da4Os

33 'America | Bernie Sanders.' Source: https://www.youtube.com/watch?v=2nwRiuh1Cug

34 'Vote Together | Bernie 2016.' Source: https://www.youtube.com/watch?v=C0wsUlzMBro

35 'For All | Bernie Sanders'. Source: https://www.youtube.com/watch?v=-HDd0GYjjz0

References

Aalberg, Toril, Esser, Frank, Reinemann, Carsten, Strömbäck, Jesper, and de Vreese, Claes H. (eds) (2017). *Populist Political Communication in Europe*. New York/London: Routledge.
Abts, Koen and Rummens, Stefan (2007). 'Populism versus Democracy'. *Political Studies*, 55(2): 405–24.
Adamidis, Vasileios (2021). 'Populist Rhetorical Strategies in the Courts of Classical Athens'. *Athens Journal of History*, 7(1): 21–40.
Addis, Maria Cristina (2020). '¿De qué hablamos cuando hablamos de populismo? El espectáculo del poder y análisis sociosemiótico de lo político'. *DeSignis*, 33: 127–42.
Akkerman, Tjitske (2003). 'Populism and Democracy: Challenge or Pathology?' *Acta Politica* 38: 147–59.
Akkeman, Tjitske, de Lange, Sarah L., and Rooduijn, Matthijs (eds) (2016). *Radical Right-Wing Populist Parties in Western Europe. Into the Mainstream?* London/New York: Routledge.
Akkerman, Agnes, Mudde, Cas, and Zaslove, Andrej (2014). 'How Populist Are the People? Measuring Populist Attitudes in Voters'. *Comparative Political Studies*, 47(9): 1324–53.
Al-Ghazzi, Omar (2021). 'We Will Be Great Again: Historical Victimhood in Populist Discourse'. *European Journal of Cultural Studies*, 24(1): 45–59.
Albertazzi, Daniele, Giovannini, Arianna, and Sedonne, Antonella (2018). '"No regionalism please, we are *Leghisti* !" The Transformation of the Italian Lega Nord under the Leadership of Matteo Salvini'. *Regional and Federal Studies*, 28(5): 645–71.
Albertazzi, Daniele and McDonnell, Duncan (eds) (2008). *Twenty-First Century Populism. The Spectre of Western European Democracy*. Basingstoke/New York: Palgrave Macmillan.
Alexander, James (2015). 'The Major Ideologies of Liberalism, Socialism and Convervatism'. *Political Studies*, 63(5): 980–94.
Alondo Aldama, Juan (2014). 'Sémiotique et politique: narrativitè et transformation'. *Recherches en communication*, 41: 61–74.
Alonso Aldama, Juan (2018). 'Régimes véridictoires et simulacres du politique'. *Actes Sémiotiques*, 118.
Anastasiou, Michaelangelo (2019). 'Of Nation and People: The Discursive Logic of Nationalist Populism'. *Javnost: The Public*, 26(3): 330–45.
Anderson, Benedict (1983). *Imagined Communities*. London: Verso.
Angenot, Marc (2010). *El discurso Social*. Buenos Aires: Siglo XXI.
Anselmi, Manuel (2017). *Populism. An Introduction*. London/New York: Routledge.
Appiah, Kwame A. (2018). *The Lies That Bind*. London: Profile Books.
Arditi, Benjamín (2005). 'Populism as an Internal Periphery of Democratic Politics'. In Francisco Panizza (ed.), *Populism and the Mirror of Democracy*, 72–98. London: Verso.
Arditi, Benjamin (2007). *Politics on the Edges of Liberalism. Difference, Populism, Revolution, Agitation*. Edinburgh: Edinburgh University Press.
Arfuch, Leonor (ed.). (2005). *Identidades, Sujetos, Subjetividades*. Buenos Aires: Prometeo.

Arrivé, Michel (2002). 'La sémiologie saussuriene, entre le *CLG* et la recherche sur la légende'. In Anne Hénault (dir.), *Questions de sémiotique*, 73–90. Paris: Presses Universitaires de France.
Arroyas Langas, Enrique and Pérez Díaz, Pedro L. (2016). 'La nueva narrativa identitaria del populismo: un análisis del discurso de Pablo Iglesias (Podemos) en Twitter'. *Cultura, lenguaje y representación*, 15: 51–63.
Aslanidis, Paris (2016). 'Is Populism an Ideology? A Refutation and a New Perspective'. *Political Studies*, 64(1): 88–104.
Badir, Sémir (2020). 'La typologie sémiotique des modalités. Une mise au point'. *Semiotica*, 234: 79–101.
Bang, Henrik and Marsh, David (2018). 'Populism: A Major Threat to Democracy?' *Policy Studies*, 39(3): 352–63.
Barbosa Gouvêa, Carina and Villas Bôas Castelo Branco, Pedro H. (2021). *Populist Governance in Brazil. Bolsonaro in Theoretical and Comparative Perspective*. Cham: Springer.
Barr, Robert (2018). 'Populism as a Political Strategy'. In Carlos de la Torre (ed.), *The Routldge Handbook of Global Populism*, 44–56. London: Routledge.
Barros, Diana Luz Pessoa de (2012). 'Directions et rôles de la sémiotique en Amérique du sud: Premières réflexions'. *Signata*, 3: 131–60.
Barros, Diana Luz Pessoa de (2017). 'Les régimes de sens et d'interaction dans la conversation'. *Actes Sémiotiques*, 120.
Barthes, Roland (1957). *Mythologies*. Paris: Seuil.
Beard, Mary (2015). *SPQR. A History of Ancient Rome*. London: Profile Books.
Bellentani, Federico and Panico, Mario (2016). 'The Meanings of Monuments and Memorials: Toward a Semiotic Approach'. *Punctum*, 2(1): 28–46.
Benveniste, Émile (1966). *Problèmes de linguistique générale, I*. Paris: Gallimard.
Benveniste, Émile (1974) *Problèmes de linguistique générale, II*. Paris: Gallimard.
Berger, Peter (1966). 'Identity as a Problem in the Sociology of Knowledge'. *European Journal of Sociology*, 7(1): 105–15.
Berger, Peter and Luckmann, Thomas (1966). *The Social Construction of Reality*. New York: Anchor Books.
Bergmann, Eirikur (2020). *Neo-Nationalism. The Rise of Nativist Populism*. Cham: Palgrave Macmillan
Bermúdez, Emilia and Martínez, Gildardo (2000). 'Hugo Chávez: La articulación de un sentido para la acción colectiva'. *Espacio Abierto*, 9(1): 53–77.
Berti, Carlo and Loner, Enzo (2021). 'Character Assassination as a Right-Wing Populist Communication Tactic on Social Media: The Case of Matteo Salvini in Italy'. *New Media & Society*, online first: 1–21.
Betz, Hans-Georg (1994). *Radical Right-Wing Populism in Western Europe*. Basingstoke: Macmillan.
Betz, Hans-Georg (2002). 'Conditions Favouring the Success and Failure of Radical Right-Wing Populist Parties in Contemporary Democracies'. In Yves Meny and Yves Surel (eds), *Democracies and the Populist Challenge*, 197–213. New York: Palgrave.
Bianchi, Cinzia (2016). 'Semiótica e ideología: modelos, remociones y perspectivas'. *DeSignis*, 26: 21–32.
Bitonte, María Elena (2008). 'La socio-semiótica como forma de pensamiento crítico'. *Perspectivas de la comunicación*, 1(2): 59–71.
Boas, Taylor C. and Gans-Morse, Jordan (2009). 'Neoliberalism: From New Liberal Philosophy to Anti-Liberal Slogan'. *Studies in Comparative International Development*, 44(2): 137–61.

Bobba, Giuliano and Legnante, Guido (2017). 'Italy. A Breeding Ground for Populist Political Communication'. In T. Aalberg et al. (eds), *Populist Political Communication in Europe*, 221–34. New York/London: Routledge.

Bobbio, Norberto (1994). *Destra e sinistra. Ragioni e significati di una distinzione politica*. Rome: Donzelli.

Bouissac, Paul (2020). *The Meaning of the Circus*. London: Bloomsbury.

Bourdieu, Pierre (1983). 'Vous avez dit "populaire"?' *Actes de la recherche en sciences sociales*, 46: 98–105.

Bourdieu, Pierre (1987). 'Les usages du peuple'. In *Choses dites*, 178–84. Paris: Minuit.

Bowman, Glenn (2005). 'Constitutive Violence and the Nationalist Imaginary: The Making of "The People" in Palestine and "Former Yugoslavia"'. In F. Panizza (ed.), *Populism and the Mirror of Democracy*, 118–43, London: Verso.

Breeze, Ruth (2017). 'Tired of Nice People? An Appraisal-Based Approach to Trump's Dichotomies'. *Cultura, Lenguaje y Representación*, 18: 7–25.

Broden, Thomas F. (2014). 'La sémiotique greimassiene et la sémiotique peirceinne: Visées, principes et théories su signe'. *Estudos Semióticos*, 10(2): 1–16.

Brubaker, Rogers and Cooper, Frederick (2000). 'Beyond "identity"'. *Theory and Society*, 29: 1–47.

Brucculeri, Maria Claudia (2009). *Semiotica per il turismo*. Rome: Carocci.

Bruner, Jerome (2002). *Making Stories. Law, Literature, Life*. Cambridge, MA/London: Harvard University Press.

Bucholtz, Mary and Hall, Kira (2005). 'Identity and Interaction: A Sociocultural Linguistic Approach'. *Discourse Studies*, 7(4–5): 585–614.

Burke, Peter and Stets, Jan (2009). *Identity Theory*. Oxford: Oxford University Press.

Canovan, Margaret (1981). *Populism*. London/New York: Harcourt Brace Jovanovich.

Canovan, Margaret (1984). '"People", Politicians and Populism'. *Government and Opposition*, 19(3): 312–27.

Canovan, Margaret (1999). 'Trust the People! Populism and the Two Faces of Democracy'. *Political Studies*, 47(1): 2–16.

Canovan, Margaret (2002). 'Taking Politics to the People: Populism as the Ideology of Democracy'. In Yves Mény and Yves Surel (ed.), *Decmoracies and the Populist Challenge*, 22–54. Cham: Palgrave Macmilla.

Caravantes, Paloma (2020). 'Tensions bewteen Populist and Feminist Politics: The Case of the Spanish Left Populist Party Podemos'. *International Political Science Review*, 42(5): 596–612.

Carpentier, Nico (2017). *The Discursive-Material Knot*. Cyprus in Conflict and Community Media Participation. New York: Peter Lang.

Casullo, María Esperanza (2019). *¿Por qué funciona el populismo?* Buenos Aires: Siglo XXI.

Casullo, María Esperanza (2020). 'The Body Speaks before It Even Talks: Deliberation, Populism and Bodily Representation'. *Journal of Deliberative Democracy*, 16(1): 27–36.

Catalano, Theresa and Waugh, Linda R. (2020). *Critical Discourse Analysis, Critical Discourse Studies and Beyond*. Cham: Springer.

Cervelli, Pierluigi (2018). 'La comunicazione politica populista: corpo, linguaggio e pratiche di interazione'. *Actes Sémiotiques*, 121.

Cervi, Laura (2020). 'Veni, vidi, Facebook-live: análisis del éxito de Matteo Salvini en Facebook'. *Revista CIDOB d'Afers Internacionals*, 124: 99–122.

Chandler, Daniel (2017). *Semiotics. The Basics*. London: Routledge.

Charalambous, Giorgios and Ioannou, Gregoris (eds) (2020). *Left Radicalism and Populism in Europe*. London/New York: Routledge.

Charaudeau, Patrick (2011). 'Réflexions pour l'analyse du discours populiste'. *Mots*, 97: 101–16.

Charaudeau, Patrick (2014). *Le discours politique. Les masques du pouvoir*. Paris: Lambert-Lucas.

Charaudeau, Patrick and Maingueneau, Dominique (2002). *Dictionnaire d'analyse du discours*. Paris: Seuil.

Charaudeau, Patrick (2020). *La manipulation de la vérité*. Paris: Lambert-Lucas.

Chumaceiro, Irma (2004). 'Las metáforas políticas en el discurso de dos líderes venezolanos: Hugo Chávez y Enrique Mendoza'. *Revista Latinoamericana de Estudios del Discurso*, 4(2): 91–113.

Cingolani, Gastón and Fernández, Mariano (2019). *Cristina, un espectáculo político*. Buenos Aires: Prometeo.

Collier, David and Gerring, John (ed.) (2009). *Concepts and Method in Social Science. The Tradition of Giovanni Sartori*. New York/London: Routledge.

Collier, David and Mahon, James E. (1993). 'Conceptual "Stretching" Revisited: Adapting Categories in Comparative Analysis'. *The American Political Science Review*, 87(4): 845–55.

Cosenza, Giovanna (2018). *Semiotica e comunicazione politica*. Bari/Rome: Laterza.

Cossarini, Paolo and Vallespín, Fernando (eds) (2019). *Populism and Passions: Democratic Legitimacy after Austerity*. New York/London: Routledge.

Courtés, Joseph (2007). *La sémiotique du langage*. Paris: Armand Collin.

Custodi, Jacopo (2021). 'Nationalism and Populism on the Left: The Case of Podemos'. *Nations and Nationalism*, 27(3): 705–20.

Dagatti, Mariano (2012). 'Aportes para el estudio del discurso político en las sociedades contemporáneas. El caso del kirchnerismo'. *De signos y sentidos*, 13: 52–82.

Dagatti, Mariano and Gómez Triben, Mariana (2020). 'Como la cigarra. Relatos de ilusión y desencanto en la campaña presidencial del Frente de todos (Argentina, 2019)'. *DeSignis*, 33: 179–203.

Dagatti, Mariano and Velázquez García-Talavera, Teresa (2022). 'Presentación'. *DeSignis*, 33: 15–22.

Damiani, Marco (2020). *Populist Radical Left Parties in Western Europe*. London/New York: Routledge.

Danesi, Marcel (2016). *The Semiotics of Emoji. The Rise of Visual Language in the Age of Internet*. London: Bloombsbury.

Danesi, Marcel (2019). *The Semiotics of Love*. Cham: Palgrave Macmillan.

Dardot, Pierre and Laval, Christian (2009). *La nouvelle raison du monde: Essai sur la société néolibérale*. Paris: La Découverte.

De Cleen, Benjamin (2017). 'Populism and Nationalism'. In Cristóbal Rovira Kaltwasser et al. (eds), *The Oxford Handbook of Populism*, 342–61. Oxford: Oxford University Press.

De Cleen, Benjamin (2019). 'The Populist Political Logic and the Analysis of the Discursive Construction of "the people" and "the elite"'. In Jan Zienkowski and Ruth Breeze (ed.), *Imagining the Peoples of Europe*, 19–42. Amsterdam: John Benjamins.

De Cleen, Benjamin and Stavrakakis, Yannis (2017). 'Distinctions and Articulations: A Discourse Theoretical Framework for the Study of Populism and Nationalism'. *Javnost: The Public*, 24(4): 301–19.

De Cleen, Benjamin, Jason Glynos and Aurelien Mondon (2018). 'Critical Research on Populism: Nine Rules of Engagement'. *Organization*, 25(5): 649–61.

De Cleen, Benjamin, Moffitt, Benjamin, Panayotu, Panos, and Stavrakakis, Yannis (2019). 'The Potentials and Difficulties of Transnational Populism: The Case of the Democracy in Europe Movement (DiEM25)'. *Political Studies*, 68(1): 146–66.

de Oliveira, Ana Claudia (ed.) (2004). *As interações sensíveis*. Saõ Paulo: Centro de Pesquisas Sociosemióticas/Estação das Letras e Cores.

de Oliveira, Ana Claudia (org.) (2013). *Sentido e interação nas práticas*. Saõ Paulo: Centro de Pesquisas Sociosemióticas/Estação das Letras e Cores.

de Oliveira, Ana Claudia (org.) (2021). *Sociossemiótica IV. Mídia e política*. Saõ Paulo: Centro de Pesquisas Sociosemióticas/Estação das Letras e Cores.

Deely, John. (2015). 'Semiotics "Today": The Twentieth-Century Founding and Twenty-First-Century Prospects'. In Peter P. Trifonas (ed.), *International Handbook of Semiotics*, 29–114. New York: Springer.

Demaria, Cristina (2006). *Semiotica e memoria. Analisi del post-conflitto*. Rome: Carocci.

Demaria, Cristina (2012). *Il trauma, l'achivo, il testimone*. Bolonia: Bononia University Press.

Demaria, Cristina (2019). *Teoria di genere. Femminismi e semiotica*. Milano: Bompiani.

Demuru, Paolo (2015). 'Malandragem vs Arte di arrangiarsi: Stili di vita e forme dell'aggiustamento tra Brasile e Italia'. *Actes Sémiotiques*, 118.

Demuru, Paolo (2017). 'Praticas de vida. Entre semiótica, comunicação e política'. *Estudos Semióticos*, 13(1): 28–39.

Demuru, Paolo (2019). 'De Greimas a Eric Landowski. A experiência do sentido, o sentido da experiência: semiótica, interação e processos sócio-comunicacionais'. Galaxia, especial 2 – Algirdas J. Greimas: 85–113.

Demuru, Paolo (2021a). 'Gastropopulism: A Sociosemiotic Analysis of Politicians Posing as "the everyday man" via Food Posts on Social Media'. *Social Semiotics*, 31(3): 507–27.

Demuru, Paolo (2021b). 'Teorias da conspiração e populismo messiânico no Brasil contemporâneo: uma perspectiva semiótico-cultural'. *Estudos Semióticos*, 17(2): 264–91.

Demuru, Paolo and Albertini, Matteo (2009). 'La politica come semiosfera e la costruzione 'in campo' dell' identità. Il caso del Partito Democratico'. *Versus*, 107–108: 101–17.

Demuru, Paolo and Pimenta Rodrigues de Oliveira, Felipe (2021). 'O corpo populista: hexis, gestos e contágio estésico na comunicação política contemporânea'. In Ana Claudia de Oliveira (org.), *Sociossemiótica IV. Mídia e política*, 193–212. Saõ Paulo: Centro de Pesquisas Sociosemióticas/Estação das Letras e Cores.

Demuru, Paolo, Pimenta Rodrigues de Oliveira, Felipe, and Cuevas Calderón, Elder (2021). 'Bodily Regimes and Meaning Production in Bolsonaro's Visual Discourse: A Socio-Semiotic Perspective'. *Comunicación y Sociedad*, e7949: 1–26.

Di Tella, Torcuato S. (1965). 'Populismo y reforma en América Latina'. *Desarrollo Económico*, 4(16): 391–425.

Di Tella, Tortuato S. (1973). 'Populismo y reformismo'. In Gino Germani, Torcuato S. di Tella, and Octavio Ianni (eds), *Populismo y contradicciones de clase en Latinoamérica*, 38–82. México: Era.

Diehl, Paula (2017). 'The Body in Populism'. In R. C. Heinish, C. Holtz-Bacha, and O. Mazzoleni (eds), *Political Populism. A Handbook*, 361–72. Baden-Baden: Nomos.

Dondero, Maria Giulia (2017). 'Du texte à la pratique: Pour une sémiotique expérimentale'. *Semiotica*, 219: 335–56.

Ducrot, Oswald and Todotov, Tzvetan (1972). *Dictionnaire encyclopédique es sciences du langage*. Paris: Seuil.

Eco, Umberto (1964). *Apocalittici e integrati*. Milano: Bompiani.
Eco, Umberto (1968). *La struttura assente*. Milano: Bompiani.
Eco, Umberto (1976). *A Theory of Semiotics*. Bloomington: Indiana University Press.
Eco, Umberto (2012). *Inventing the Enemy and Other Occasional Writings*. Boston/New York: Houghton, Mifflin & Harcourt.
Eisenstadt, Shmuel N. (1998). 'Modernity and the Construction of Collective Identities'. *International Journal of Comparative Sociology*, 39(3): 138–58.
Ekström, Mats and Morton, Andrew (2017). 'The Performances of Right-Wing Populism: Populist Discourse, Embodied Styles and Forms of New Reporting'. In Mats Ekström and Julie Firmstone (eds), *The Mediated Politics of Europe*, 289–316. Cham: Palgrave Macmillan.
Ekström, Mats, Patrona, Marianna, and Thornborrow, Joanna (2018). 'Right wing Populism and the Dynamics of Style: A Discourse-Analytic Perspective on Mediated Political Performances'. *Palgrave Communications*, 4: 1–11.
Escudero Chauvel, Lucrecia (2005). 'Identidad e identidades'. *Estudios*, 17: 51–7.
Escudero Chauvel, Lucrecia (2016). 'La Ideología en *Tratatto di Semiotica Generale* de Umberto Eco. Una puesta en perspectiva'. *DeSignis*, 26: 61–77.
Escudero Chauvel, Lucrecia (2019). 'El pueblo de la web. Consecuencias de la mediatización y transformación de la esfera pública'. *DeSignis*, 31: 209–40.
Fabbri, Paolo (1973). 'Le comunicazioni di massa in Italia: sguardo semiotico e malocchio della sociologia'. *Versus*, 5: 57–109.
Fabbri, Paolo (1998). *La svolta semiotica*. Bari-Roma: Laterza.
Fabbri, Paolo (2019). 'Identidades colectivas'. *DeSignis*, 31: 285–9.
Fabbri, Paolo (2021). *Biglietti d'invito per una semiotica marcata*. Milano: Bompiani.
Fabbri, Paolo and Marcarino, Aurelia (1985). 'Il discorso politico'. *Carte Semiotiche*, 1: 9–22.
Fairclough, Isabela and Fairclough, Norman (2012). *Political Discourse Analysis. A Method for Advanced Students*. London/New York: Routledge.
Fairclough, Norman (1989). *Language and Power*. Edinburgh: Longmane.
Fairclough, Norman (1992). *Discourse and Social Change*. Cambridge: Polity Press.
Fatala, Norma (2013). 'El lugar del otro en la construcción discursiva de los sujetos colectivos'. *E/C*, 15–16: 206–10.
Fechine, Yvana (2020). 'Passions et présence dans le populisme numérique brésilien'. *Actes Sémiotiques*, 123.
Fechine, Yvana (2021). 'Paixões e presença no populismo digital: o caso do presidente brasileiro Jair Bolsonaro'. In Ana Claudia de Oliveira (org.), *Sociossemiótica IV. Mídia e política*, 151–92. Saõ Paulo: Centro de Pesquisas Sociossemióticas/Estação das Letras e Cores.
Fernández Vázquez, Guilllermo (2017). 'Los olvidados de Marine Le Pen'. *CTXT*, 15 March 2017. Retrieved from https://ctxt.es/es/20170315/Politica/11575/Frente-Nacional-Marine-Le-Pen-Emmanuel-Macron-olvidados-Francia.htm.
Filc, Dani (2015). 'Latin American Inclusive and European Exclusionarypopulism: Colonialism as an Explanation'. *Journal of Political Ideologies*, 20(3): 263–83.
Finchelstein, Federico and Urbinati, Nadia (2018). 'On Populism and Democracy'. *Populism*, 1(1): 15–37.
Floch, Jean-Marie (1986). *Les formes de l'empreinte*. Périgeux: Pierre Fanlac.
Floch, Jean-Marie (1990). *Sémiotique, Marketing et Communication*. Paris: Presses Universitaires de France.
Floch, Jean-Marie (1995). *Identités visuelles*. Paris: Presses Universitaires de France.

Floch, Jean-Marie (2002). 'Introduction. Quelques Concepts fondamentaux en sémiotique générale'. In A. Hénault (dir.), *Questions de sémiotique*, 103–19. Paris: Presses Universitaires de France.
Fontanille, Jacques (1999). *Sémiotique et littérature. Essais de méthode*. Paris: Presses Universitaires de France.
Fontanille, Jacques (2008). *Pratiques sémiotiques*. Paris: Presses Universitaires de France.
Fontanille, Jacques (2011). *Corps et sens*. Paris: Presses Universitaires de France.
Fontanille, Jacques (2015). *Formes de vie*. Liège: Presses Universitaires de Liège.
Fontanille, Jacques (2020). 'Populisme: le grand chambardement sémiotique?' *Actes Sémiotiques*, 123.
Fontanille, Jacques and Perusset, Alain (2021). 'Les formes de vie entre pratiques et cultures, styles et idéaux de vie'. *Estudos semióticos*, 17(2): 89–103.
Freeden, Michael (1996). *Ideologies and Political Theory: A Conceptual Approach*. Oxford: Oxford University Press.
Freeden, Michael (2013). 'The Morphological Analysis of Ideology'. In M. Freeden, L. T. Sargent, and M. Stears (eds), *The Oxford Handbook of Political Ideologies*, 148–73. Oxford: Oxford University Press.
Frege, Gottlob (2008). 'Über Sinn und Bedeutung'. In *Funktion, Begriff, Bedeutung. Fünf logische Studien*, 23–46. Göttingen: Vandenhoeck & Ruprecht.
Fukuyama, Francis (2018a). 'The Populist Surge'. *The American Interest*, 13(4). Retrieved from https://www.the-american-interest.com/2018/02/09/the-populist-surge/.
Fukuyama, Francis (2018b). *Identity*. London: Profile Books.
García Agustín, Óscar (2020). *Left Wing Populism. The Politics of the People*. Bingley: Emerald Publishing.
García-Marín, Javier and Luengo, Óscar G. (2019). 'Populist Discourse in the 21st Century. The Definition of Otherness on Twitter in the Cases of Spain, Bolivia and Venezuela'. In Encarnación Hidalgo-Tenorio et al. (eds), *Populist Discourse. Critical Approaches to Contemporary Politics*, 81–99. London/New York: Routledge.
Geertz, Clifford (1973). *The Interpretation of Cultures*. New York: Basic Books.
Gerbaudo, Paolo (2018). 'Social Media and Populism: An Elective Affinity?' *Media, Culture & Society*, 40(5): 745–53.
Germani, Gino (1965). *Política y sociedad en una época de transición*. Buenos Aires: Paidós.
Germani, Gino (1973). 'Democracia representativa y clases populares'. In Gino Germani, Torcuato S. di Tella, and Octavio Ianni, *Populismo y contradicciones de clase en Latinoamérica*, 12–37. México: Era.
Gerring, John (2012). *Social Science Methodology. A Unified Framework*. Cambridge: Cambridge University Press.
Gherlone, Laura (2020). 'In the Footsteps of the Semiotic School of Moscow-Tartu / Tartu-Moscow: Evaluations and Perspectives'. *Semiotica*, 235: 229–41.
Giannitrappani, Alice (2009). *Viaggiare: istruzioni per l'uso. Semiotica delle guide turistiche*. Pisa: ETS.
Giannitrappani, Alice (2013). *Introduzione alla semiotica dello spazio*. Rome: Carocci.
Glynos, Jason and Howarth, David (2007). *Logics of Critical Explanation in Social and Political Theory*. London: Routledge.
Goertz, Gary (2006). *Social Science Concepts. A User's Guide*. Princeton/Oxford: Princeton University Press.
Goffman, Erving (1956). *The Presentation of Self in Everyday Life*. Edinburgh: University of Edinburgh.

Gonçalves, Daniela Norcia and Martynuk, Valdenise Leziér (2021). 'Sémiotique greimassiene au Brésil: Production de sens dans les Organisations'. *Revue Française des Sciences de l'information et de la communication*, 21. https://journals.openedition.org/rfsic/10470.
Greimas, Algirdas J. (1986). *Sémantique structurale*. Paris: Presses Universitaires de France.
Greimas, Algirdas J. (1970). *Du sens I*. Paris: Seuil.
Greimas, Algirdas J. (1983). *Du sens II*. Paris: Seuil
Greimas, Algirdas J. (1984). 'Sémiotique figurative et sémiotique plastique'. *Actes Sémiotiques*, 6(60): 5–24.
Greimas, Algirdas J. and Courtés, Joseph (1982). *Semiotics and Language. An Analytical Dictionary*. Bloomington: Indiana University Press.
Greimas, Algirdas J. and Ricoeur, Paul (1989). 'On Narrativity'. *New Literary History*, 20(3): 551–62.
Greimas, Algirdas J. and Fontanille, Jacques (1991). *Sémiotique des passions*. Paris: Seuil.
Grimson, Alejandro (2019) *¿Qué es el peronismo?* Buenos Aires: Siglo XXI.
Grugel, Jean and Riggirozzi, Pía (eds) (2009). *Governance after Neoliberalism in Latin America*. New York: Palgrave Macmillan.
Gualda, Ricardo (2019). 'Hugo Chávez's Contemporary Latin American Populist Discourse'. In Marcia Macaulay (ed.), *Populist Discourse. International Perspectives*, 59–88. Cham: Palgrave Macmillan.
Hall, Stuart and Du Gay, Paul (2011). *Questions of Cultural Identity*. London: Sage.
Halliday, Michael A. K. (1978). *Language as Social Semiotic*. London: Edward Arnold.
Harvey, David (2005). *A Brief History of Neoliberalism*. Oxford: Oxford University Press.
Hawkins, Kirk A. (2009). 'Is Chávez Populist? Measuring Populist Discourse in Comparative Perspective'. *Comparative Political Studies*, 42(8): 1040–67.
Hawkins, Kirk A. and Rovira Kaltwasser, Cristóbal (2019). 'Introduction. The Ideational Approach'. In Kirk A. Hawkins, Ryan A. Carlin, Levente Littvay, and Cristóbal Rovira Kaltwasser (eds), *The Ideational Approach to Populism. Concept, Theory, and Analysis*, 1–24. London/New York: Routledge.
Heinisch, Reinhard C., Holtz-Bacha, Christina, and Mazzoleni, Oscar (eds) (2017). *Political Populism: A Handbook*. Baden-Baden: Nomos.
Hénault, Anne (2002a). 'Saussure et la théorie du Langage'. In Anne Hénault (dir.), *Questions de sémiotique*, 53–72. Paris: Presses Universitaires de France.
Hénault, Anne (dir.) (2002b). *Questions de sémiotique*. Paris: Presses Universitaires de France.
Hénault, Anne (2012). *Les enjeux de la sémiotique*. Paris: Presses Universitaires de France.
Hennessy, Alistair (1969). 'Latin America'. In Ghita Ionescu and Ernest Gellner (eds), *Populism. Its Meanings and National Characteristics*, 28–61. London: Weidenfeld & Nicolson.
Hermet, Guy (1997). 'Populisme et nationalisme'. *Vingtième Siècle*, 56: 34–47.
Hestbaek Andersen, Thomas, Boeriis, Morten, Maagero, Eva, and Seip Tonnessen, Elise (2015). *Social Semiotics. Key Figures, New Directions*. London/New York: Routledge.
Hidalgo-Tenorio, Encarnación, Benítez-Castro, Miguel Ángel, and De Cesare, Francesca (eds) (2019). *Populist Discourse. Critical Approaches to Contemporary Politics*. London/New York: Routledge.
Hjarvard, Stig (2013). *The Mediatization of Culture and Society*. London/New York: Routledge.

Hjelmslev, Louis (1961). *Prolegomena to a Theory of Language*. Madison: The University of Wisconsin Press.
Hobsbawm, Eric and Ranger, Terence (1987). *The Invention of Tradition*. Cambridge: Cambridge University Press.
Hodge, Bob (2014). *Teaching as Communication*. London/New York: Routledge.
Hodge, Robert and Kress, Gunther (1988). *Social Semiotics*. Ithaca: Cornell University Press.
Hodge, Robert and Kress, Gunther (1993). *Language as Ideology*. London: Routledge.
Hofstadter, Richard (1969). 'North America'. In Ghita Ionescu and Ernest Gellner (eds), *Populism. Its Meanings and National Characteristics*, 9–27. London: Weidenfeld & Nicolson.
Howarth, David (2005). 'Populism or Popular Democracy? The UDF, Workerism and the Struggle for Radical Democracy in South Africa'. In Francisco Panizza (ed.), *Populism and the Mirror of Democracy*, 202–23. London: Verso.
Howarth, David, Norval, Aletta J., and Stavrakakis, Yannis (eds) (2000). *Discourse Theory and Political Analysis. Identities, Hegemonies and Social Change*. Manchester/New York: Manchester University Press.
Howarth, David and Stavrakakis, Yannis (2000). 'Introducing Discourse Theory and Political Analysis'. In David Howarth, Aletta J. Norval, and Yannis Stavrakakis (eds), *Discourse Theory and Political Analysis. Identities, Hegemonies and Social Change*, 1–23. Manchester/New York: Manchester University Press.
Howarth, David and Torfing, Jacob (ed.) (2005). *Discourse Theory in European Politics. Identity, Policy and Governance*. Basingstoke: Palgrave Macmillan.
Hubé, Nicolas and Truan, Naomi (2016). 'France. The Reluctance to Use the Word *Populism* as a Concept'. In Aalberg, Toril et al. (eds), *Populist Political Communication in Europe*, 181–94. New York/London: Routledge.
Ionescu, Ghita (1969). 'Eastern Europe'. In Ghita Ionescu and Ernest Gellner (eds), *Populism. Its Meanings and National Characteristics*, 97–121. London: Weidenfeld & Nicolson.
Ionescu, Ghita and Gellner, Ernest (eds) (1969). *Populism. Its Meanings and National Characteristics*. London: Weidenfeld & Nicolson.
Ivaldi, Gilles (2016). 'A New Course for the French Radical Right? The Front National and 'de-Demonisation'. In Tjitske Akkerman, Sarah L. de Lange, and Matthijs Rooduijn (eds), *Radical Right-Wing Populist Parties in Western Europe. Into the Mainstream?*, 225–46. London/New York: Routledge.
Iyengar, Shanto, Sood, Gaurav, and Lelkes, Yphtach (2012). 'Affect, Not Ideology. A Social Identity Perspective on Polarization'. *Public Opinion Quarterly*, 76(3): 405–31.
Jagers, Jan and Walgrave, Stefaan (2007). 'Populism as Political Communication Style: An Empirical Study of Political Parties' Discourse in Belgium'. *European Journal of Political Research*, 46: 319–45.
Jakobson, Roman (1963). *Essais de linguistique générale, I: Les fondatios du langage*. Paris: Minuit.
Katsambekis, Giorgios and Kioupkiolis, Alexandros (eds) (2019). *The Populist Radical Left in Europe*. London/New York: Routldge.
Katsambekis, Giorgios and Stavrakakis, Yannis (2017). 'Revisiting the Nationalism/Populism Nexus: Lessons from the Greek Case'. *Javnost: The Public*, 24(1): 391–408.
Kharbouch, Ahmed (2018). 'Manipulation et contagion: le discours ambivalent du populisme politique'. *Actes Sémiotiques*, 121.
Knight, Alan (1998). 'Populism and Neo-Populism in Latin America, Especially Mexico'. *Journal of Latin American Studies*, 30(2): 223–48.

Knight, Kathleen (2006). 'Transformations of the Concept of Ideology in the Twentieth Century'. *American Political Science Review*, 100(4): 619–26.
Krastev, Ivan (2007). 'The Populist Moment'. *Critique & Humanism*, 23: 107–13.
Kress, Gunther (2001). 'Sociolinguistics and Social Semiotics'. In Paul Cobley (ed.), *The Routledge Companion to Semiotics and Linguistics*, 66–82. London: Routldge.
Kress, Gunther (2010). *Multimodality: A Social Semiotic Approach to Contemporary Communication*. London/New York: Routledge.
Kress, Gunther and van Leeuwen, Theo (2001). *Multimodal Discourse*. London: Bloomsbury.
Kurunmäki, Jussi and Marjanen, Jani (2018). 'Isms, Ideologies and Setting the Agenda for Public Debate'. *Journal of Political Ideologies*, 23(3): 256–82.
La Nación (2015). 'Cristina Kirchner, sobre la marcha por Nisman: 'A ellos les dejamos el silencio, siempre les gustó el silencio''. 11 February 2015. Retrieved from https://www.lanacion.com.ar/politica/cristina-kirchner-sobre-la-marcha-por-nisman-a-ellos-les-dejamos-el-silencio-siempre-les-gusto-el-silencio-nid1767655/.
Labov, William (1972). *Sociolinguistic Patterns*. Philadelphia: University of Pennsylvania Press.
Laclau, Ernesto (1977). *Politics and Ideology in Marxist Theory*. London: Verso.
Laclau, Ernesto (1991). *Emancipations*. London: Verso.
Laclau, Ernesto (ed.) (1994). *The Making of Political Identities*. London: Verso.
Laclau, Ernesto (2000). 'Foreword'. In David Howarth, Aletta J. Norval, and Yannis Stavrakakis (eds), *Discourse Theory and Political Analysis. Identities, Hegemonies and Social Change*, x–xi. Manchester/New York: Manchester University Press.
Laclau, Ernesto (2005a). *On Populist Reason*. London: Verso.
Laclau, Ernesto (2005b). 'Populism: What's in a Name?' In Francisco Panizza (ed.), *Populism and the Mirror of Democracy*, 32–49. London: Verso.
Laclau, Ernesto and Mouffe, Chantal (2001). *Hegemony and Socialist Strategy*. London: Verso.
Lakoff, George (2016a). 'Understanding Trump's Use of Language'. *Huffpost*, 24 August 2016. Retrieved from https://www.huffpost.com/entry/understanding-trumps-use-_b_11675280.
Lakoff, George (2016b). 'Understanding Trump'. *Huffpost*, 22 July 2016. Retrieved from https://www.huffpost.com/entry/understanding-trump_b_11144938?1469216981.
Lancioni, Tarcisio (2015). 'Appareils de Capture. Pour une sémiotique de la Culture'. *Actes Sémiotiques*, 118.
Lancioni, Tarcisio and Marsciani, Francesco (2007). 'La pratica come testo: per una etnosemiotica del mondo quotidiano'. In Gianfranco Marrone, Nicola Dusi e Giorgio Lo Feudo (eds), *Narrazione ed esperianza. Intorno a una semiotica della vita quotidiana*, 59–69. Rome: Meltemi.
Landowski, Eric (1976). 'La mise en scène des sujets de pouvoir'. *Langages*, 43: 78–89.
Landowski, Eric (1983). 'Simulacres en Construction'. *Langages*, 70: 73–81.
Landowski, Eric (1984). 'Les chantiers sociaux de la sémiotique'. *Langage et société*, 28(2): 141–9.
Landowski, Eric (1985). 'Eux, nous et moi: régimes de visibilité'. *Mots*, 10: 9–16.
Landowski, Eric (1989). *La societé reflechie. Essais de socio-sémiotique I*. Paris: Seuil.
Landowski, Eric (1997). *Presences de l'autre. Essais de socio-sémiotique II*. Paris: Presses Universitaires de France.
Landowski, Eric (2004). *Passions sans nom. Essais de socio-sémiotique III*. Paris: Presses Universitaires de France.

Landowski, Eric (2005). *Les interactions risquées*. Limoges: Presses de l'Université de Limoges.
Landowski, Eric (2012). 'Régimes de sens et styles de vie'. *Actes Sémiotiques*, 115.
Landowski, Eric (2013). 'Une sémiotique à refaire?' *Galaxia*, 26: 10–33.
Landowski, Eric (2014). 'Sociossemiótica: uma teoria geral do sentido'. *Galáxia*, 27: 10–20.
Landowski, Eric (2017). 'Interactions (socio) sémiotiques'. *Actes Sémiotiques*, 120.
Landowski, Eric (2018). 'Populisme et esthésie'. *Actes Sémiotiques*, 121.
Landowski, Eric (2019). 'Politiques de la sémiotique'. *Rivista Italiana di Filosofia del Linguaggio*, 13(2): 6–25.
Landowski, Eric (2020) 'Critique sémiotique du populisme'. *Punctum*, 6(2): 155–66.
Ledin, Per and Machin, David (2020). *Introduction to Multimodal Analysis*. London: Bloomsbury.
Lévi-Strauss, Claude (1958). *Anthropologie structurale*. Paris: Plon.
Lévi-Strauss, Claude (2010). *L'identité*. Paris: Presses Universitaires de France.
Lobaccaro, Luigi (2022). 'La semiotica cognitiva in Italia: origini, diramazioni, evolucioni'. In Gianfranco Marrone and Tiziana Migliore (eds), *Cura del senso e critica sociale. Ricognizione della semiotica italiana*, 61–94. Milano: Mimesis.
Lorusso, Anna Maria (2008). *Umberto Eco. Temi, problemi e percorsi semiotici*. Rome: Carocci.
Lorusso, Anna Maria (2015). *Cultural Semiotics*. Basingstoke: Palgrave Macmillan.
Lotman, Juri (2005). 'On the Semiosphere'. *Sign Systems Studies*, 33(1): 205–29.
Lotman, Yuri M. (1990). *Universe of the Mind. A Semiotic Theory of Culture*. London/New York: I.B. Tauris.
Lotman, Yuri M. (2009). *Culture and Explosion*. New York: De Gruyter.
Lowndes, Joseph (2005). 'From Founding Violence to Political Hegemony: The Conservative Populism of George Wallace'. In Francisco Panizza (ed.), *Populism and the Mirror of Democracy*, 144–71. London: Verso.
Macaulay, Marcia (2019a). 'Bernie and the Donald: A Comparison on Left- and Right-Wing Populist Discourse'. In Marcia Macaulay (ed.), *Populist Discourse. International Perspectives*, 165–95. Cham: Palgrave Macmillan.
Macaulay, Marcia (ed.) (2019b). *Populist Discourse. International Perspectives*. Cham: Palgrave Macmillan.
MacDonald, Laura and Ruckert, Arne (eds) (2009). *Post-Neoliberalism in the Americas*. Basingstoke: Palgrave Macmillan.
Machin, David (2007). *Introduction to Multimodal Analysis*. London: Bloomsbury.
MacRae, Donald (1969). 'Populism as an Ideology'. In Ghita Ionescu and Ernest Gellner (eds), *Populism. Its Meanings and National Characteristics*, 153–65. London: Weidenfeld & Nicolson.
Madisson, Mari-Liis and Ventsel, Andreas (2020). *Strategic Conspiracy Narratives: A Semiotic Approach*. London/New York: Routledge.
Madrid, Raúl L. (2008). 'The Rise of Ethnopopulism in Latin America'. *World Politics*, 60(3): 475–508.
Madrid, Raúl L. (2012). *The Rise of Ethnic Politics in Latin America*. Cambridge: Cambridge University Press.
Maingueneau, Dominique (2009). *Les termes clés de l'analyse du discourse*. Paris: Points.
Maingueneau, Dominique (2017). *Discours et analyse du discours*. Paris: Armand Colin.
Malasevic, Siniša (2006). *Identity as Ideology. Understanding Ethnicity and Nationalism*. New York: Palgrave Macmillan.

Manetti, Giovanni (2013). *In principio era il segno. Momenti di storia della semiotica nell'antichità classica*. Milano: Bompiani.
Mangano, Dario (2022). 'Semiotica del cibo'. In Gianfranco Marrone and Tiziana Migliore (eds), *Cura del senso e critica sociale. Ricognizione della semiotica italiana*, 279–304. Milano: Mimesis.
Manning, Paul (2012). *The Semiotics of Drink and Drinking*. London: Continuum.
Marrone, Gianfranco (2001). *Corpi sociali*. Turin: Einaudi.
Marrone, Gianfranco (2007). 'Introduzione. Un nodo teorico: narrazione, esperienza, quotidianità'. In Gianfranco Marrone, Nicola Dusi e Giorgio Lo Feudo (eds), *Narrazione ed esperienza. Intorno a una semiotica della vita quotidiana*, 7–14. Rome: Meltemi.
Marrone, Gianfranco (2016). *Semiotica del gusto*. Milano: Mimesis.
Marrone, Gianfranco (2022). *Gustoso e saporito. Introduzione al discorso gastronómico*. Milano: Bompiani.
Marrone, Gianfranco and Migliore, Tiziana (eds) (2022). *Cura del senso e critica sociale. Ricognizione della semiotica italiana*. Milano: Mimesis.
Marsciani, Francesco (2007). *Traciatti di etnosemiotica*. Milano: Franco Angeli.
Mazzarino, Giuseppe (2022). 'Etnosemiotica. Storia, teorie e proposte per una prospettiva di studio dei fenomeni socio-culturali'. In Gianfranco Marrone and Tiziana Migliore (eds), *Cura del senso e critica sociale. Ricognizione della semiotica italiana*, 95–124. Milano: Mimesis.
Mazzoleni, Gianpietro and Schulz, Winfred (1999). '"Mediatization" of Politics: A Challenge for Democracy?' *Political Communication*, 16(3): 247–61.
Mazzoleni, Gianpietro, Stewart, Julianne, and Horsfield, Bruce (ed.) (2003). *The Media and Neo-Populism. A Contemporary Comparative Analysis*. Westport/London: Praeger.
Mazzolini, Samuele and Borriello, Arthur (2021). 'The Normalization of Left Populism? The Paradigmatic Case of Podemos'. *European Politics and Society*, online first.
Mazzucchelli, Francesco (2010). *Urbicidio. Il senso dei luoghi tra distruzioni e ricostruzioni nella ex Jugoslavia*. Bolonia: Bononia University Press.
McCallum-Bayliss, Heather (2019). 'Donald Trump is a Conqueror: How the Cognitive Analysis of Trump's Discourse Reveals his Worldview'. In Encarnación Hidalgo-Tenorio et al. (ed.), *Populist Discourse. Critical Approaches to Contemporary Politics*, 242–58 London/New York: Routledge.
Meléndez, Carlos and Rovira Kaltwasser, Cristóbal (2017). 'Political Identities: The Missing Link in the Study of Populism'. *Party Politics*, 25(4): 520–33.
Minogue, Kenneth (1969). 'Populism as a Political Movement'. In Ghita Ionescu and Ernest Gellner (eds), *Populism. Its Meanings and National Characteristics*, 197–211. London: Weidenfeld & Nicolson.
Moffitt, Benjamin (2014). 'How to Perform Crisis: A Model for Understanding the Key Role of Crisis in Contemporary Populism'. *Government and Opposition*, 50(2): 189–217.
Moffitt, Benjamin (2016). *The Global Rise of Populism. Performance, Political Style, and Representation*. Stanford: Stanford University Press.
Moffitt, Benjamin (2017). 'Transnational Populism? Representative Claims, Media and the Difficulty of Constructing a Transnational "people"'. *Javnost: The Public*, 24(4): 409–25.
Moffitt, Benjamin and Tormey, Stefaan. (2014). 'Rethinking Populism: Politics, Mediatisation and Political Style'. *Political Studies*, 62: 381–97.

Montoro, Juan Manuel and Moreno Barreneche, Sebastián (2021a). 'Towards a Social Semiotics of Geo-cultural Identities. Theoretical Foundations and an Initial Semiotic Square'. *Estudos Semióticos*, 17(2): 121–43.

Montoro, Juan Manuel and Moreno Barreneche, Sebastián (2021b). 'Identidad latinoamericana y sistemas de transporte: notas para una semiótica de las identidades geo-culturales'. *DeSignis*, 34: 67–82.

Moreno Barreneche, Sebastián (2019). 'Populism and the Reshaping of the Political Imaginary'. *Im@go*, 14: 37–53.

Moreno Barreneche, Sebastián (2020a). 'La democracia y sus otros. Una contribución desde la semiótica al debate sobre la erosión democrática'. *Revista de Estudios Sociales*, 74: 12–22.

Moreno Barreneche, Sebastián (2020b). 'Sentido, relaciones e interacciones. Intersecciones entre el pensamiento relacional y la sociosemiótica'. *Andamios*, 44: 15–37.

Moreno Barreneche, Sebastián (2020c). 'Mind the Gap! On the Discursive Construction of Collective Political Identities'. *Punctum*, 6(2): 11–27.

Moreno Barreneche, Sebastián (2020d). 'Polarización política y fanatismo "blando": una hipótesis semiótica'. *DeSignis*, 33: 143–58.

Moreno Barreneche, Sebastián (2020e). 'From a Biological Entity to a Social Monster. A Semiotic Construction of the Coronavirus during the COVID-19 Pandemic'. *Fuori Luogo*, 7(1): 105–15.

Moreno Barreneche, Sebastián (2022). 'The Imaginary Construction of the Political Future'. *Versus*, 134: 143–64.

Morris, Charles (1938). *Foundations of the Theory of Signs*. Chicago: Chicago University Press.

Morris, Charles (1964). *Signification and Significance*. Cambridge, MA: MIT Press.

Mouffe, Chantal (2005a). *On the Political*. London: Routledge.

Mouffe, Chantal (2005b). 'The "End of Politics" and the Challenge of Right-Wing Populism'. In Francisco Panizza (ed.), *Populism and the Mirror of Democracy*, 50–71. London: Verso.

Mouffe, Chantal (2013). *Agonistics. Thinking the World Politically*. London: Verso.

Mouffe, Chantal (2018). *For a Left Populism*. London: Verso.

Mudde, Cas (2004). 'The Populist Zeitgeist'. *Government and Opposition* 39(4): 541–63.

Mudde, Cas (2007). *Populist Radical Right Parties in Europe*. Cambridge: Cambridge University Press.

Mudde, Cas (2017). 'Populism. An Ideational Approach'. In Cristóbal Rovira Kaltwasser et al. (eds), *The Oxford Handbook of Populism*, 27–47. Oxford: Oxford University Press.

Mudde, Cas (2018). 'How Populism Became the Concept that Defines Our Age'. *The Guardian*. Retrieved from https://www.theguardian.com/commentisfree/2018/nov/22/populism-concept-defines-our-age.

Mudde, Cas and Rovira Kaltwasser, Cristóbal (2013). 'Exclusionary vs. Inclusionary Populism: Comparing Contemporary Europe and Latin America'. *Government and Opposition*, 48(2): 147–74.

Mudde, Cas and Rovira Kaltwasser, Cristóbal (2017). *Populism: A Very Short Introduction*. Oxford: Oxford University Press.

Müller, Jan-Werner (2016). *What Is Populism?* Philadelphia: University of Pennsylvania Press.

Navaja de Arnoux, Elvira (2008). *El discurso latinoamericanista de Hugo Chávez*. Buenos Aires: Biblios.

Ochoa Espejo, Paulina (2017). 'Populism and the Idea of the People'. In Cristóbal Rovira Kaltwasser et al. (eds), *The Oxford Handbook of Populism*, 607–28. Oxford: Oxford University Press.

Orriols, Lluis and Cordero, Guillermo (2016). 'The Breakdown of the Spanish Two-Party System: The Ursurge of Podemos and Ciudadanos in the 2015 General Election'. *South European Society and Politics*, 21 (4): 469–92.

Ortner, Sherry B. (1973) 'On Key Symbols'. *American Anthropologist*, 75(5): 1338–46.

Ostiguy, Pierre (2017). 'Populism. A Socio-Cultural Approach'. In Cristóbal Rovira Kaltwasser et al. (eds), *The Oxford Handbook of Populism*, 73–97. Oxford: Oxford University Press.

Ostiguy, Pierre, Panizza, Francisco, and Moffitt, Benjamin (2021). *Populism in Global Perspective. A Performative and Discursive Approach*. London/New York: Routledge

Oswald, Michael (ed.) (2022). *The Palgrave Handbook of Populism*. Cham: Palgrave Macmillan.

Panizza, Francisco (2005). 'Introduction. Populism and the Mirror of Democracy'. In Francisco Panizza (ed.), *Populism and the Mirror of Democracy*, 1–31. London: Verso.

Panizza, Francisco (2017). 'Populism and Identification'. In Cristóbal Rovira Kaltwasser et al. (eds), *The Oxford Handbook of Populism*, 406–24. Oxford: Oxford University Press.

Paolucci, Claudio (2012). 'Sens et Cognition: La narrativité entre sémiotique et Sciences Cognitives'. *Signata*, 3: 299–316.

Paolucci, Claudio (2017). *Umberto Eco. Tra ordine e avventura*. Milano: Feltrinelli.

Paolucci, Claudio (2020). *Persona. Soggettività nel linguaggio e semiotica dell'enunciazione*. Milano: Bompiani.

Paolucci, Claudio (2021a). 'The Distinction between Semantics and Pragmatics The Point of View of Semiotics'. *Intercultural Pragmatics*, 18(3): 293–307.

Paolucci, Claudio (2021b). *Cognitive Semiotics. Integrating Sings, Minds, Meaning and Cognition*. Cham: Springer.

Pappas, Takis S. (2019a). *Populism and Liberal Democracy. A Comparative and Theoretical Analysis*. Oxford: Oxford University Press.

Pappas, Takis S. (2019b). 'On Populism, Planets, and Why Concepts Should Precede Definitions and Theory-Seeking'. *Sociologica*, 13(2): 19–22.

Pariser, Eli (2012). *The Filter Bubble. What the Internet Is Hiding from You*. London: Penguin.

Peñamarín, Cristina (2020). 'Fronteras afectivas de la esfera pública y semiótica pragmática'. *Cuadernos de Información y Comunicación*, 25: 61–75.

Pereira, Gustavo (2019). *Imposed Rationality and Besieged Imagination*. New York: Springer.

Perusset, Alain (2020). *Sémiotique des formes de vie*. Louvaine-la-Neuve: De Boeck.

Pezzini, Isabella (ed.) (1991). *Semiotica delle passioni*. Bologna: Esculapio.

Pezzini, Isabella (2001). *Lo spot elettorale*. Rome: Meltemi.

Pozzato, Maria Pia (1994). 'L'analisi del testo e la cultura di massa nella socio-semiotica'. In Roberto Grandi (ed.), *I mass media fra testo e contesto*, 175–226. Milano: Lupetti.

Pozzato, Maria Pia (2007). 'Ruolo e rilevanza dei modelli narrativi nella semiotica attuale'. In Gianfranco Marrone, Nicola Dusi e Giorgio Lo Feudo (eds), *Narrazione ed esperienza. Intorno a una semiotica della vita quotidiana*, 70–9. Rome: Meltemi.

Prentoulis, Marina (2021). *Left Populism in Europe. Lessons from Jeremy Corbyn to Podemos*. London: Pluto Press.

Priester, Karin (2007). *Populismus. Historische und aktuelle Erscheinungsformen*. Frankfurt/New York: Campus.
Rastier, François (2001): *Arts es Sciences du texte*. Paris: Presses Universitaires de France.
Reinemann, Carsten, Aalberg, Toril, Esser, Frank, Stömbäck, Jesper, and de Vreese, Claes H. (2017). 'Populist Political Communication: Toward a Model of Its Causes, Forms, and Effects'. In Toril Aalberg et al. (eds), *Populist Political Communication in Europe*, 12–25. New York/London: Routledge.
Remedi, Gustavo (2019). 'La esfera pública plebeya en América Latina: prácticas subalternas, usos y significaciones'. *Encuentros Latinoamericanos*, 3(2): 2–9.
Reyes, Oscar (2005). 'Skinhead Conservatism: A Failed Populist Project'. In Francisco Panizza (ed.), *Populism and the Mirror of Democracy*, 99–117. London: Verso.
Ricoeur, Paul (1990). *Soi même come un autre*. Paris: Seuil.
Rooduijn, Matthijs (2014). 'The Nucleus of Populism: In Search of the Lowest Common Denominator'. *Government and Opposition*, 49(4): 572–98.
Rosanvallon, Pierre (2006). *La contre-démocratie. La politique à l'âge de la défiance*. Paris: Seuil.
Rosanvallon, Pierre (2020). *Le siècle du populisme. Histoire, théorie, critique*. Paris: Seuil.
Rovira Kaltwasser, Cristóbal (2012). 'The Ambivalence of Populism: Threat and Corrective for Democracy'. *Democratization* 19(2): 184–208.
Rovira Kaltwasser, Cristóbal, Taggart, Paul, Ochoa Espejo, Paulina, and Ostiguy, Pierre (eds) (2017). *The Oxford Handbook of Populism*. Oxford: Oxford University Press.
Salmon, Christian (2008). *Storytelling. La machine à fabriquer des histories et à formater les esprits*. Paris: La Découverte.
Sanders, Karen B., Berganza, Rosa, and De Miguel, Roberto (2016). 'Spain: Populism From the Far Right to the Emergence of Podemos'. In Toril Aalberg et al. (eds), *Populist Political Communication in Europe*, 249–60. New York/London: Routledge.
Santaella Braga, Lucia (2002). 'Introduction: La mise en œuvre de la sémiotique de Peirce. Difficultés et stratégies'. In Anne Hénault (dir.), *Questions de sémiotique*, 433–44. Paris: Presses Universitaires de France.
Sartori, Giovanni (1970). 'Concept Misformation in Comparative Politics'. *American Political Science Review*, 64(4): 1033–53.
Sartori, Giovanni (1984). 'Guidelines for Concept Analysis'. In Giovanni Sartori (ed.), *Social Science Concepts: A Systematic Analysis*, 15–48. Beverly Hills: Sage.
Saul, John (1969). 'Africa'. In Ghita Ionescu and Ernest Gellner (eds), *Populism. Its Meanings and National Characteristics*, 112–51. London: Weidenfeld & Nicolson.
Saussure, Ferdinand de (1959). *Course in General Linguistics*. New York: Columbia University Press.
Savage, Ritchie (2018). *Populist Discourse in Venezuela and the United States*. Cham: Palgrave Macmillan.
Scavino, Dardo (2020). 'El "nosotros" político: un 'yo" caracterizado'. *DeSignis*, 33: 159–65.
Schmitt, Carl (1932). *Der Begriff des Politischen*. Munich: Duncker & Humblot.
Schoor, Carola (2021). 'Probing into Populism's Core: An Analysis of the Semio-Linguistic Structure Underlying Populism'. *Critical Discourse Studies*, 18(2): 226–44.
Sclafani, Jennifer (2018). *Talking Donald Trump. A Sociolinguistic Study of Style, Metadiscourse and Political Identity*. London/New York: Routledge.
Searle, John (1995). *The Construction of Social Reality*. London: Penguin.
Sebeok, Thomas (1994). *Signs*. Toronto: University of Toronto Press.

Sebreli, Juan José (2008). *Comediantes y mártires: ensayo contra los mitos*. Buenos Aires: Debate.
Sedda, Franciscu and Demuru, Paolo (2018a). 'Da cosa si riconosce il populismo? Ipotesi semiopolitiche'. *Actes Sémiotiques*, 121.
Sedda, Franciscu and Demuru, Paolo (2018b). 'Social-ismo. Forme dell'espressione politica nell'era del populismo digitale'. *Carte Semiotiche*, Annali 6: 130–45.
Sedda, Franciscu and Demuru, Paolo (2019). 'La rivoluzione del linguaggio social-ista: umori, rumori, sparate e provocazioni'. *Rivista Italiana di Filosofia del Linguaggio*, 13(1): 26–40.
Selg, Peeter and Ventsel, Andreas (2020). *Introducing Relational Political Analysis*. London: Palgrave.
Shields, James (2013). 'Marine Le Pen and the "New" FN: A Change of Style or of Substance?' *Parliamentary Affairs*, 66: 179–96.
Sigal, Silvia (2006). *La Plaza de Mayo. Una crónica*. Buenos Aires: Siglo XXI.
Sigal, Silvia and Verón, Eliseo (2003). *Perón o muerte*. Buenos Aires: Eudeba.
Somers, Margaret (1994). 'The Narrative Constitution of Identity: A Relational and Network Approach'. *Theory and Society*, 23: 605–49.
Sorrentino, Paolo (2022). 'Semiotica della cultura: sguardo glocale e definizioni semiopolitiche'. In Gianfranco Marrone and Tiziana Migliore (eds), *Cura del senso e critica sociale. Ricognizione della semiotica italiana*, 125–64. Milano: Mimesis.
Stanley, Ben (2008). 'The Thin Ideology of Populism'. *Journal of Political Ideologies*, 13(1): 95–110.
Staufer, Simon J. (2021). 'Donald Trump, Bernie Sanders and the Question of Populism'. *Journal of Political Ideologies*, 26(2): 220–38.
Stavrakakis, Yannis (2005). 'Religion and Populism in Contemporary Greece'. In Francisco Panizza (ed.), *Populism and the Mirror of Democracy*, 224–49. London: Verso.
Stavrakakis, Yannis (2017). 'How Did "Populism" Become a Pejorative Concept? And Why Is This Important Today? A Genealogy of Double Hermeneutics'. *Populismus Working Papers*, 6: 1–23.
Stavrakakis, Yannis and Katsambekis, Giorgios (2014). 'Left-Wing Populism in the European Periphery: The Case of SYRIZA'. *Journal of Political Ideologies*, 19(2): 119–42.
Stavrakakis, Yannis, Katsambekis, Giorgios, Nikisianis, Nikos, Kioupkiolis, Alexandros, and Siomos, Thomas (2019). 'Extreme Right-Wing Populism in Europe: Revisiting a Reified Association'. *Critical Discourse Studies*, 14(4): 420–39.
Stewart, Angus (1969). 'The Social Roots'. In Ghita Ionescu and Ernest Gellner (eds), *Populism. Its Meanings and National Characteristics*. 180–96. London: Weidenfeld & Nicolson.
Taggart, Paul (2000). *Populism*. Buckingham/Philadelphia, PA: Open University Press.
Taggart, Paul (2017). 'Populism in Western Europe'. In Cristóbal Rovira Kaltwasser et al. (eds), *The Oxford Handbook of Populism*, 248–65. Oxford: Oxford University Press.
Taguieff, Pierre (1995). 'Political Science Confronts Populism: From a Conceptual Mirage to a Real Problem'. *Telos*, 103: 9–43.
Tajfel, Henri (1982). 'Social Psychology of Intergroup Relations'. *Annual Review of Psychology*, 33: 1–39.
Tamm, Marek and Torop, Peeter (ed.) (2022). *The Companion to Juri Lotman. A Semiotic Theory of Culture*. London: Bloomsbury.
Tarchi, Marco (2008). 'Italy: A Country of Many Populisms'. In Daniele Albertazzi and Duncan McDonnell (eds), *Twenty-First Century Populism. The Spectre of Western European Democracy*, 84–99. New York: Palgrave Macmillan.

Tarragoni, Federico (2021). 'Populism, an Ideology Withouth History? A New Genetic Approach'. *Journal of Political Ideologies*, online first: 1–22.
Taylor, Charles (2004). *Modern Social Imaginaries*. Durham/London: Duke University Press.
Terracciano, Bianca (2019). 'Il sovranismo è servito: la retorica salviniana del buono made in Italy'. *E/C*, 27: 162–74.
Theocharis, Yannis (2015). 'The Conceptualization of Digitally Metworked Participation'. *Social Media + Society*, 1(2): 1–14.
Tiercelin, Claudine (2002). 'La sémiotique philosophique de Charles Sanders Peirce'. In Anne Hénault (dir.), *Questions de sémiotique*, 15–52. Paris: Presses Universitaires de France.
Traini, Stefano (2006) *Le due vie della semiotica. Teorie strutturali e interpretative*. Milano: Bompiani.
Urbinati, Nadia (1998). 'Democracy and Populism'. *Constellations*, 5(1): 110–24.
van Deth, Jan (2004). 'A Conceptual Map of Political Participation'. *Acta Politica*, 49: 349–67.
van Leeuwen, Theo (2005). *Introducing Social Semiotics*. London/New York: Routledge.
van Leeuwen, Theo (2021). *Multimodality and Identity*. London/New York: Routledge.
Ventsel, Andreas (2011). 'Hegemonic Signification from Cultural Semiotics Point of View'. *Sign Systems Studies*, 39(2–4): 58–87.
Ventura Bordenca, Ilaria (2022). "Sociosemiotica: teorie, esplorazioni e prospettive". In Gianfranco Marrone and Tiziana Migliore (eds), *Cura del senso e critica sociale. Ricognizione della semiotica italiana*, 24–59. Milano: Mimesis.
Verón, Eliseo (1983). 'Il est là, je le vois, il me parle'. *Communications*, 38: 98–120.
Verón, Eliseo (1987). 'La palabra adversativa. Observaciones sobre la enunciación política'. In: Eliseo Verón et al. (eds), *El discurso político. Lenguajes y acontecimientos*, 13–26. Buenos Aires: Hachette.
Verón, Eliseo (1988). *La semiosis social*. Barcelona: Gedisa.
Verón, Eliseo (1989). 'Semiótica y teoría de la democracia'. *Revista de Occidente*, 92: 130–42.
Verón, Eliseo (1994). 'Mediatización, comunicación política y mutaciones de la democracia'. *Revista Semiósfera*, 2: 5–36.
Verón, Eliseo (1997). 'Esquema para el análisis de la mediatización'. *Diálogos de la comunicación*, 48: 10–17.
Verón, Eliseo (1998). 'Mediatización de lo político. Estrategias, actores y construcción de los colectivos'. In: G. Gauthier, A. Gosselin, and J. Mouchon (eds), *Comunicación y política*, 220–36. Barcelona: Gedisa.
Verón, Eliseo (2013). *La semiosis social 2*. Buenos Aires: Paidós.
Verschueren, Jef (2001). 'Pragmatics'. In Paul Cobley (ed.), *The Routledge Companion to Semiotics and Linguistics*, 83–94. London: Routldge.
Verschueren, Jef (2012). *Ideology in Language Use*. Cambridge: Cambridge University Press.
Vilas, Carlos M. (2004). '¿Populismos reciclados o neoliberalismo a secas? El mito del neopopulismo latinoamericano'. *Revista de Sociología e Política*, 22: 135–51.
Villegas, Juan (2020). *Diario de la grieta*. Buenos Aires: Galerna.
Violi, Patrizia (2014). *Paessagi della memoria*. Milano: Bompiani.
Violi, Patrizia (2017). 'Due vie per la semiotica o un incrocio di sguardi? Algirdas Greimas e Umberto Eco a confronto'. *Entornos*, 30(1): 25–33.
Violi, Patrizia (2019). 'Story of a counter monument: Doris Salcedo's *Fragmentos* in Bogotá'. *Punctum*, 5(2): 62–71.

Walicki, Andrzej (1969). 'Russia'. In Ghita Ionescu and Ernest Gellner (eds), *Populism. Its Meanings and National Characteristics*, 62–96. London: Weidenfeld & Nicolson.

Wendt, Alexander (1992). 'Anarchy Is What States Make of it: The Social Construction of Power Politics'. *International Organization*, 46(2): 391–425.

Weyland, Kurt (2001). 'Clarifying a Contested Concept: Populism in the Study of Latin American Politics'. *Comparative Politics*, 34(1): 1–22.

Weyland, Kurt (2017). 'Populism. A Political-Strategic Approach'. In Cristóbal Rovira Kaltwasser et al. (eds), *The Oxford Handbook of Populism*, 48–72. Oxford: Oxford University Press.

Wiles, Peter (1969). 'A Syndrome, not a Doctrine: Some Elementary Theses on Populism'. In Ghita Ionescu and Ernest Gellner (eds), *Populism. Its Meanings and National Characteristics*, 166–79. London: Weidenfeld & Nicolson.

Wodak, Ruth (2015). *The Politics of Fear. What Right-Wing Populist Discourses Mean*. London: Sage.

Wodak, Ruth and Fairclough, Norman (2013). *Critical Discourse Analysis*. London: Sage.

Wodak, Ruth, KhosraviNik, Majid, and Mral, Brigitte (2013). *Right-Wing Populism in Europe. Politics and Discourse*. London: Bloombsbury.

Wodak, Ruth and Meyer, Andreas (2001) *Methods of Critical Discourse Analysis*. London: Sage.

Worsley, Peter (1969). 'The Concept of Populism'. In Ghita Ionescu and Ernest Gellner (eds), *Populism. Its Meanings and National Characteristics*, 212–50. London: Weidenfeld & Nicolson.

Zienkowski, Jan (2017). *Articulations of Self and Politics in Activist Discourse*. Cham: Palgrave Macmillan.

Zienkowski, Jan and Breeze, Ruth (eds) (2019). *Imagining the Peoples of Europe*. Amsterdam/Philadelphia: John Benjamins.

Zienkowski, Jan, Östman, Jan-Ola, and Verschueren, Jef (eds) (2011). *Handbook of Pragmatics Highlights, 8: Discursive Pragmatics*. Amsterdam: John Benjamins.

Index

actorialization 72, 75–7, 84–6, 90, 103
addressee 67–8, 93, 109, 115, 130, 136, 158–60
   counter-addressee 67, 136
   para-addressee 67–8
   pro-addressee 67, 130, 136, 158
aesthesia/aesthesic 70, 104, 106–8, 110, 171, 184
affect/affective 73, 82, 104, 107, 118, 178
anti-establishment 74, 140
Argentina 3–4, 9–10, 53, 66, 75, 101, 127, 138, 150–1, 153–5, 182
articulation 6, 9, 15, 16, 25, 27–30, 35, 36, 51, 53, 55, 58, 63, 66, 67, 71, 74, 77–9, 83, 90, 91, 97, 98, 102, 111, 122, 123, 128, 131, 133, 143, 144, 151, 153, 155, 158, 166, 179
attire 56, 57, 65, 66, 102, 103, 106, 108, 118, 158, 171, 172
axiologization 72, 75, 77, 83–7, 90, 92, 94, 96, 98, 103, 109, 113, 116, 117, 126, 127, 131, 132, 137, 145, 158, 160

Barthes, Roland 43, 47
binary scheme 82, 84, 97, 154
body 33, 57, 75, 106–8, 119, 140
Bolivia 3, 101, 117, 150, 151, 153, 155–7, 164, 187
Bolsonaro, Jair 18, 70, 123, 138–40, 144, 153, 186
Brazil 3, 9, 17, 53, 75, 102, 138–40, 182, 186
bricolage 50, 63, 122, 130, 140

Canovan, Margaret 10, 25, 28, 31, 88–9, 96, 105
Cárdenas, Lázaro 3, 9, 101, 150
'chain of equivalences' 91, 109, 116, 117, 133, 146, 148, 161, 164, 165, 185, 187

Chávez, Hugo 3, 17, 101, 102, 108, 115–18, 138, 145, 150, 151, 157, 166, 172, 183, 184
cognitive 1, 5, 6, 19, 31, 33, 47, 52, 58, 73, 75, 76, 81, 93, 95, 105–7, 132, 140, 173, 178, 184
collectives 68, 103
conceptual definitions 19–22
constructivism 46, 181
'contest over meaning' 17, 18, 59, 60, 65, 67, 78–9, 87, 102, 103, 119
crisis 25, 31–3, 106, 134–5, 139, 141, 147–8, 157, 158, 160, 161, 187
   crisis of confidence 18
Critical Discourse Analysis (CDA) 27–8, 40, 56–7, 71, 103, 180
cultural Semiotics 48, 49, 51, 54, 70, 71, 95
cultural unit, meaning of 64, 65, 72, 76, 85, 95

de Saussure, Ferdinand 29, 41–3, 45, 47, 48, 53, 54, 64–6, 71, 179, 180
débrayage 44, 45
deep structures 15, 44, 51, 56, 68, 69, 74, 75, 78, 82, 84, 90, 102, 113, 129, 185
definition of, populism 22–4
demagoguery 2, 4, 23, 24, 69, 70, 94, 172, 178
democracy 2, 6, 7, 9, 10, 13, 18, 20, 23–5, 27, 29, 32, 36, 69–70, 87, 88, 91, 124, 143, 144, 146, 147, 149, 151, 152, 155, 158, 159, 161, 166, 171, 172, 174
dichotomization 74, 82–7, 136, 172
discourse, populism 28–31
discourse analysis 28, 31, 63, 179
discourse-theory 17, 25, 29, 55–7, 63–6, 70–1, 105, 125, 170, 174, 181
discursive construction 17, 29, 30, 45, 59, 74–8, 82, 87, 99, 103, 109, 116, 129, 156, 159, 160

discursive practice   1, 5, 7, 11, 15, 16, 37, 47, 78, 91, 98, 101, 105, 121, 125, 126, 137, 139, 140, 143, 145, 146, 150, 155, 162, 165, 171, 173, 177–9
dysphoric/negative axiologization   77, 84, 117, 137, 158

Eco, Umberto   x–ix, 41–3, 45–6, 52, 64, 66, 84, 110, 132, 179, 180
effect of sense   32, 58, 73, 106–8, 114, 115, 118, 119, 130, 131, 136, 158, 159
elite   ix, 13, 16, 25–7, 30, 33, 36, 44, 81, 83, 86, 94, 96, 97, 107, 128, 141, 147, 149, 156, 162, 172, 180, 184
elitism   13, 26, 33, 36, 94, 114, 178
emotion/emotional   26, 34, 47, 48, 51, 58, 73, 75, 78, 95, 104, 105, 111, 119, 123, 130–2, 135, 140, 159, 171, 173, 184
emplotment   84, 166
empty signifier   89–92, 94, 125, 167
enemy   ix, 15, 30, 37, 62, 67, 74, 83–7, 94, 96–8, 102, 109–11, 116, 126, 131, 138, 153, 160, 174, 182
enunciation   27, 44–5, 52, 57, 58, 67–8, 71, 101, 103, 104, 115, 118, 119, 128–30, 133, 136, 154, 166, 170, 182
Essex school of discourse analysis   ix, 29, 30, 66, 71, 170
establishment   11, 12, 30, 35, 43, 44, 83, 85, 97, 98, 110, 117, 122, 124, 125, 131, 135–41, 144–6, 148, 149, 158, 165, 184, 187
euphoric/positive axiologization   77, 87
Europe/European   2, 3, 8, 10, 16, 25, 28, 43, 49, 50, 58, 70, 75, 92, 108, 112, 123, 127, 128, 138, 145, 147, 148, 150, 157–9, 162, 182, 188
European Union/EU   96, 112, 125, 127, 128, 147

Facebook   103, 108, 114, 115
Fernández (de Kircher), Cristina   3, 127, 146, 150, 151, 153–5, 157, 162, 166, 187
figurativization   72, 75, 77–8, 84–6, 90, 103
Floch, Jean-Marie   49–51, 180

Fontanille, Jacques   49–51, 107, 179, 180
forms of life   46, 51, 76, 114, 146, 150, 179
frame   1, 5, 6, 15, 18, 30–2, 70, 81, 93, 106, 111, 132, 143, 144, 174, 177, 179, 184
France   3, 17, 49, 50, 101, 128–33, 135, 148, 157, 185
Front National   3, 128–33
Fujimori, Alberto   3, 9, 101, 138, 150

generalization   25, 72, 75, 76, 84–6, 90, 103
gesture/gestures   37, 56, 57, 102–4, 107, 108, 171, 172
globalization   98, 123, 141, 143, 146–50, 165, 166, 186
Greece   2, 3, 11, 16, 101, 147, 148, 157
Greimas, Algirdas J.   x, 41–51, 53, 54, 57, 64, 66, 68, 72–4, 76, 77, 79, 93, 107, 132, 158, 171, 174, 178–80, 182

Halliday, Michael   46, 48, 52–3
hegemony   47, 63–7, 71, 79, 147, 182
history of, populism   10–12
Hjelmslev, Louis   42–4, 48, 64, 66, 75, 180

ideational approach   16, 25, 35–7, 58
identification   5, 18, 36, 58, 61, 73–4, 77, 84, 85, 90, 95, 104–6, 111, 127, 130, 139, 152, 156
identity (excl. 'collective')   12, 17, 29, 30, 48, 58, 60, 63, 72–4, 76, 84, 91–3, 95–8, 103, 104, 113, 119, 124, 127, 128, 138, 156, 182, 183
  collective identity/identities   11, 15, 17, 36, 56, 58–61, 65, 67, 68, 71–8, 81, 83–7, 91, 93, 95–8, 102, 108–10, 112–15, 125–7, 130, 133, 136, 146, 147, 152, 155, 156, 163, 164, 170, 173, 182
ideology   1, 5, 6, 8, 10, 16, 20, 24–8, 30, 33, 34, 36, 47, 52, 58, 71, 81–3, 86, 108–10, 121, 122, 132, 162, 165, 172, 173, 179
Iglesias, Pablo   3, 101, 145, 157–62, 188
Instagram   103, 108

interactions   1, 31, 39, 46, 48, 50–1, 53, 55, 57, 62, 67–70, 75, 89, 104, 106, 108, 110, 113, 115, 119, 171, 173, 182
Italy   3, 17, 49, 51–2, 101, 112–15, 178, 180

Kirchnerism   153, 173

Laclau, Ernesto   x, 7, 9, 10, 17, 24, 25, 27–31, 55–7, 60, 63–7, 70, 71, 79, 82, 83, 88, 89, 91–2, 97, 98, 103, 105, 125, 129, 143, 146, 148, 151, 164, 166, 170, 173–5, 178, 181, 182, 187
Landowski, Eric   18, 48–51, 53, 57, 68–71, 79, 98, 104, 108, 110, 114, 180
  interactional regimes   50–1, 104
  political regimes   69–70, 104
Le Pen, Marine   3, 17, 96, 101, 112, 128–37, 139, 140, 159, 166, 172, 185, 187
leader/leadership   x, 9, 15, 32–4, 37, 70, 101–4, 123, 124, 128, 133, 139, 141, 150, 153, 154, 157, 159, 162, 164, 172, 187
  populist leader   17, 37, 56, 85, 98, 99, 101–2, 104–19, 121, 130, 131, 135, 136, 139, 156, 158, 162, 164, 166, 171, 179, 183, 186
left-wing, populism   143–67
Lega (Nord)   3, 106, 112
Lévi-Strauss, Claude   43
linguistics   2, 39, 40, 42, 48, 49, 52, 56, 64, 169, 179, 180
Lotman, Juri   54–5, 57, 66, 70, 71, 95, 125, 180, 182

manipulation   50, 68–70, 110, 116, 119
  of semiotic resources   7, 67, 68
Mélenchon, Jean-Luc   3, 5, 96, 101, 148, 157
Menem, Carlos   3, 9, 101, 138, 150
Morales, Evo   3, 101, 117, 138, 146, 150, 151, 153, 155–7, 159, 163–4, 187–8
Mouffe, Chantal   2, 17, 27, 29, 30, 55–67, 69–71, 73, 75, 77, 79, 85, 90, 103, 124, 129, 143–51, 164–6, 173, 181, 186, 187

Mudde, Cas   2, 4, 13, 25–8, 31, 35, 36, 86, 90, 92, 119, 122, 128, 173
Mujica, José 'Pepe'   93–4, 127, 138, 151–2, 155, 157, 166, 186, 187
music   32, 33, 56, 129, 131–3, 135, 136, 152, 153, 159, 162, 171, 172, 186, 187

narodni/narodnitchestvo   11, 16, 23–4, 178
narrative scheme   44, 57, 77, 79, 93, 178
narrativity   52
  principle of narrativity   52, 77
nationalism   9, 20, 36, 82, 92, 93, 113, 122, 124–7, 132, 133, 140, 152, 183, 189
nativism   93, 122–4, 140
neoliberalism   143, 146–50, 165, 186

Object of Value   45, 79, 82, 84, 85, 93, 131, 158
oligarchy/oligarchs   83, 96, 98, 145, 149, 150, 155, 165

patriotism   124, 189
Peirce, Charles Sanders   41–3, 47, 53, 66
performance/performative/performativity   x, 1, 5, 6, 9, 14–17, 19, 28, 30–3, 35–7, 39, 56–8, 61, 67–70, 77, 78, 90, 93, 97, 98, 102–9, 111–16, 118, 119, 121, 124, 128, 134, 138–40, 143, 145, 146, 150–7, 162, 163, 165, 166, 169–74, 179, 184, 185
Perón, Juan Domingo   3, 9, 10, 101, 117, 138, 150, 153
Peronism   138, 153, 173
plebeian/s   88, 94, 109, 113, 114, 138, 146, 149–57, 165–7, 172, 186, 189
plebeianism   151–2, 167
pluralism   6, 13, 26, 85, 87, 178
Podemos   3, 17, 127, 143, 145, 147, 148, 157–62, 164, 166, 172, 188–9
polarization   82, 87, 139, 154, 172
the political/*le politique*   7, 27, 29, 32, 35, 57–72, 73, 75, 77–9, 81, 82, 85, 87, 90, 97, 98, 101, 104–6, 111, 114, 119, 124, 126, 137, 144, 147, 150, 162, 175
Populist Narrative Structure   15–17, 30, 37, 74, 78, 83–5, 94–6, 98–9, 101–2, 105–11, 113, 115, 116, 121–8,

131–41, 143–8, 150–3, 155, 156, 158–60, 162, 163, 165–7, 171–5, 177, 179, 182, 183, 187, 188
practice/practices (excl. 'discursive')   7, 10, 18, 27, 33, 35, 39, 44, 46–7, 49–51, 53, 55–7, 61, 63, 65–7, 69, 72, 76, 89, 90, 93, 95, 102, 103, 107, 114, 115, 118, 121, 123, 127, 149, 179, 180, 182

right-wing, populism   121–41

Salvini, Matteo   3, 17, 101, 102, 108, 112–15, 118, 138, 139, 184
Sanders, Bernie   3, 4, 17, 101, 143, 145, 148, 158, 162–6, 186, 189
semiotic resources   7, 33, 35, 37, 52, 53, 55, 56, 58, 60, 61, 63, 67, 68, 76, 79, 83, 90, 94, 102–8, 110, 113, 115, 118, 121, 129, 130, 133, 135, 140, 145, 152, 153, 159, 171–3
social media   15, 32, 46, 56, 57, 67, 102–4, 108, 111, 113–15, 118, 138, 158
Sociolinguistics   48, 49
South/Latin America   xii, 3, 4, 8, 9, 11, 16, 17, 23, 42, 49, 50, 53–5, 115–18, 123, 127, 138–40, 143, 145, 146, 148, 150–7, 160, 163, 166, 177, 182, 186–8

Spain   3, 17, 101, 147, 148, 157–62, 166, 188
style of, populism   31–3
SYRIZA   3, 97, 145, 147, 148, 157, 188

text/textual   1, 44, 45, 51, 54–6, 114, 122, 128–33, 135–7, 144, 153, 155, 159–64, 171, 172, 174
Trump, Donald   3, 4, 17, 70, 83, 85, 86, 89, 92, 94, 101, 102, 108–14, 134–9, 153, 159, 163, 164, 166, 172
Twitter   108, 114, 156, 158

United States of America   3, 4, 11, 16, 17, 23, 43, 74, 90, 101, 108–11, 116, 123, 127, 134–8, 143, 147, 148, 157, 162–5, 182, 183
Uruguay   75, 93–4, 126–7, 138, 151, 152, 157, 181
US People's party   11, 108, 134, 162, 165

valorization   27, 36, 77, 96
van Leeuwen, Theo   52–3, 183
Vargas, Getúlio   3, 9, 101, 117, 138, 150
Venezuela   3, 17, 101, 115–18, 183
Verón, Eliseo   17, 42, 43, 46, 47, 53–4, 57, 63, 65–8, 71, 103, 130
virtual   99, 105, 113, 121, 156

xenophobia   122, 124, 132

www.ingramcontent.com/pod-product-compliance
Lightning Source LLC
Chambersburg PA
CBHW062225300426
44115CB00012BA/2225